The Youth Effect

A Hormone Therapy Revolution

Ronald L. Brown, M.D.

Fine Books Publishing Company
St. Augustine, Florida

Many of the anecdotes that appear in this book are summaries of actual patient histories. Individuals' names and other characteristics have been changed to protect their identity. Nevertheless, they do reflect actual circumstances in the lives of patients whom I have seen in the past 10 years. Should an individual recognize, or think that you recognize, your story in this book, the similarities are coincidental unless I have received your specific permission to use your story.

Graphic Design: Margaret F. Kemp

Content Editor: Melissa Block

Copy Editor: Roberta W. Waddell

Dust Jacket Design: O_2 IDEAS

Produced by **FINE BOOKS PUBLISHING COMPANY** L.L.C.
St. Augustine, Florida

Printed by Taylor Publishing Company, Dallas, Texas

To my wife of 34 years, Susan Kennedy Brown.

Your enduring patience, tolerance, understanding and love sustain me and are a shining example for all you encounter.

Foreword

I am a radiologist who specializes in breast imaging. I am also a patient of Ronald Brown. Hormone replacement has risks and benefits, and I sought his opinion for help not only for myself, but for my patients.

There are so many conflicting messages regarding hormone replacement therapy not only in the popular press, but also in the medical literature. Even doctors are confused by it all, and we expect you to make your own choice!

It is true that whether you start hormone replacement or not, you are making a decision. I believe the best decision is an informed decision. It is important to understand why hormone replacement may make good sense and when it may not. Not all hormones are equal. There is a difference in the biochemical types and in their function. The requirements for hormones vary during an individual's lifetime and with her (or his) physiological needs. What works for your friend or relative may not be the best choice for you. On the other hand, an uninformed choice to avoid hormone replacement may put you at risk for other health problems, which may require the use of medications that might be avoided with the appropriate hormone replacement therapy. In other words, if you want to age gracefully, I encourage you to do your homework!

Over the years, I have been fortunate to have Dr. Brown as my own personal source of information on these matters. Now, so do you.

Everyday I see women suffering through "the change of life," and they are fearful of hormone replacement – although they may know that it could help relieve their symptoms and improve the quality of their lives. This book takes a simple, clear, level-headed, research-based approach to describing the pros and cons of bio-identical HRT, both for menopausal symptoms and the consequences of aging; shows why it's different from traditional hormone replacement; and helps to guide you to making your own best choice.

Dr. Brown has methodically synthesized all of the information to date on the subject. He has carefully applied that knowledge to helping thousands of patients like myself. The book covers more than hormones for women (and men); it also helps you to integrate a truly healthful diet, exercise regimen, and supplement plan into your life for that total "Youth Effect."

As a physician, a breast imaging expert, and as a woman who continues to benefit greatly from Dr. Brown's approach to bio-identical hormone replacement therapy, I value the opinions of this book's author highly. I encourage you to discover what he has to say.

To your best health,
Laurene Mann, M.D.
Metrolina Women's Breast Center, P.A.

Acknowledgments

A work such as this does not get finished without considerable help and input from others. Without the considerable writing skills and research assistance of Melissa Block, I would still be floundering to put out a readable manuscript. For her help, I will be forever grateful. Others whom I must thank for making this book a reality are: Nancy Kesler, who provided me with the finest transcription service I've ever had; Bobby Waddell who provided her skillful editing skills at a critical point; Peggy and Ted Kemp of *Fine Books Publishing Company* whose guidance and expertise brought about the final, actual product.

In one way or another, my wife, Susan, has had a daily role in making this book happen. Thanks for gently nudging me when I needed it.

A special thanks to my good friends John Zimmerman, Margaret Rainey, and Luther Cochrane who convinced me that a book of my own was a worthy venture. They also provided needed encouragement, moral support and literary expertise. John's awesome staff at *O2 Ideas* also provided me with design work that is the best in the business.

One doesn't get to a point in a career where a book is meaningful without the experience, knowledge, wisdom, and clinical acumen imparted by many mentors. For these things I'd like to thank my past teachers, attendings, fellow residents, and partners for their many contributions. In particular, I would like to thank Dr. Peter Van Dorsten, my friend and original mentor. He is a true Pied Piper who has inspired and trained many OB/GYN physicians in the past 30 plus years. And Dr. Bill Stallworth who was my partner and taught me the art of being passionate about caring for the whole patient.

There have been a number of courageous pioneers and innovators who have paved the way for the rest of us to follow and take up the banner of bioidentical hormone replacement therapy. Particularly, I'd like to acknowledge the invaluable contributions of the late Dr's Robert Greenblatt, Don Gambrell, and John Lee.

Everyone needs moral support, and I've certainly been blessed with a family that has backed me through thick and thin. Thanks and all my love to Spencer, Margaret and my mother, Dot. My nurse of 24 years, Lynda Evans, is essentially family to me. Our patients are only too aware of her caring, steadfast attitude and join me in being blessed by her presence.

Lastly, I want to thank all of my patients through the years who have taught me everything and allowed me to partake in their lives, deliver their babies, and share the good times and the tough times.

Contents

Introduction

Tommy and Amy are close family friends of ours. We've known them for more than twenty years, and I delivered two of their three children. Amy is one of the sweetest, kindest, most loving people I have ever met. She has always had a very calm demeanor—even labor didn't seem to put this most serene person out of balance.

When Amy became menopausal a few years ago, she didn't want to discuss it. She didn't want to talk about any of the symptoms she was experiencing as a result of her decreasing hormone levels. I could see, during the approximately two years of her change, that she was having some degree of discomfort, but I was reluctant to bring it up. She seemed quite sensitive about the subject. Tommy, who had become a patient of mine, tried for some time to coax Amy into seeing me for counseling about hormone replacement therapy (HRT). She wanted nothing to do with it; she insisted there was nothing wrong with her, and made it clear she didn't want it brought up again.

Tommy confided in me that Amy had become a different person. He and their children were all painfully aware of her increasingly ill moods and irrational flares of temper. My wife and I had both seen small examples of this, but we weren't present for any of these fireworks displays Tommy had reported to me in confidence. Despite my concern, and my strong conviction that I could be of help to her, I knew I couldn't press the issue with her until she was ready and willing to discuss it. Then, it hit the fan.

On one Saturday afternoon, I was at Tommy and Amy's home to help them prepare a going-away party for a mutual friend that evening. There were live lobsters, their claws banded, wandering around on the kitchen floor as we prepared pots to cook them in. Tommy was trying to make a phone call on their portable phone but was having difficulty making a connection and hearing the person on the other end. Frustrated, he complained about the difficulty in finding a good portable phone and asked Amy why she couldn't have bought a more reliable model.

Without a word, Amy snatched the phone from Tommy's hand and hurled it against the kitchen wall, cracking it into a number of pieces. Then, spouting expletives, Amy stormed over to its remains and picked up the largest piece, which she proceeded to throw back onto the tile floor as hard as she could—not once, but twice. Imagine the scene: normally sweet, pleasant, petite Amy standing there steaming over 100 splintered telephone pieces, with lobsters scurrying about on the floor, the boiling pots on the stove also pouring steam into the air, and Tommy and I standing there, agape and speechless.

It seems that was a wakeup call for Amy because the following week she came in to see me, armed with the results of some lab work that indicated significant deficiencies in *all* her ovarian hormones. We discussed her options, and she agreed that a good starting point would be subcutaneous (just below the skin) pellets of estradiol and testosterone. She also began taking a progesterone capsule every night at bedtime.

According to Amy, and her family and friends, she was back to her old self in *less than two days*. She told me, "The first night after having the pellets put in, I slept better than I had in at least five years." Soon afterwards, she had more energy and sex drive—better than she could ever remember having. Then, within two weeks, her hot flashes, night sweats, and vaginal dryness, which she had told no one about, went away completely. And her sweet disposition returned. She was definitely back to being the Amy we all knew and loved.

She has now been on subcutaneous HRT pellets for over two years. She looks and feels great. She's playing the best golf of her life—and she found a portable phone that works just fine.

While it might seem quite novel, I hear stories like this—stories of reborn happiness and fulfillment—every day. The point I want to make here and throughout this book is: To a large extent, you, me, everyone is who they are and what they are *because of hormones*. Having optimal levels of all the hormones makes for a healthier, happier, and probably longer life. Since many of the less welcome changes that come with aging result from lower-than-optimal hormone action in the body, maintaining the desired optimal levels in the years following the menopausal change (in women) and the andropausal change (in men) may require the use of hormone replacement therapy.

Hormone replacement therapy (HRT) has been around for more than six decades. In the past several years, it has received a lot of bad press. This negative information has come from a number of scientific studies that have precisely, and consistently, defined the offending agent—namely the combination hormone therapy Prempro. Prempro contains Premarin (estrogens derived from horse urine) and Provera, a progestin (a synthetic, chemically altered form of the hormone progesterone).

However, a gross and misguided generalization that *all women's HRT is bad*—even hormones other than those damned by the scientific studies—has evolved from these specific studies. Additionally, this misinformation has been propagated by a willing press and by those who stand to profit from your doctor and you not understanding what the real truth is.

What This Book Contains

The whole purpose of this book is to clear up the waters that have been thoroughly muddied by the drug companies. Facts *support* the use of the right kind of HRT, and those facts demonstrate that this particular kind of HRT, *bio-identical hormone replacement therapy* (BHRT), is not only beneficial, *it is safe.* BHRT uses only hormones that are exact replicas of hormones made in the human body. They are made from plants, and molecularly they are carbon copies. Your body doesn't know the difference.

I can summarize the reasons for this in a few simple sentences, and I'm going to do so here. The reason the book doesn't end on page nine is the prevailing negativity surrounding HRT. In light of the confusing and often frightening press you may have seen on this subject, it will require three hundred or so additional pages to offer and clearly explain thorough scientific support for the advice you'll receive here

Here are the four basic tenets of female hormone replacement therapy (HRT). As you'll see by the studies I describe throughout this book, these are not conjecture, opinion, or wishing/hoping/praying. They are the facts.

The Four Basic Tenets of Female HRT

1. Hormone replacement for women, even the *bad* stuff (including Prempro), has significant health benefits, including reduced bone loss and reduced risk of colon cancer.
2. Any estrogen taken by mouth engenders some increased cardiovascular risk (that is, risk of blood-clot formation, heart attacks,and strokes). Estrogen therapy that is not delivered by mouth—that is absorbed into the body through the skin, for example—does not carry these same risks.
3. Progestins, the synthetic version of progesterone that is found in Prempro, significantly increase cardiovascular risk and the risk of breast cancer. Progesterone, the hormone that is made in the body and is found in bio-identical hormone replacement therapy, does not increase the risk of either. It may even decrease the risk of both.
4. Testosterone is the forgotten female hormone. It's very important to a woman's health and well-being, and for the prevention of age-related diseases, including osteoporosis.

I start out being reasonably certain that I'll need to justify my position in order to convince you—the educated healthcare consumer who has been reading all the scary HRT press—that bio-identically replacing those hormones in which you have become deficient is a beneficial step. This is why I've written this book for you.

I will delve into all all the HRT options and give you the pros and cons of each therapy. I'll end by giving you a look at what I believe the future options will be—you should know that the options available today are far better than those of thirty years back, and in another thirty years, none of the current options will be what they are today.

No discussion of HRT would be complete without a discussion of what many women fear most—breast cancer. Here, you will get the real story about the role that HRT plays in this dreaded disease, and I will elaborate on what you can do to significantly lower your risk of being diagnosed with it.

After that, I will tackle men's HRT. It's pretty simple because it comes down to one hormone: testosterone. Yes, men do become deficient in testosterone. That change of life is called the andropause, and it is much more common than you probably think. I'll explain the reasons why optimal testosterone levels are so beneficial, and give you options for therapy.

Testosterone replacement can be boiled down to two basic tenets, which I'll explain fully in the chapters dedicated to men's health.

The Two Basic Tenets of Testosterone Replacement for Men

1. Testosterone replacement therapy has significant health benefits for aging men.
2. Bio-identical testosterone, when not given orally, and when given in a dose adequate to relieve the symptoms of deficiency, does not increase the risk of heart disease, prostate cancer, or any other adverse event.

Men fear prostate cancer the way women fear breast cancer. Fortunately, there is much that can be done to lower the risk. I'll tell you how to maximize the odds that you—or the man in your life if you read those chapters on his behalf—will never hear the dreaded words, "You have prostate cancer."

In the closing chapters, I discuss other, non-hormone-replacement ways to stay healthy longer, and then I veer slightly off-message to give you a physician's perspective on the ways in which your healthcare is being dictated to you by the economic forces of medicine. The bottom line is that ***you***—not your insurance company, a drug company, the government, or even your doctor—are responsible for your own health. You must take charge of your own health and make decisions that positively influence your well-being. No one besides you yourself can do this. It's all up to you.

To help you go in this direction, The Ultimate Physical in the Appendix details exactly how to proactively protect your health well into those seasoned-citizen years. This is the kind of work-up that will optimally gauge your level of health now and, if needed, show you what can be done to improve it, both in the short- and long-term. It includes rapidly improving health technology that you can utilize to prevent disease, or diagnose it years before it manifests itself.

How the Information in this Book Can Help You

Most of my patients come to me because they are having outright symptoms that they recognize, either through their own research or due to the advice of a friend already in the know, as potentially signifying hormone imbalances. Not many people know the breadth and depth of these symptoms, or how many of the common signs of aging can be traced back to changes in hormone levels that are, in fact, a natural part of aging.

I strongly believe there are also a great many people who aren't experiencing anything besides so-called normal, natural aging, and I believe they too can benefit enormously from the use of bio-identical hormone replacement—if not today, then years or decades in the future. This does not mean that normal, natural aging is a disease, or that menopause or andropause are disease states. It means there are methods available to fortify, strengthen, and protect your body from the risk of disease states—a risk that increases exponentially after the fifth decade of life. And if you are truly proactive, starting with bio-identical hormone replacement as soon as your hormone levels begin to change substantially, you can expect to remain physiologically younger and healthier than your calendar years would predict.

The drug companies haven't researched or created bio-identical hormones on any noticeable scale because natural hormones cannot be patented and therefore cannot yield the enormous profits that drug companies have become accustomed to. But when you apply *natural* therapies like BHRT in an effort to maintain youth and prevent illness, you can almost entirely eliminate risk and derive huge benefits from them.

Will you look and feel like you're back in your twenties when you get on a bio-identical hormone replacement program in the years around menopause? Probably not, unless you have a very, very good plastic surgeon, some stellar genes, or a combination of the two. Will you look and feel like a vibrantly healthy, youthful-looking you? Yes. And that's what you and I are after here. It isn't magic I'm performing, it's simply replacement of the hormones your body stops making in adequate amounts as you age.

I have been prescribing hormone replacement therapy to women for thirty years. From my vantage point, I can tell you that not many women are going to stick with a regimen every day for the rest of their lives unless they experience a noticeable change in their quality of life, in the way they feel from day to day. As an example, the compliance rate with pharmaceutical HRT, such drugs as Premarin and Provera, hovers down around 10 percent, but since shifting to a bio-identical approach in my practice, my continuation rates have soared to easily over 90 percent. And this is even after the terrible press that HRT received in the wake of the Women's Health Initiative (WHI) Study.

In my work with over 1000 women and the hundreds of men who have followed my bio-identical HRT regimen, which may differ from other BHRT regimens in other books on bio-identical hormones, I hear the same refrain over and over: "*I've never felt so good in all my life.*"

1

Successful Aging

A Physician's Perspective

Every human being is the author of his own health or disease.

Sivananda

When Adam and Eve made the fateful decision to eat the apple, our best shot at immortality went down the tubes. Since then, prophets, seers, scientists, and lunatics have been looking for ways to outwit the aging process. Stories and myths involving the fountain of youth, the elixir of life, and universal panaceas have been found in every culture throughout history.

In the early 1500s, the Spanish explorer Juan Ponce de León discovered what he thought was the fountain of youth in St. Augustine, Florida. You can still visit the place where it was supposed to be, which is now a tourist attraction. Although there's no evidence that this fountain of youth is the real deal, it doesn't keep some of the thousands who visit it each year from drinking the water in hopes of turning back the clock.

Not everyone agrees that turning back the clock is a good idea. Well-respected authorities on the aging process and health argue that people should embrace the aging process, which is, after all, a natural thing. These naturalists suggest that aging is not something that should be interfered with, but needs to be accepted.

The reality is, we've been running plenty of interference with the body's aging process for hundreds of years. We now treat all kinds of disease processes that would unquestionably have been fatal only a century ago. In the year 1800, life expectancy in the United States was twenty-eight years. In 1900, it was forty-eight, and right now it is at eighty. This enormous increase in life expectancy didn't happen by accident. It has been brought about by scientific discoveries that have made for longer lives, and, most people would agree, for better and more comfortable lives. In 1900, the two major causes of death were pneumonia and diarrhea. The twentieth century saw rapid advances in basic medical care and hygiene that propelled a huge improvement in public health. Thanks to sterile techniques, antimicrobial therapy (antibiotics), immunizations, and many other scientific advances, the major causes of death are now cancers, cardiovascular disease (heart attacks and strokes), and neurological diseases (Alzheimer's disease, Parkinson's disease). These are diseases of older people—of aging.

You may have to accept the reality of chronological aging, but there are some choices when it comes to *biological* aging. If you accept the diseases of aging as unpreventable, incurable, and final, then you are accepting biological aging as inevitable. The truth is that biological aging is a process over which everyone has a considerable amount of control. The physical changes of aging originate at the cellular level, and if you understand the causes and effects of those changes, you have the tools to prevent age-related diseases.

It is imperative to do everything possible to keep America's aging population healthy—we owe it to our children and grandchildren, because otherwise the world will be overrun with disabled people in nursing homes in the very near future. Who wants to be stuck in a world where 80 percent of the population is over sixty-five and most of them are disabled or chronically ill?

The question, then, is this: What is the best way to keep the less desirable, age-related cellular metabolic changes from happening? Is it taking patented drugs, which *abnormally alter* cellular metabolism, to try and bring about something positive? Or is it restoring *normal* cellular metabolism by eating well, exercising regularly, taking certain vitamins and supplements, avoiding environmental hazards, and judiciously using bio-identical hormone replacement therapy, which consists of hormones that are exact replicas of the hormones naturally cranked out by people during their physical prime?

Personally, I think the answer is obvious, but you should decide for yourself. This book will give you the information you need to make that decision.

Theories of Aging

As you read this, many a head is bowed over a microscope or a computer monitor, the brain inside busily working to try and figure out that key to unlock the fountain of youth, the genetic clues that could rewind the aging clock once and for all—or that could, at least, help the majority remain in hale and hearty good health right up until the day they kick the bucket.

Unlocking these secrets could make or break the entire civilization over the next few decades, as increasing numbers of older people become increasingly vulnerable to the disease and disability that will make their lives and healthcare difficult. So far, the research has uncovered a lot of theories, most of which overlap, and all of which probably play a role in the big picture of the aging process.

Genetic theories propose that aging and death appear to be programmed into body cells, and that extending life beyond 100 years or so will require the development of genetic therapies, stem-cell therapies, and the like.

Genetic studies of the aging process have also revealed a role for telomere shortening. Telomeres are chains of nucleotide bases at the ends of DNA, that appear to work as a sort of aging clock. Each time the cell divides, more chunks of telomere are sheared away by an enzyme called *telomerase*. When the telomeres are gone, the cell knows it's time to self-destruct. Over time, cellular aging adds up to aging of the whole body, inside and out. Lengthening telomeres could prolong the healthy lifespan of individual cells. Interestingly, chronic psychological stress has been found to acclerate the speed with which telomeres shorten, helping to explain the connection between stress, accelerated aging, and age-related disease.

The wear-and-tear theory proposes that insults from the environment, such as junk food, toxic chemicals, and ultraviolet rays, are what causes cells to age because the aging body loses the ability to repair those insults. Waste-accumulation theories dictate that accumulation of wastes produced during the body's normal processes clog the works of cells.

Both above theories interrelate with the free-radical theory of aging. Free radicals are electrons that are spun off of atoms during normal cellular metabolism. Free-radical damage has been strongly implicated in most of the diseases related to aging. When produced in excess, free radicals damage proteins, fats, and genetic material in the cells, setting the stage for loss of function at the tissue and organ levels. Antioxidants, such as vitamin E, selenium, and coenzyme Q_{10} protect against aging by neutralizing these free radicals.

Immune theories, which posit that gradual changes in immune function predispose the body to chronic inflammation, have also been implicated in the aging process.

The Neuroendocrine Theory of Aging

The above theories certainly have merit, and can describe certain aspects of the age-disease connection, but the most likely candidate to explain why people get sick and infirm as they age is the neuroendocrine theory. It appears to be the *most likely* reason why humans and other animals undergo the well-known physical changes that make eighty-year-old grandmothers and grandfathers look and feel so different from their grandsons and granddaughters.

This most promising theory about aging, which looks as though it can provide a common denominator for many of the other theories, was first developed back in the 1960s by Vladimir Dilman, Ph.D., and Ward Dean, M.D.

They proposed that age-related changes in the *hypothalamus,* the part of the brain that is the master controller of hormone production throughout the body, cause alterations in the body's hormonal balance, as well as in the balance of *neurotransmitters,* chemicals that act as messengers within the nervous system and play a substantial role in mood and clarity of thought.

As people get older, hormone levels begin to shift, with the balance of the hormones that orchestrate reproduction—estrogen, progesterone, and testosterone—changing most dramatically. These changes accelerate in the late forties and early fifties, altering hormone levels in ways that impact the body at the cellular level.

Every cell in the body has receptors for every single one of the hormones the body produces. Hormones are complex molecules that *dock* at receptor sites and trigger a change in the way the cell operates. When glands cease to produce enough hormones to optimally stimulate these receptors, bad things start to happen. The cells don't function as well as they once did. The function of the tissues those cells make up is compromised until, eventually, entire organism's systems are affected, and disease results.

As I said in the Introduction, people's hormones don't decline because they age, *people age because their hormones decline.* This concept—that the drop in hormones *precedes* the less desirable changes related to aging—is well understood today. It follows, therefore, that by maintaining hormones at youthful levels, it is possible to slow the biological aging process.

There is also much that can be done to slow down many of the non-hormonal causes of aging and age-related diseases, and I will address some practical, preventive measures throughout this book. But my specialty is in dealing with hormone imbalances that come with aging.

Aging and Hormonal Change in Humans

For most people who have had children in their late twenties and thirties, once they've thoroughly raised them and set them free, they are in their late forties or fifties, through about sixty, the exact time during which their hormone levels start to change dramatically. In terms of the grand scheme of the species, people of these ages seem to have become obsolete, but happily, human civilization has evolved in firm opposition to this obsolescence. Those who are fifty or more tend to want to hang around for as long as possible, and there is no question that their families and the world will benefit if they stick around for a few more decades to grandparent and otherwise impart their hard-earned wisdom to the world.

Once their reproductive lives are over, women's hormone production drops quite abruptly over the span of a few years, culminating in menopause—the complete cessation of menstrual periods and the hormonal fluctuations that create that cycle. The abruptness of the female change makes hot flashes, mood swings, and night sweats common. In men, the reproductive hormone levels change more gradually during these years, so the consequences of declining hormones tend to affect men in a general, more gradual way, often, allowing the changes that result to be written off as the inevitable consequences of aging.

As the body's production of the hormones that orchestrate reproduction (and a lot of other important physiological processes) dwindles, the characteristic signs of aging begin to show. This relative deficiency of hormones leads to changes at the cellular level; and, with every year that passes after the reproductive life is over, people become more vulnerable to the diseases that lead to disability or death.

Is this natural? Not really. No other species has these problems as they age. The human birthright is to live out its lifespans as healthy, productive, busy, joyful creatures. There are many reasons why human beings don't, as a matter of course, enjoy that birthright, and they include an unhealthy diet, lack of exercise, toxins in the environment, and constant stress, usually, adding up over the course of a lifetime.

Hormone replacement therapy isn't the answer to all these problems, but as you age, this therapy can provide you with an easy, safe, and comprehensive approach to fortifying your resistance to the adverse effects of contemporary life.

Bio-Identical Hormones Benefit Vivian

My patient Vivian is a shining example of the benefits of bio-identical hormone replacement therapy (BHRT) even when it's begun late in life. At age eighty-four, she came to me through her daughter and son-in-law, also my patients, also using BHRT, and seeing me is clearly a priority because they drive an hour and a half to get to my Charlotte office.

I started Vivian on an estrogen patch, low-dose testosterone, and oral progesterone. Her visits are paying off—she looks amazing, like a woman in her sixties. One day in my office, her daughter said to me, "She looked great for her age before she went on BHRT, but she looks even better now." And, more importantly from my point of view, she *feels* as great as she looks.

But...Is It Really Natural or Safe to Replace Hormones?

If the body's ability to make certain hormones naturally wanes with age, is it not reasonable to assume that is just the way it's supposed to be? And, if that's the way it was intended, who are we to mess with Mother Nature's plan?

In line with this, I am asked several times a week, "Why should I use hormone replacement?" Frankly, I love hearing the question, and I love answering it. To me, the answer is the very essence of the philosophical argument for preventive medicine.

My answer begins with *Yes*, the natural production of sex hormones (estrogen, progesterone, and testosterone) *does* wane with time. If you live long enough, you will outgrow your body's ability to naturally make optimal amounts of these hormones. But if you consider why you had these hormones in the first place—to procreate and propagate the species – then why on earth would you even need them after age fifty or so?

Testosterone Levels

Interestingly, some men have more than adequate testosterone levels and sperm production well into their eighties. If a man has no symptoms indicating a lack of testosterone (described in detail in Chapter 9), he may not need additional amounts of the hormone. Some women, too, will have adequate testosterone activity throughout their lives. But every woman who lives past her early fifties will enter menopause, where her levels of estrogen and progesterone will drop dramatically.

The answer here is that the sex hormones have a large role

in the much bigger scheme of overall health. A decreasing hormone effect is a causal factor in the aging process and can lead to such diseases as dementia, heart disease, and osteoporosis, among many others.

Now, think about the usual ways of treating these infirmities and disease processes that go with aging—drugs, heart bypass surgery, joint replacement surgery, drugs, chemotherapy, radiation therapy, and more drugs. Do you honestly believe these treatments and invasive surgeries are a more logical complement to Mother Nature's plan than hormone replacement? As you read on, I think you'll realize that the appropriate HRT approach makes far more biological sense than the current measures employed by mainstream medicine because it's a gentle preventive measure rather than a slash-and-burn invasion or a pharmaceutical onslaught.

Every drug made by the drug companies is devised to somehow chemically alter your normal metabolism. That's how drugs work. When a drug is prescribed, there is supposed to be some benefit, and I don't argue that this is usually the case when a drug is used to help an ill person; but, if you take a drug, you should understand you are abnormally altering your body's own inherent mechanisms. So, the next time you hear someone carping about how unnatural hormone replacement is, ask them whether three or more prescription drugs a day—ironically, to treat the conditions that arise from decreased-hormone effect—is what Mother Nature had in mind.

If you're deficient in a hormone, any hormone, and it gets replaced with just enough of it to move your body into a normal range for a person who has not yet reached menopause, that hormone replacement is restoring *normal* cellular metabolism, not altering it abnormally. Restoring normal metabolism to all your cells makes you feel and look better, improves your resistance to chronic disease, and helps you to lead a longer, happier life. Hormone replacement creates this effect—what I like to call *The Youth Effect*—at your body's most basic, cellular level.

If this is true, why wouldn't you opt for these benefits of HRT? Well, you might ask, isn't a considerable risk involved? Most people think so, and considering the press HRT has gotten in recent years, this mindset is understandable. But this question of risk—how much, what kind—has been misrepresented in the news media and by many physicians who don't understand some of the distinctions between the *types, dosages,* and *delivery methods* that I will detail in these pages.

Consider that the difference between a car that drives beautifully and a car that won't drive at all might be a tiny malfunction in some miniscule piece of machinery. The difference between a deadly poison and a valuable drug can be a matter of a few atoms in the molecule of each. These distinctions may seem small at first, but they're important. So too it is with different types of HRT—the type, dosage, and delivery method of a hormone all matter far more than you (or your doctor) might think.

The end result of all the bad HRT press is that a lot of people are scared to use HRT for its most promising indication: to prevent disease. Hormones can prevent disease, whereas drugs treat problems created by hormone deficiency. This is not the case with *all* diseases, of course, but it is with most of those age-related bugaboos many fear most, including Alzheimer's disease, arthritis, heart disease, skin aging, and even some types of cancer.

After a factual presentation of the real scientific information on HRT that is contained in this book, I hope you will see the truth for yourself. And when you do, I think you will agree with me that properly administered HRT is not dangerous, and that its benefits are enormous.

Monica—Another Beneficiary of Bio-Identical HRT

When I first saw Monica, she was fifty-three years old. She had hit menopause at age fifty, with irregular periods in the years leading up to it. For at least six years, anxiety, depression, hot flashes, lack of libido, mood swings, night sweats, trouble sleeping, vaginal dryness, and fairly extreme problems with memory, concentration, and focusing on tasks had all been issues for her.

Her gynecologist had put her on birth control pills when her periods became irregular. The month following, she had gained five pounds and had struggled with bloating and depression, plus, for the first time in her life, she was having panic attacks. After a month, she stopped the pill and the problems resolved, with

Monica vowing she'd never again take oral contraceptives because the cure was worse than the disease.

As the months passed, however, she had increasing symptoms of hormone imbalance. She started seeing doctors—an internist, an OB/GYN, a psychologist, a sleep-medicine specialist, and a psychiatrist. A bone-mineral-density (BMD) test she had during this time yielded troubling information. She had *osteopenia,* a loss of bone mass that is a predecessor of osteoporosis, and was prescribed a bone-building drug called Fosamax (alendronate sodium). Also of note: Monica had been divorced in her late forties and had been recently laid off from her job after working there for twenty-six years. She was not a happy camper.

By the time Monica got to me, as a referral from a friend of hers, she was calling herself a zombie, adding, "I feel like I'm walking around in a haze." After her oral-contraceptive experience, and after all the negative press about female HRT, she was nervous about trying hormone replacement. But, she said, "I figure I couldn't feel worse, even if the hormones killed me."

At the time, she was taking a long laundry list of prescriptions: Fosamax, Celexa (an antidepressant/anti-anxiety drug), Wellbutrin (an antidepressant), Xanax (a sedative), Ambien (a sleeping pill), and Dexedrine (an amphetamine-like stimulant). Is it any wonder the woman didn't feel like herself? For the life of me, I don't know how anyone could function under the influence of all those drugs. She's not alone. Approximately 75 percent of the women I see are on some sort of antidepressant or anti-anxiety drug given to them by their doctor to treat what are actually symptoms of hormone deficiency.

I can assure you of one thing: Monica *never* had a deficiency of Fosamax, Celexa, Xanax, Ambien, or Dexedrine—*all her symptoms were due to a deficiency of one or more hormones.* No one had ever performed a hormone assay (a test that measures levels of hormones) to see whether her hormones might have something to do with her initial complaints...because, well, you know, menopause is a *normal* transition, and those hormone replacement pills are just too dangerous, right? Wrong!

Monica's doctors were really barking up the wrong tree. As medication after medication was prescribed, everyone lost track of which issues were part of Monica's physiology, and which were the side effects of drugs. Some of the drugs were prescribed to modulate side effects of other drugs—a practice that's a lot more common than you might think in establishment medicine.

Happily, Monica is now on bio-identical hormone replacement therapy, using subcutaneous pellets, a method I prefer for a large number of my patients (for reasons I'll discuss later). Since she had developed a dependency on more than one of the drugs, it took a while for her to clear them all out of her life, but over a period of months, she was able to successfully discontinue all her medications. She now has a new, better-paying job as a securities analyst and is engaged to marry a man she calls "the love of my life."

Win the Aging-Gracefully Game with BHRT

In my opinion, the practice of bringing patients into hormone balance as they age is a slam-dunk. It's a sort of cellular tune-up, a way of addressing a broad swath of age-related changes with a single therapy. In the game of pushing back the clock, it will gain more points in your favor than any other anti-aging therapy known so far.

Properly administered bio-identical hormone replacement improves your appearance, your health, your resistance against disease, and the length of your lifespan because *it does not abnormally alter your internal chemistry or physiology.* In fact, with balanced bio-identical HRT, your body is literally made younger, because your individual cells' normal chemistry and physiology are restored to a more youthful, healthy state. This is something your body perceives and handles as natural.

To be honest, everyone wants to feel good. Even hypochondriacs want to feel good—they just can't admit it. This kind of hormone replacement will make you feel better and look better, and will bring you improved health. It will help you resist chronic disease and live a longer (maybe even happier) life. Isn't that what everyone wants? The only reason you wouldn't do something that provided all these benefits is some perception that they entail risks outweighing those benefits.

Those who nay-say BHRT would have you believe that all hormone replacement therapy is dangerous and bad for you. They say recent studies have proven that the risks of prescription HRT—hormone drugs, such as Premarin and Prempro—are significant, and that the benefits just don't warrant their use. Such nay-sayers can be heard quite vocally grumbling about how the medical community just won't let go of HRT despite its risks—haven't people learned enough to just forget the whole idea of pharmaceutical hormone replacement? Isn't it time to move on?

In these pages, I'll make the case for BHRT from the standpoint of a clinician who has been prescribing hormones for thirty years to thousands of my patients who are happy with the outcome. (The stories of some are sprinkled throughout the book.) Over the years, I've come to believe that the risks of *not* using BHRT are far greater than the risks of using it, and I believe that history will bear me out. When this therapy finally catches on, it's inevitable that scientific research will show how those who do nothing will be more at risk for age-related diseases than those who go the BHRT route. The risk of using pharmaceutical alternatives to BHRT is also much greater than any risk you accept in trying this wonderful, safe therapy, without nearly the benefit.

My goal here is to enable you to see through the muddied waters that have been stirred by those who have a vested interest in the status quo, even if hanging on to that status quo means preventing you from attaining your best state of health and youthfulness. The vision of doctors and laypeople alike have been clouded by bad science, conflicts of interest, hype, and media misinterpretations of science (both bad science and good). The time has come to clear up the murkiness, and that's why I decided I had to write this book.

Because hormones have such far-reaching effects throughout your body, replacing them will also have far-reaching effects on the health of your cardiovascular system, your brain, bones, skin, libido, and every other part of your being.

Keep in mind, however, that while this book is primarily about hormones, you should also eat well, exercise, and take supplements to promote better health and longevity. I'll address these other topics after I've gotten all the hormone talk out of the way.

2

Understanding Bio-Identical Hormone Replacement Therapy

After all is said and done, what is achieved with bio-identical hormone replacement therapy is a return of your body, at the cellular level, to a normal, everyday physiological state in which your body functions at its peak, and where its resistance to disease is enhanced.

In order to understand the benefits and risks of hormone replacement therapy, you need to understand what hormones are and how they work. A very basic knowledge of hormones' biochemistry and physiology will show you that, although the postmenopausal/postandropausal state is a normal transition and not a disease state, it does leave you *functionally deficient* in youthifying hormones, such as estrogen, progesterone, and testosterone, and this functional deficiency increases your vulnerability to disease.

> Biochemistry is the chemistry of living things.
>
> Physiology is the study of an organism's processes and functions.

This chapter will educate you about the ways in which your hormones work when you are in the prime of your life—the time when you probably have the most energy (both physical and mental), the best sex, and the greatest resistance to health problems. You'll also gain a simple and straightforward understanding of the normal, everyday workings of certain hormones.

I'll start with some general information on the male and female hormones and their roles in maleness, femaleness, and the other things that make human beings tick. Then, I'll delve more deeply into the roles of steroid hormones in the health and reproduction of each gender. (*See* Figure 2.2)

Hormone Basics

Hormones are microscopic, bioactive substances made and secreted by *endocrine glands.* Once produced, they are released from those glands and carried in the bloodstream to target tissues. There, they have effects specific to each particular hormone.

The word hormone comes from the Greek word *horman,* which means *to set in motion.* The hormones that are the focus of this book are, in the years before the change, produced primarily in the reproductive glands—estrogen, progesterone, and testosterone in the ovaries of women, and testosterone in the testicles of men—but they affect the entire body, from the top of the head to the tips of the toes.

Once hormones reach their target tissues, they bind to specialized receptors in those tissues—receptors designed specifically as docking sites for that hormone.

> Tissues and Cells
>
> Tissues are groups of similar cells joined to perform the same function.
>
> Cells are the structural and functional units of all living organisms. They are sometimes referred to as the building blocks of life.

There, they trigger some sort of biological activity within the cells that make up that tissue. That's the short, simple story of hormones.

What makes the picture more complex is that this biological activity varies, depending on three factors:

1. Which hormone is being discussed;
2. Which kind of cells are the hormone's target;
3. The specific way in which that hormone interacts with, and alters the function of, those particular cells.

The human body is home to numerous endocrine glands and the hormones produced by them, and they all have a role in the normal function of the human organism. Although some hormones are not essential for survival, their absence or a deficiency will cause significant alterations in the appearance and function of the body.

For instance, a lack of *growth hormone* in early life leads to dwarfism; less-than-ideal levels of estrogen in teenage girls leads to poor development of female characteristics; low testosterone in males can affect fertility, body composition, and potency; low progesterone levels make a pregnancy hard to maintain. While not essential for life, such hormones are extremely important as they allow the body to function in its most optimal state (the sex hormones fall into this category).

Hormones are potent. They work in microgram (a millionth of a gram) or even picogram (a trillionth of a gram) concentrations. (The cap of a Bic pen weighs about a gram. So does a dollar bill.) When replacing hormones, as long as the right hormone is used in the right amount in order to achieve a balance resembling that of a healthy forty-year-old, their potency can be used to definite advantage.

One Big Happy Hormone Family

On its grandest scale, the endocrine or hormonal system is made up of intricate interrelationships among all the hormone-producing glands of the body. No hormone or gland flies solo, they are all interwoven and interdependent. When there is a problem with one gland's output of hormone, either too much or too little, it often leads to a malfunctioning of other hormonal mechanisms.

This is why, when replacing a deficient hormone, balancing the hormones can be a tricky business. It's not just about introducing a single hormone in a predetermined amount in each person, but, it's also about striking a balance between all the hormones—that's what is most healthful for that particular person's body as a whole. This lack of balance is one of the drawbacks of giving roughly the same dose of the same hormones to every woman—the one-size-fits-all approach that has been used in women's hormone replacement therapy in the past.

Table 2.1

Hormones—Where They're Made, What They Do

Hormone	**Gland of Origin**	**Job in the Body**
Melatonin	Pineal gland	Secreted when night falls; promotes deep rejuvenative sleep; powerful antioxidant
Luteinizing hormone	Pituitary gland	In women, stimulates estrogen production in ovary and induces ovulation; in men, acts on testes to stimulate testosterone production
Follicle-stimulating hormone	Pituitary gland	In women, FSH stimulates the maturation of ovarian follicles; in men, it acts on Sertoli cells, participating in the regulation of sperm production
Adreno-corticotropic hormone	Pituitary gland	Stimulates cortisol production in adrenal glands

Growth hormone (also: prolactin, melanocyte-stimulating hormone, oxytocin, vasopressin)	Pituitary gland	Growth hormone is an anabolic hormone that promotes growth of lean tissue (i.e. muscle), encourages use of stored fat for energy
Thyroid-stimulating hormone	Pituitary gland	Stimulates thyroid gland to make its hormones
Insulin, glucagon	Pancreas	Maintains blood-sugar balance
Triiodothyronine and thyroxine (T_3 and T_4)	Thyroid gland	Controls the body's metabolic rate
Cortisol (also: aldosterone)	Adrenal gland	Produced in response to stress; aids in fight-or-flight reactions
Dehydroepiandrosterone (DHEA)	Adrenal gland	DHEA is a hormone precursor (raw material) that can be transformed into estrogen, progesterone, and testosterone in the body
Estradiol, progesterone, testosterone	Ovaries	Hormones that orchestrate reproduction, libido, menstrual cycles, pregnancy, and many other body functions in women
Testosterone	Testes	In men, the hormone that allows for sperm production and creates libido, and has many other effects in the body

Vive la Difference—Some Hormones Make People Men, Others Women

Everyone, whether a man or a woman, makes the same hormones, they're just made in different proportions. It's misleading to call estrogen a female hormone or testosterone a male hormone. Men even make a small amount of progesterone, although they never have to concern themselves with gestation.

The Progesterone Effect

Research has found that progesterone plays a role in tender fathering behavior. A rise in a man's progesterone levels brings out his more sensitive, emotional, feminine side. Just watching a romantic film can increase a man's progesterone levels by about 10 percent.

The presence of all of these hormones in the bodies of both men and women provides clues that their jobs go beyond facilitating each gender's role in reproduction. These hormones are designed as checks and balances on one another's activity in the body in ways that are similar in both genders.

Early in fetal development, the reproductive organs of male and female fetuses are indistinguishable from one another. Twelve weeks following conception, the differences become more visible, although it takes an expert eye to see the difference even at that stage, as any non-physician who has attempted to deduce her or his child's gender from looking at an early second-trimester ultrasound well knows.

A penis and a clitoris grow from the exact same bud of tissue; a penis is, essentially, a clitoris under the influence of testosterone. The exact same fetal tissue that differentiates into the ovaries in girls will, when testosterone is involved, transform into testicles within a boy-fetus's body and descend around the seventh or eighth month of Mom's pregnancy. Uterus and prostate also develop from the same tissues early in fetal life. These differences are created, even at this most early stage of human life, by the action of sex hormones.

Infancy and childhood are relatively calm in terms of sex hormone activity, but it's still easy to see how the balance of sex hormones in males and females affects babies and kids. "He's all boy," you might hear yourself saying as your three-year-old son or grandson amuses himself by beating a tree stump with a baseball bat. "She's such a *girl,*" you might muse as your five-year-old daughter or granddaughter spends twenty minutes changing her clothes before kissing her baby doll goodbye and heading off to kindergarten. Despite the best of intentions to ignore gender biases and expectations, it is easy to spot when a boy is acting like a girl, or vice versa.

I've heard many a parent who, before having kids, was committed to avoiding the imposition of social expectations about gender roles on their offspring. They buy toy trucks for their daughters...who then turn them into doll strollers. They buy baby dolls for their sons, who turn them into projectiles. It's undeniable, and it's part of biology. It's hormones in action. Hormones on the brain. *Vive la difference!*

Hormones Can Make You Happy or Unhappy

Many of the people who come to me for help are mired in mood swings, depression, anxiety, or a combination of these. Many have never had these problems before their hormones took the downward shift characteristic of menopause and andropause.

A big part of *The Youth Effect* is to help bring out the positive emotions that come with great hormone balance. Replacing testosterone in a man who is deficient often has dramatic effects on his mood, and can even lift him from depression. In women with low testosterone, replacement boosts mood, libido, and energy levels. Estrogen replacement in women enhances mental sharpness and alertness.

None of my patients ever came to me with an antidepressant deficiency, so I'd rather give them what they're lacking to relieve sadness, low energy, and depression, than another drug.

In both men and women, the hormones FSH (*follicle-stimulating hormone*) and LH (*luteinizing hormone*) play similar roles in both sexes once puberty sets in, and a closer look more at this most important interrelationship between the *pituitary* gland, which sits at the base of the brain, and the ovaries (in women) and testes (in men) is indicated.

Hypothalamus and Pituitary—Your Body's HVAC System

The hypothalamus is the brain of the endocrine system, and it is situated next to its most important helper, the pituitary gland. Both reside at the base of the brain.

In response to releasing factors made by the hypothalamus in both men and women, the pituitary releases FSH (follicle stimulating hormone) and LH (luteinizing hormone) into the bloodstream. They circulate around the body until they reach their target tissues, the ovaries (in women) and testes (in men). There, they stimulate the production of sex hormones in their appropriate balance. Once the levels of those hormones reach a certain point, a feedback system shuts the LH/FSH signals down.

This system works much the same as your home heating and air conditioning system (HVAC). Think of your hypothalamus/pituitary unit as the thermostat. The thermostat sends a message (FSH/LH) to the heat pump (ovary or testes), which leads to the production of heat or air conditioning (estrogen or testosterone). The heat or AC is then circulated through the house (body). When the temperature in the air matches the temperature on the thermostat, the thermostat shuts down the heat-pump's production of heat or AC; when the hypothalamus/pituitary detect appropriate levels of hormone in the bloodstream, they turn off the signal to make more hormone. When the temperature moves outside the comfort range—as soon as there is inadequate hormone output—that thermostat starts kicking out more signals that it's time to fire up the heat or AC again.

When the ovaries or testicles are unable to keep up with the demands of that thermostat, as happens with most postmenopausal women and some andropausal men, things can go a bit haywire in your body, even with your body's actual thermostat, as any woman who's had hot flashes can attest. (*See* Figure 2.1 for a simple depiction of this system.)

Figure 2.1

The Making of Estrogen, Progesterone, and Testosterone

Hypothalamus/pituitary senses low testosterone and estrogen in circulating blood.

↓

Hypothalamus/pituitary produces more FSH and LH

↓

FSH and LH go to testes or ovaries

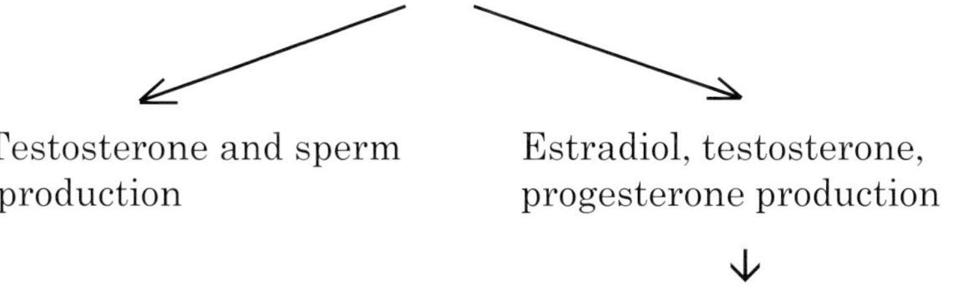

↓

Ovulation, and menstrual cycle

FSH and LH are also called *gonadotrophins*, because their role in the body is to stimulate cells in the *gonads* (ovaries/testes) to produce their own hormones. Once the ovaries and testes respond by pumping hormones out into the circulation, rising blood levels of those hormones serve as signals to the hypothalamus and pituitary that it's time to cool it with the *make-your-Hormones* messages.

Men's FSH/LH pattern is steady, with levels about the same from day to day throughout the month. Over the period of each day, levels tend to rise highest in the morning. A spike in FSH/LH stimulation in the early morning causes testosterone production to peak at that time, hence the morning erection (when a man stops having morning erections, his testosterone production has probably fallen below optimal levels.)

In premenopausal women, FSH/LH secretion changes cyclically over the span of her monthly menstrual cycle. Estradiol and progesterone both fluctuate dramatically over the course of the cycle.

Estrogen, Progesterone, and Testosterone—A Closer Look

Here are a few things you probably didn't know about sex hormones.

Chemically, estrogen, progesterone, and testosterone are all derived from the same molecule—cholesterol. (Other hormones, including growth hormone, insulin, and thyroid hormone, are made from proteins or the building blocks of proteins, *peptides* and *amino acids*.) Most people think of cholesterol as something to be banished from a healthy body, but without adequate cholesterol, you could not exist. Cholesterol is a very important building block of your cells, your hormones, and your body as a whole.

Cholesterol is a *sterol*, an immediate precursor of a *steroid* molecule. Chemically, cholesterol is a molecule built from atoms of carbon, hydrogen, and oxygen, which can be arranged in different ways, with added carbon, hydrogen, and oxygen, to make the various steroid hormones. Every hormone discussed in depth in this book is known as a steroid hormone, and all these hormones have the same basic molecular structure. If you look at diagrams of the steroid hormones, you will see that the difference between them is almost imperceptible.

Don't worry about understanding this diagram completely; I supply it here only so you can see how the smallest molecular changes turn one hormone into another. The letters over the arrows denote the action of an enzyme on the hormone before the arrow, transforming it into the version after the arrow.

Enzymes can act on a steroid hormone and transform it, with just a few nips and additions of atoms here and there, into another steroid hormone that has a totally different biological activity. A double bond here or a group of atoms there is the only difference between two hormones, such as estrogen and testosterone, which make the difference between a man and a woman.

Figure 2.2

The Steroid Hormone Cascade

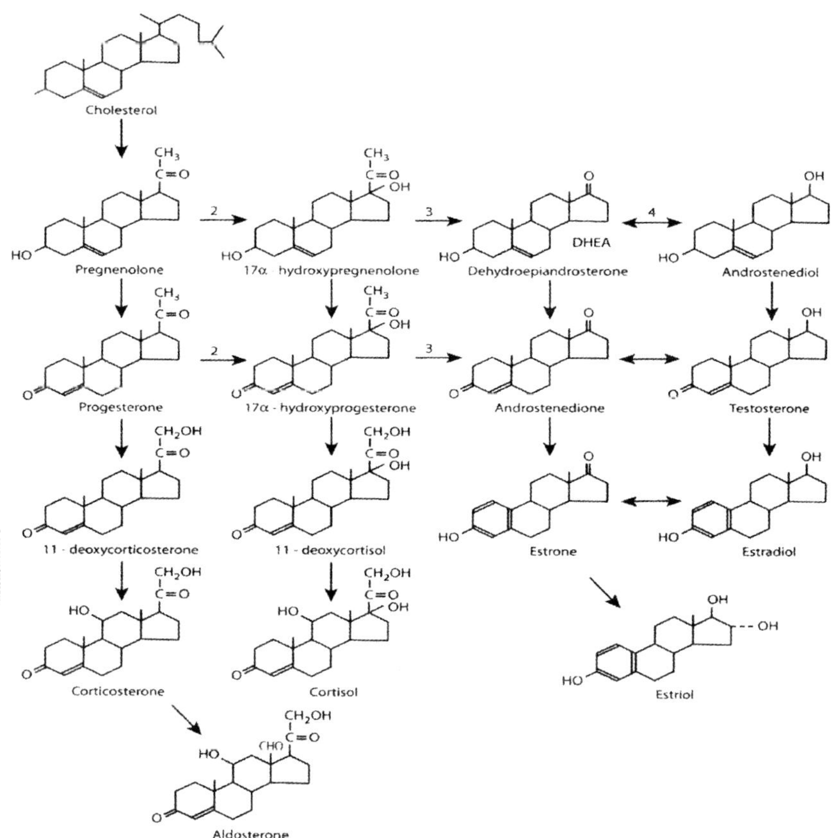

Where the Hormone Meets the Receptor

One more technical detail to cover is how the hormone exerts its action on the cell itself. This part is easy to understand, and that's good because it's one of the most important aspects of endocrinology for you to grasp as you consider becoming an educated user of bio-identical HRT.

First of all, you need to understand that almost every cell in your body has receptors for estrogen, progesterone, and testosterone. This means that all three of these hormones have unique effects on most of your cells.

Picture the receptor as a lock on the cell. This lock is a different shape for each hormone, so it can only be opened by the key that is the specific hormone for that receptor. The very presence of all of these hormone receptors is a powerful illustration of the importance of adequate hormone levels in the body.

Each hormone influences what happens within the cell, affecting variables, such as growth, division, maturation, and death. Cells from different parts of the body have differing numbers of receptors for each individual hormone.

For example, women's breast tissue has lots of estrogen receptors. Estrogen has *proliferative* effects, meaning that it stimulates cells to grow and (sometimes) multiply; the abundance of estrogen receptors in the breast means that more estrogen causes proliferation in the breast. This is why a woman's breasts start to bud and grow at puberty, and why they get larger during pregnancy. The uterine lining also harbors a great many estrogen receptors, so it is exquisitely sensitive to relatively tiny increases in estrogen concentration, such as those that occur with the menstrual cycle.

There are also plenty of progesterone and testosterone receptors present in breast tissue. With normal physiological levels of all three hormones, the progesterone and testosterone receptors in breast tissue cells have the effect of *down-regulating*—turning down—the growth-stimulating effect of the estrogen receptors.

Bio-Identical Defined

Getting a firm grasp on the concept of *bio-identical,* a term I've been freely tossing around up to this point, and which I've defined in brief, is key to reaping the benefits of *The Youth Effect*. What is a bio-identical hormone? How can you tell whether the hormone you're using is bio-identical? And why should you use it instead of a non-bio-identical hormone?

I would like to turn to the hormone, insulin, to help answer these questions.

The Story of Insulin

Everyone knows that insulin is the hormone missing in those with type 1 diabetes (formerly known as juvenile-onset diabetes). Unless they get insulin shots to control their blood sugar, their health will rapidly deteriorate, and they will fall into a coma and die. Insulin, the hormone made by the pancreas that facilitates the movement of sugars from the bloodstream into the cells to be burned for energy, is an example of a hormone that is absolutely essential for life.

Insulin was discovered by two young Canadian researchers, Drs. Banting and Best, in 1922. Before that time, a diagnosis of insulin-dependent diabetes was almost sure to be a cause of death. Children with diabetes were extremely underfed in an effort to keep them alive, but with insulin injections, people with diabetes were suddenly able to eat enough to sustain themselves and live much longer lifespans. It was an incredible medical success story.

From 1922 until about 1980, a span of almost sixty years, all insulin was extracted from sheep, cattle, and pigs. The insulin molecules from the animals and from humans are not exact carbon copies in terms of their molecular structure; in other words, the animal insulin is not *bio-identical* to the insulin made in the human body. Fortunately, it worked OK; there was no way to extract insulin from a living person, and insulin from cadavers doesn't work. Then, in 1980, recombinant DNA technology allowed bio-identical human insulin to be made for the first time.

Contrary to what most laypeople—and some doctors—believe, *human* insulin *doesn't come from humans*. Human insulin is not really human, but it is bio-identical. It is synthesized from bioengineered *E. coli* bacteria, but it is the same exact molecule as the molecule made in the pancreas of a healthy human being. It's a little different from sheep insulin, which is a little different from cattle insulin, which is a little different from pig insulin. Human beings who require insulin are, today, always given synthetic, bio-identical insulin.

Insulin is an excellent model of bio-identical hormone replacement therapy (BHRT). No one thinks twice about giving it to a patient who makes insufficient amounts of that vital hormone, but there is a lot of scuttlebutt about giving some other bio-identical hormones, such as estrogen, progesterone, and testosterone, to people whose bodies have become deficient in those hormones.

The reason for this is, most of the hormone-replacement drugs that have been FDA-approved, prescribed by most doctors, and used on a broad scale in millions of women are *non-bio-identical.* They're not a good fit. They're square pegs in round holes, and the body doesn't know exactly how to handle them. This is why they have all those scary side effects you've been hearing about in the media.

One of my patients told me that a friend of hers, who had also been a patient of mine, had stopped using her BHRT. "I'm so worried about her," I was told. "She's gaining all this weight and feeling terrible, and she won't even go to the doctor because she can't bear the thought of having to get on the scale with all the weight she's gained, but she says she won't go back on the hormones."

I had to find out what was going on, so I sat down with the ex-patient and her husband. The husband told me that they just didn't feel comfortable or safe taking non-FDA-approved hormones.

I told them, "Well, they may not be FDA-approved, but they've been in our bodies since our species first walked the earth. If it weren't for these exact same hormones, none of us would even be here." If that's not adequate evidence of safety or efficacy, I don't know what is. As is discussed later in this book, FDA approval is *not* the last word on the safety of any substance, drug, hormone, or food. Besides, a lot of the bio-identical hormones I use are, in fact, FDA-approved, and those I prescribe that *don't* have FDA approval come from the exact same sources as the ones that are FDA-approved.

The risk-to-benefit equation with BHRT tips powerfully in the direction of benefit, because bio-identical hormones are *the exact same substances made by the human body.* When the production of those hormones tapers off, you begin to age more quickly and your risk of age-related disease rises. When you receive the hormones you're low in, in ways that match the body's natural production of those substances, your body doesn't know the difference between bio-identical HRT and its own hormones. It can use them in exactly the way it uses the hormones that you made plentifully in your youth—and that helped keep you young.

Your Own Hormones' Identical Twins

You can liken bio-identical HRT to having an organ transplant from an identical twin. If you have end-stage kidney failure and need a kidney transplant, you have two options: you go into a national data bank and hope that someone, somewhere, some generous soul who is a close enough tissue match will volunteer to offer you a kidney. The other, more usual, avenue is to ask relatives to be tested, since there is more chance of their being a close match.

In both these scenarios, there is still the problem of the kidney being rejected. There are always subtle discrepancies between the tissues of two people who are not exactly the same. The kidney recipient has to cope with the possibility that his or her immune system will target the new organ as foreign and begin to attack it. However, if you are fortunate enough to have an identical twin willing to donate a kidney, you won't have to worry about rejection at all. Both identical twins are formed from the same egg and sperm and share all their genes in common. Your body recognizes the kidney of a twin as self, and the transplanted kidney performs as if it had been yours to start with.

Bio-identical HRT is like a transplant from an identical twin. Your body recognizes the hormone molecules as self. The BHRT then acts in the body as if it were made by the body's own glands, and there is no problem with rejection—a state of affairs that manifests with synthetic hormones as increased risk of adverse side effects and such potential health concerns as cancer and heart disease.

Sure, your body *can* utilize non bio identical hormones to a certain extent, but non-bio-identical hormones aren't recognized by the body as self. They are not recognized as natural to the body's makeup. For that reason, your body doesn't have the same capability to metabolize non-bio-identical hormones that it does with your own hormones. (Metabolize, in this context, means to break down and get rid of, by way of the liver, urinary tract, and bowel.) Your body cannot tell the difference between your own endogenous (made in your body) hormone and the bio-identical replacement hormone, and both are metabolized in exactly the same fashion.

Consider the fact that every other hormone given to people, *except* women's hormone replacement therapy, is a bio-identical hormone. Why is that? Because the drug companies, which make the synthetic hormones that have long been considered the gold standard of treatment for the postmenopausal lack of hormones in women, have a very powerful hold on how doctors prescribe, and what you, as a consumer, believe about medications. Drug companies created the patentable estrogen and progestin drugs that are now believed to be more risky than beneficial. They didn't do this with natural, bio-identical hormones because there wasn't much money to be made with substances that couldn't be patented.

Imitating the Body's Natural Hormone Delivery Systems

The insulin model can also serve to teach the importance of the right hormone delivery system, a system that is *physiologic,* or as close as possible to the one employed naturally by the human body.

> Physiologic Hormone Replacement
>
> This term describes the use of a hormone delivery system that matches, as closely as possible, the body's natural way of delivering a hormone to the tissues that need it.

Since about 1980, we have used human (bio-identical) insulin, and that has been a real boon to all those with diabetes. But a subset of people with insulin-dependent *brittle diabetes* have a very difficult time controlling their blood sugars and insulin levels, even with frequent blood-sugar testing and three to four shots of insulin per day. Before 1990, these people often had to be hospitalized to get their blood sugars under control.

Then, the insulin pump was invented. This is a pager-sized device that holds a small vial of insulin, which gets pumped through a small tube and a tiny, indwelling catheter into the subcutaneous fat—usually in the abdomen. Very small doses of insulin are dispensed all day, on demand, depending on blood-sugar levels.

These small doses imitate the physiological action of the pancreas, and blood glucose and insulin levels are maintained in a much tighter range. Those on the pump have been able to live a more normal lifestyle, with fewer trips to the doctor and fewer hospitalizations. Plus, they have a significantly lower incidence of cardiovascular disease, strokes, blindness, or kidney disease.

This kind of delivery system does bio-identical hormones one better. An exact replica of the human body's version of the hormone is getting into the body and the tissues in a more physiologic way. This should be the standard for all hormone replacement therapy.

New Hope for the Right Kind of HRT

I fervently hope that, in the near future, doctors will overcome their prejudices and understand the logic and literature that support BHRT. I have yet to sit down with an open-minded physician who didn't get it by the time we finished our discussion. The logic is compelling.

Early in these kinds of conversations, I often hear comments, such as, "Well, I don't much believe in those bio-identical hormones," or, "They're not proven safe and effective, so I avoid them." What these doctors don't realize is that the commonly prescribed hormone drugs Synthroid, Humalin, and Androgel (transdermal testosterone) are also BHRT. So are estradiol patches (Vivelle, Climara) and oral progesterone (Prometrium). These are all bio-identical and FDA-approved. If you consider these safe and effective, it would seem reasonable to assume that the compounded forms of testosterone, estrogen, and progesterone—exactly the same molecules, from the same sources as FDA-approved Androgel, estradiol patches, and Prometrium—would be safe and effective as well. In fact, using a bio-identical hormone formulated by a compounding pharmacy would appear to be even safer than the one-size-fits-all dosing that is generally used with FDA-approved hormones. Compounding enables physicians to fine-tune dosages to the needs of individuals.

Compounding Pharmacies

What They Are, What They Make, and How

In compounding pharmacies, medicines are dispensed as they are in any other pharmacy, but they can also be made to order to suit the needs of individuals. Customized prescription medications can be ordered by physicians from these pharmacies, according to the specific needs of their individual patients.

The pharmaceutical lobby, with lots of help from a media that doesn't understand hormone replacement, does its best to convey to the public the idea that compounded medicines are somehow less safe than ready-made, one-size-fits-all medicines. But the truth is that all pharmacists learn how to compound medicines as a core part of their college curriculum. These pharmacies are licensed in all fifty states by their state boards of pharmacy, and the compounded medicines they prepare are safe and effective.

If your doctor prescribes bio-identical hormones from a compounding pharmacy, that pharmacist uses precisely prescribed doses of United States Pharmacopoeia (USP)-certified, plant-derived (usually from soy), bio-identical hormones (although the drug companies don't publicize it, these hormones are also made by them, just as the *non*-bio-identical hormones are). The pharmacist combines the hormone with appropriate base material for optimal absorption into skin, mucous membranes, or the GI tract (depending on the mode of delivery). Compounding pharmacies can also package hormones in individual, pre-measured doses.

Any state-licensed compounding pharmacy can make bio-identical hormone replacement products. Some are higher caliber than others, but it is highly unlikely that any compounding pharmacy products would ever pose any danger to you. Any difference in quality that I've seen between compounding pharmacies has had more to do with small concerns, such as their creams not being homogenized enough and separating in the jar, or not having labeled syringes available for easy measuring of doses.

Somewhere in the neighborhood of 500,000 women in the United States alone are believed to be using some form of bio-identical hormone after menopause. When Wyeth, the company that makes Premarin and Prempro, filed a petition to the FDA suggesting that investigation and government regulation of bio-identical hormones were necessary to protect women's health, around 30,000 letters were received from women using these hormones during the 180-day comment period. No one was going to take away their hormones—period. In response, L.D. King, the executive director of the International Academy of Compounding Pharmacists, said:

> "The response to Wyeth's citizen petition is unprecedented and very telling...On the one hand, Wyeth and a small number of paid allies support restricting patients' access to bio-identical hormones.On the other hand, you have literally thousands of patients who are justifiably scared that Wyeth's campaign will rob them of hormone treatments on which they and their physicians rely to treat pain and discomfort. This imbalance should make it easy for FDA to deny Wyeth's petition...It's not about patient health, but Wyeth's wealth."

Don't buy into the fear-mongering around compounded hormones. Compounding pharmacies are closely regulated by state pharmacy boards. They have excellent quality control. Every compounding pharmacy I use regularly submits samples of their products to outside labs for analysis, to ensure that they're doing everything right. The hormones used in compounding are made in laboratories and labeled USP (United States Pharmacopoeia); to earn the USP label, they have to meet exacting standards.

Further, *even if a compounding pharmacist accidentally makes a batch of BHRT for you that is too strong, it's not going to hurt you long-term.* It isn't going to give you a heart attack or cause a tumor to spring up in your breast like a ghoul out of a grave in a bad horror movie. You might grow a little extra hair if your testosterone is too high (and it will go away when you reduce the dose), or you might find yourself feeling snappish or *off* with too much estrogen, but using a too-high dose of a natural hormone for a month—even six months—does not pose any serious risk...unlike many of the drugs that have been FDA-approved and used by millions of people. The push to get rid of compounding pharmacies is not about your safety—it's about Wyeth-Ayerst's solvency.

When you get your BHRT prescription, your doctor will probably ask you what pharmacy you would like to use. She or he may already use a trusted pharmacy; if not, you can refer him or her to one of the pharmacies listed in the Resources section in back.

Unfortunately, hormone replacement therapy has had a somewhat checkered history. This history, longer than you may think, has culminated in huge disagreements over the risks and benefits of this therapy and what forms of it might be safer than others. Providing some historical highlights of female hormone replacement can give a more comprehensive perspective on how it has been done wrong ...and how it can be done just right.

3

A Quick Trip Through the History of Women's HRT

There's more to the HRT story than meets the eye. Its history extends back a long, long way, to at least the eleventh century A.D.

Written records from Chinese physicians of that time tell us that preparations made from the urine of teenage boys and girls were used to restore sexual prowess and promote longer, more vigorous life in aging people. Eating animal glands, either as medicinal preparations or in foods, has been advocated for at least 150 years, and is still practiced in some parts of the world. Judging from its famous annual testicle-cooking festival, it would seem that Serbia is at the forefront of modern gonad cuisine.

Adrenal glands, brains, liver, and sweetbreads (thymus or pancreas) have all been served up as food at various points throughout history. Eating the hormone-soaked placenta—the afterbirth that follows the baby out of the mother's body—is a common ritual in animals believed to support the mother's fast recovery and her production of nutrient-rich milk. (If you're interested in how a human being might consume her own placenta, you can actually find instructions for cooking or dehydrating human placenta on the Internet.)

Today's medical use of ovarian hormones for replacement of deficiencies dates back to approximately 1935. Because I have been prescribing hormones since the early 1970s, I've had a front-row seat from which to watch a good deal of the evolution of present-day hormone replacement therapy. In this chapter, I'll focus on the history of HRT in women. (*See* Chapter 9 for HRT in men.)

An HRT Timeline

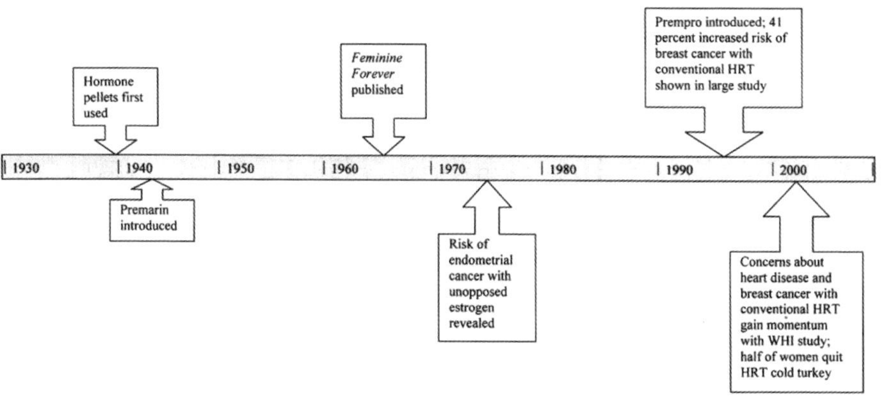

1939—Publications First Describe Use of Subcutaneous Hormone Pellets

The use of subcutaneous (just under the skin) hormone pellets in humans dates back to about 1935. An article from the *Journal of Science* in 1939 describes the use of subcutaneous hormone pellets in humans, the first such report in print. In 1949, Dr. Robert Greenblatt reported the use of these same pellets in an article in the *American Journal of Obstetrics and Gynecology*. At that point, he had been using these pellets for HRT since 1941.

1942—Premarin is First Introduced

The first commercially available estrogen compound was Premarin, introduced in 1942 by Wyeth Pharmaceutical Company. It was, and still is, created by extracting estrogens from the concentrated urine of pregnant mares (*pre*gnant–*mar*es'–ur*in*e). Today, to the dismay of animal activists everywhere, tens of thousands of thirsty, pregnant mares stand in narrow stalls with funnels strapped to their vulvas to collect their concentrated urine.

Premarin contains over forty identifiable hormonal structures, some of which are very similar to those made in the human body, and others that are quite different. Somehow, Wyeth-Ayerst has been successful at suppressing competition from those who would make generic versions of the drug, despite laws that allow generic competitors after a drug has been on the market for seven years. Sixty-five years later, Premarin is still considered by many to be the gold standard for estrogen replacement.

For the first twenty years of its existence, however, the idea of hormone replacement didn't quite catch on. Enter Robert Wilson, M.D., who did for Premarin what the *Harry Potter* books did for children's passion about reading. Like J.K. Rowling, Dr. Wilson accomplished his end through the written word.

1966: Feminine Forever is Published

In 1966, Robert Wilson, M.D., a gynecologist, authored *Feminine Forever*. This book advocated that all women take Premarin at menopause and for the remainder of their lives. In it, Dr. Wilson called menopausal women "castrates" and called menopause a "horror of living decay":

> "It was quite late in the evening, toward the end of my consulting hours, when my receptionist told me there was a man in the waiting room who wished to see me. Male patients being a rarity in a gynecologist's practice, I agreed to talk to him, even though he had come without an appointment. A skinny man in his fifties with a sharp and sallow face slid rather furtively through the door. His manner was an unpleasant mixture of embarrassment and aggressiveness. For a while he just fidgeted; then, 'Doc, they tell me you can fix women when they get old and crabby...She's driving me nuts. She won't fix meals. She lets me get no sleep. She picks on me all the time. She makes up lies about me. She hits the bottle all day. And we used to be happily married.
>
> " 'She's been to three doctors already,' he contin-

ued. 'They all tell her it's the change and nothing can be done about it. Now she tells me to get out and never come back. But I won't. It's my home. And if anyone's going, she is.' He reached into his back pocket—in those days shoulder holsters were still unknown—and quietly laid a .32 automatic on the edge of my desk.

" 'If you don't cure her, I'll kill her.'

"I looked at him doubtfully. 'You think that would be better for you?' I asked cautiously, my mind reeling with all I had heard about armed madmen in doctors' offices. But I was wrong. The man was completely rational.

" 'I got advanced T.B.,' my visitor explained. 'I was x-rayed again just last week. My doctor tells me that I have less than a year to live. I want to die in peace—and I can't if she's around.'

"...Fortunately no calamity occurred. I accepted his wife as a patient and she responded well to intensive twice-a-week estrogen injections. Her disposition improved noticeably after three weeks, and soon she was very busy taking care of her sick husband. I heard no more from him directly. He died on schedule and I received an invitation to his elaborate funeral. His widow felt genuine grief at his death.

"...I have often been haunted by the thought that—except for the tiny stream of estrogen which I passed into her body through the hypodermic needle—this woman might have died a violent death at the hands of her own husband...Outright murder may be a relatively rare consequence of menopause, though not as rare as most of us might suppose."

In 2003, Dr. Wilson's son, Ronald Wilson, stepped forward to state that his father's pro-Premarin campaign had been comfortably financed by Wyeth, the maker of the hormone drug. Wyeth had paid Wilson to write *Feminine Forever,* and had also financed speaking tours and the opening of a Park Avenue office for this enterprising doctor.

Dr. Wilson believed in what he preached. He really believed

that Premarin injections were the magic bullet that would keep women youthful, desirable, and happy, and that its calming effect on crazed menopausal women would keep families from breaking apart.

His book sold 100,000 copies its first six months in print, and was published in seventeen countries.

1975: Endometrial-Cancer Risks of Unopposed Estrogens Revealed

As more and more doctors began to prescribe Premarin, they and their patients discovered that it did get rid of hot flashes and some other adverse symptoms of the change of life.

In the Summer 2004 issue of the online magazine *Dissent,* writer Carl Elliot tells us that women were thrilled with the effects of estrogen therapy. Many who had read Dr. Wilson's book insisted that their physicians prescribe it. And men seemed pretty pleased in the bargain:

> "Men were happy, too. In fact, the pharmaceutical industry often advertised estrogen to doctors in a way that emphasized its benefits for men. 'Menrium treats the menopausal symptoms that bother him the most,' said the advertisements from Roche. Ayerst ran ads with the tag line, 'He is suffering from menopause because of her.' Because menopause was thought to be associated with depression and anxiety, some pharmaceutical companies bundled estrogen into a single pill alongside a minor tranquilizer. Wallace Laboratories marketed Milprem, a combination of estrogen and Miltown, while Roche produced a combination of estrogen and Librium."

Word spread, and by the early 1970s, when I was in medical school, it had become the standard to treat menopausal symptoms with whatever oral dose of Premarin it took to reduce a woman's hot flashes. Certainly, there was some concern about long-range consequences of such therapy, but at the time little restraint was exercised. The therapy's benefit seemed to outweigh whatever risks there might be...until 1975, when a series of studies revealed a many-fold increase in the risk of endometrial (uterine) cancer in women who had taken estrogen replacement therapy. This risk was estimated at between four and fifteen times that of a woman who did not use estrogens postmenopausally.

It turned out that a relationship between Premarin and endometrial cancer had been suspected for some time. Several investigators had been quietly studying the effect of using a synthetic progestin, Provera, with Premarin to see if its progestational effect would protect the lining of the uterus from cancerous changes. Sure enough, it did, and virtually every possible regimen that could be devised showed an equal degree of safety. Instead of crashing and burning forever as a result of the endometrial-cancer scandal, Premarin rose from the ashes with the help of the synthetic progestins.

From that point forward, every woman with a uterus got two prescriptions—an estrogen plus a progestin—instead of one. From 1975 through 1995, several competing products were introduced that contained different estrogens and progestins. All these hormone drugs were proprietary, patented chemicals. In this twenty-year window, drug companies spent millions upon millions of dollars funding research. Their goal was to provide an unbreakable case in favor of HRT's benefits for bone, bowel, brain, heart, and reproductive health. Many studies even attempted to frame these HRT drugs as cancer preventives.

1995—Prempro is Introduced

In 1995, after the FDA gave approval for Wyeth to combine Premarin and Provera in a single pill, Prempro and Premphase came to the market. This made the HRT drugs easier for women to take and doctors to prescribe. Shortly thereafter, other companies received approval for their combination of estrogen and proprietary progestin. It wasn't long before doctors and patients could choose from more than twenty different options for traditional HRT, many of which contained hormones that were a far cry from the body's natural forms of estrogen and progesterone.

Over the years, scattered reports of increased incidence of breast cancer in women who took HRT had surfaced. Drug companies were at the ready with their studies revealing no increased risk, and occasionally they were even able to come up with a study showing a *decreased* risk of breast cancer with pharmaceutical HRT.

They had me convinced. I was right up there with the others, prescribing Prempro and Premphase and other HRT drugs left and right, until later in 1995.

1995: Nurses' Health Study Shows 41-Percent Increased Risk of Breast Cancer with Conventional HRT

In 1995, the landmark Nurses' Health Study, involving over 40,000 nurses, was published. This study revealed a 41-percent increase in the risk of breast cancer in women who took HRT for more than ten years.

This was pretty big stuff, and it was at that juncture I began to change my thinking about HRT. Of course, the drug companies were quick to point out that this study, albeit large, was uncontrolled and retrospective, so you really could not draw any solid conclusions from it.

Terms Used in Studies

1. Uncontrolled means there was no control group that did not take hormones. Comparing a group using a drug to a group not using that drug better clarifies the effects of that drug.
2. Retrospective refers to a study that looks back in time, using the medical records of study subjects, rather than following subjects' progress in real time during the course of the study.
3. A placebo-controlled study includes a control group, which is given a placebo instead of the drug being tested.

Their campaign seemed to work, at least on most physicians. I didn't see a lot of doctors changing their prescribing habits. Still, a lot of women who stayed informed about breaking health news began to question the safety of traditional HRT. They wondered whether the line that the benefits really did outweigh the risks was just that—a line designed to get them to buy into long-term use of a drug that might actually be harming them.

At that point in my own medical practice, I started looking for other HRT options. I discovered bio-identical hormones, and as soon as I understood how they worked and how they were safe, I moved in that direction. I will forever be thankful I saw the light when I did. I only wish I 'd seen it earlier.

1995–2002—The Salad Days of Premarin/Progestin HRT

Before 2002, the few studies that demonstrated no cardiovascular benefit (prevention of heart disease and strokes) with HRT were written off as biased. Some studies were said to have enrolled an inordinately high percentage of smokers; others were disregarded because they used high doses of hormones instead of the much lower doses generally used in hormone pills for post-menopausal women.

The overwhelming force of scientific opinion was still that Premarin/progestin HRT was safe and effective preventive medicine against heart disease and osteoporosis.

One series of studies, the Postmenopausal Estrogen-Progestin Interventions (PEPI) Trial, involved 875 healthy women ages forty-five to sixty-five. PEPI yielded a lot of promising information about the effects of estrogens and progestins on heart and bone health. Overall, the evidence from these studies showed that estrogen replacement (ERT) raised the good cholesterol (HDL), lowered the bad cholesterol (LDL), reduced the constriction of blood vessels, and decreased fibrinogen (a clotting factor—high levels make blood stickier and more likely to clot, blocking blood flow). Early studies of large groups of women found a reduced risk of heart disease in women who took ERT compared to those who did not; other research looked promising in terms of the use of ERT to prevent second heart attacks in women who had already had one.

One thirty-six-month evaluation found that women who took placebo instead of hormones lost an average of 1.8 percent of their spinal bone density and 1.7 of their hip bone density, while women on estrogens or estrogens plus progestins had a 3.5–5-percent increase in spine bone density and an average 1.7-percent increase in hip bone density. Pretty compelling evidence for HRT as prevention of a leading cause of debility in older women.

The number of subjects participating in some of the pro-HRT studies was quite large, numbering in the tens of thousands. The results and conclusions drawn from those studies were convincing to the medical community.

Why Does Having More Subjects Make A Study More Reliable?

Imagine flipping a coin ten times; you might expect roughly half heads and half tails, but you wouldn't think much of it if you got eight of one and two of the other. That's just chance. But if you flip the coin 100 times, you're far more likely to get a more exact 50/50 split of heads and tails; if you don't, you might start thinking some other influence could be at play. If you flip the coin 1,000 times, you're even more apt to end up with a 50/50 split; even more so with 10,000 or 100,000 times, and on and on. So, the more subjects in the study, the less likely it is that the results are due to chance, and the more reliable its results are.

Overall, the future of HRT for the prevention of heart disease in menopausal women—the number-one cause of death in this population—looked rosy indeed. Most studies found that the risk of heart disease was either dramatically reduced or unchanged by female hormone replacement therapy. The heart-protective effects seemed most pronounced in women on estrogens only (who didn't have a uterus), but Prempro looked like a safe bet, too. Some researchers piped up with concerns that progestins might counter estrogen's benefits to the heart, but the tide of combined HRT's popularity drowned out their voices. And so, in spite of growing evidence that progestins *would* cancel out the heart-protective effects of estrogen, and without adequate counter-evidence that they wouldn't, doctors kept on prescribing Prempro and other HRT regimens to millions of women.

The benefits of HRT were found to extend far beyond heart protection. Estrogen was, according to the thrust of most research on the subject, believed to prevent and help to manage:

1. Alzheimer's disease
2. Colon cancer
3. Postmenopausal osteoporosis
4. Short-term menopausal complaints, such as hot flashes and night sweats
5. Skin aging
6. Urogenital atrophy (vaginal dryness)

These benefits were all attributed to the estrogen component of HRT; progestins' only purpose in the mix was to protect the endometrium.

At this point, the American Heart Association (AHA) and almost every other governing body in medicine agreed with the recommendation of taking postmenopausal HRT to protect the bones, brain, colon, and heart. No small wonder that by 2002, some 22 million American women were on HRT.

2002—Concerns about Heart Disease and Breast Cancer Risk with HRT Gain Momentum

In January, 2002, the so-called HERS (Heart and Estrogen/Progestin Replacement) study was published. It was a prospective, placebo-controlled study of Prempro versus placebo in women started on the drug or a placebo following a heart attack. The women on Prempro had a twofold increased chance over the placebo of having a second heart attack within the first year of therapy. This finding caused the AHA to withdraw their endorsement of HRT for prevention of heart disease in postmenopausal women.

All this leads us up to July 2002, when the Women's Health Initiative (WHI) Study results hit the presses. These results, and the media's hyped-up reporting of them, would almost totally overhaul the public's perception of HRT. It made the drugs' benefits look far less worth the risks—more risk of breast cancer, and more risk of cardiovascular disease—the kinds of diseases the drugs were supposed to protect against.

I do not intend to promote the use of horse estrogens and progestins. I did say, in the Four Tenets of women's HRT in the Introduction, that *even Prempro and similar drugs do have some benefits*—but those benefits are not worth the risks found with these drugs, in light of the safe alternatives described in this book. In this and the next chapter, my aim is to clear the air about what the studies really mean, and how their meaning impacts what I recommend. I will make it clear to you that the difference between bio-identical estrogens and progesterone and Prempro is as big as the difference between night and day—no matter how often others lump them all together as *hormone replacement therapy*.

4

The Women's Health Initiative

"Hype Fomenting Hysteria"

...[t]he report by the WHI investigators was preempted by a press conference that prejudged the meaning of the data for patients and physicians. Media reports glossed over the protection offered by HT [hormone therapy] against osteoporosis, colon cancer, and mortality in users versus controls to emphasize the risks of breast cancer and cardiovascular disease (CVD). It was a classic case of hype fomenting hysteria.

Don Gambrell, M.D.

On July 9, 2002, the Women's Health Initiative (WHI) Study was halted prematurely. It was supposed to last until 2005, but after a little over five years, some unacceptable risks had surfaced that could not be ignored. This huge, National Institutes of Health-sponsored study had followed all the rules dictating the ideal scientific evaluation of a drug's safety and effectiveness.

The 16,000 or so women in that study who had been given the hormone replacement drug Prempro—a combination of conjugated estrogens from horse urine (Premarin) and a synthetic progestin (Provera)—received a letter from the study's organizers saying they should stop taking the study medication because a significant increase in the risk of breast cancer had been found in women on the drug. After 5.2 years, there was a 26-percent increased incidence of breast cancer in the group on Prempro over the placebo group.

There was also a significant increase in the incidence of cardiovascular disease (heart attacks, strokes, and deep vein thrombosis) in the women taking Prempro. This was a real shocker because most women who had chosen to use this form of HRT had been told it would protect them against cardiovascular disease.

As in most of the previous studies, there were some benefits with HRT, including a reduced risk of colon cancer and hip fracture. But the breast cancer and cardiovascular issues overshadowed these benefits. Women on Prempro were judged to have a 1.26-fold relative increase in risk, which amounts to eight additional cases of invasive breast cancer per 10,000 women using the medicine. The increase in heart-attack risk was a little less dramatic—an additional seven episodes for every 10,000 women on the drug.

Relative Risk

The relative risk of developing a disease, for people using a medication (such as Prempro), can be figured out by first looking at the overall incidence of the disease in the population, and then looking at the incidence of the disease in the people who used the medication. Dividing one of the rates by the other yields something called a *risk ratio*—a measure of relative risk.

To illustrate: Take a disease that has a normal occurrence of 50 cases per 100,000 people in the general population. If 65 people per 100,000 people using a particular drug are found to have this disease, divide 65 by 50 and get a relative risk of 1.3. That's a 30 percent increased risk of that disease in people taking the drug.

If the incidence of the disease is *lower* in those on the drug than in the general population—if, for example, the trends were reversed, with 65 per 100,000 in the general population having the disease, and 50 per 100,000 of those using the drug having the disease—the relative risk is .77, or about a 23 percent *decreased* risk.

The increases in breast cancer and heart-attack risk with Prempro are not very substantial compared to the significance of the smoking-lung cancer link: a woman who smokes has twelve times the risk of lung cancer compared to one who does not smoke—a 12-fold increase. Women who took unopposed estrogens before the 1980s had a similarly huge increase in their risk of endometrial cancer, between four and fifteen times the risk compared to women with intact uteruses who did not take unopposed estrogens. The increases in breast cancer and heart-disease risk with Prempro don't even come close to this magnitude. Still, it is unacceptable, particularly if you are one of those unlucky fifteen who might not have gotten these diseases if you had not used these drugs.

Putting the WHI Into Perspective

Aproximately half of the women in the United States who were using HRT stopped cold turkey in 2002, and they did so regardless of which type they were taking. (More than a dozen pharmaceutical HRT preparations are available.) The phone of every OB/GYN physician in the country was tied up for days, even weeks, as women demanded to know how this could have happened.

Wyeth, the maker of Prempro, wasn't too happy either, and neither were its stockholders. The stock's price fell by more than one-third soon after the study was halted and the story hit the papers.

WHI was probably the biggest medical news of that year. And, as the media likes to do, they really played up the gloom and doom, obscuring important truths in the process. How can a drug seem so wonderful one day and so horrible the next? Why is it so hard to get the straight story from the media, whose very purpose is to inform us about issues important to our health and well-being?

The WHI story is an excellent path towards answering these questions. I want you to understand what went wrong with the WHI and how people can learn to trust HRT again as long as it's *bio-identical* and *physiologic*.

As the hype and hysteria raged over the Prempro arm of the WHI, another arm of the study, known as WHI-2, continued. Its outcome would prove to be quite different.

WHI-2—Estrogen-Only HRT Does Not Increase Breast Cancer Risk

The WHI-2 arm of the study that continued after the Prempro arm of the WHI was halted involved 10,000 women who were given estrogen but not progestins, which they were judged not to need because their uteruses had been removed. This arm of the study was discontinued after 6.8 years of treatment.

Corroborating some forty other studies on estrogen only, WHI-2 found no increased incidence of breast cancer. In fact, there was a slight *decrease* in breast cancer incidence in the women on estrogen only. No increase in heart attacks or strokes was found; but, consistent with almost all other studies on oral estrogen, there was a significant increase in the incidence of *deep vein thrombosis* (DVT, a type of abnormal blood clotting in veins).

The difference between WHI-1, stopped in 2002 because of excess breast cancer cases in women on Prempro vs. women on placebo, and WHI-2, where women took only Premarin with no progestin, was the *progestin*. The women who got only estrogens did not have an increased incidence of heart disease or strokes, and the risk of breast cancer did not rise. Although the WHI-2 results don't help women who have not had a hysterectomy, they give a figurative slap upside the head about the role of progestins and oral estrogens in the risks and benefits of pharmaceutical HRT.

Studies variously show that in postmenopausal women, estrogen replacement—when administered in the appropriate way, a subject I'll get to later—either does not raise the risk of heart disease, or it actively helps to lower that risk. *But progestins* (not progesterone, but progestins—horses of quite different colors), *are known to have adverse effects on cardiovascular health.* When you add progestins in, you can negate health-promoting effects for the heart that might otherwise come from ERT (estrogen replacement therapy).

And when you give estrogen orally instead of with a cream, a patch, or another mode that bypasses the digestive system, you further offset some of estrogen's potential benefits to cardiovascular health.

As the WHI-2 results were revealed, the media continued to cloud the issue. On Valentine's Day, 2006, an article entitled "Final Estrogen Report Finds No Heart Disease Benefit" appeared in *USA Today*. On the very same day, the *Wall St. Journal's* headline read, "Estrogen's Heart Benefits Gain Support." Both articles concerned the same analysis of the estrogen-only arm of the WHI study that was published in the *Archives of Internal Medicine*. Reading the conflicting conclusions of these articles doesn't help to clarify the issues, much less help you decide what to do for your own health.

The Conclusions of the WHI Writing Group—If a Tree Falls in the Forest...

You know that old question: If a tree falls in the forest and no one is there to hear it, does it make a sound? Similarly, if the authors of an $800 million study on hormone replacement therapy conclude that bio-identical hormones might well be the safe alternative to Prempro, but no one reports that in the media, was such a conclusion really arrived at?

Of course. I've got it in writing. Here's what the WHI writing group (the people conducting the study and reporting on its findings) said in the concluding remarks of their published study: ***"It remains possible that [the use of] transdermal estradiol with progesterone, which most closely mimics the normal physiology and metabolism of endogenous sex hormones, may provide a different risk/benefit profile."***

In the context of this report, and knowing the widespread implications it would have on women taking HRT, it would appear that the WHI writing group *was making a pitch for women to consider using bio-identical HRT.* Unfortunately, this conclusion was never publicized. It was essentially buried beneath the mound of hype and hysteria heaped on all HRT because of the shortcomings of Prempro.

On September 18, 2002, two months after the first WHI study was reported, the Women's Health Advisory Board, composed of six of the leading reproductive endocrinologists in the world, sent a letter to every doctor in the United States who prescribes hormones. The letter pleaded with us to ***stop Premarin and Prempro and start using transdermal estradiol and individualize the therapy, because of the obvious risk differences.***

When I talk to physicians about BHRT, I love to quote these two references because I think they are the most compelling arguments for the use of bio-identical hormones. In fact, I don't think I can define BHRT any better than the authors of the WHI report defined it in their conclusion: ***"...transdermal estradiol with progesterone...which most closely mimics the normal physiology and metabolism of endogenous sex hormones."***

This is exactly the kind of BHRT regimen this book is addressing.

If You're Convinced that BHRT May Be for You...

...You may want to skip over the rest of this chapter, or just skim it, and move on to the chapters on specific hormones.

If you aren't yet convinced of the safety of BHRT—if the media hype and hysteria have got you flustered enough to need further convincing—I invite you to explore the rest of this chapter in depth.

What's in the rest of this chapter? It's evidence from scientific research studies that further cement the case for BHRT and the glaring differences between it and conventional HRT. It addresses the specific flaws of the Women's Health Initiative, showing you in simple, clear detail the reasons why so many people—M.D.s included—have come to a huge misunderstanding about hormone replacement therapy.

If you decide to show this book to your doctor, the next few pages may be the most important for him or her to read.

Understanding WHI's Flaws

Before the WHI, plenty of evidence had already shown a link between combined estrogen/progestin HRT and breast cancer, and a link between this form of HRT and heart disease. Those links weren't well-publicized because the evidence seemed contradictory until the WHI study. Besides, the drug companies had too much at stake for this information to be spelled out clearly to the world at large—until an enormous, well-publicized study made the truth impossible to ignore.

The WHI study was the most expensive, well-designed, informative study ever done on women and hormones. Unfortunately, as with any scientific study, it has some important flaws that explain why such different interpretations are not only possible, but probable.

For now, I want to look at how flaws in the WHI affected the relationship between heart disease and HRT. Later on, I will address the issue of HRT and breast cancer in great detail

Flaw One—Non-Bio-Identical Hormones

The HRT used in the WHI study was a combination pill containing Premarin (conjugated equine estrogens) and Provera (medroxyprogesterone acetate, also known as MPA), a synthetic progestin. *Using these non-bio-identical hormones instead of bio-identical versions is like trying to unlock a door with a key that doesn't quite fit.* You can get the key into the lock, and maybe turn it a little, and if you jimmy it around enough, it might get the door open, but the job would be a lot easier if you used the key that was actually designed to open the door. Plus, using the wrong key over and over again can eventually damage the lock.

Flaw Two—Oral Estrogens Increase Clotting Factors

Remember the Second Tenet of female HRT? *Any estrogen*

taken by mouth engenders some increased cardiovascular risk (that is, risk of blood-clot formation, heart attacks, and strokes). Estrogen therapy that is not delivered by mouth—that is absorbed into the body through the skin, for example—does not carry these same risks.

The route taken to administer estrogen can make an enormous difference in both its safety and its effectiveness. When you swallow estrogen in a pill, its benefits and risks may be altogether different from those achieved by administering it through the skin (transdermally), under the tongue (sub-lingually), or with a pellet (subcutaneously). These latter routes of administration are more physiological—a closer approximation to the way the body's own hormones are delivered—than oral administration.

As researchers have explored this issue, a definite cardiovascular benefit of estrogen (when unaccompanied by progestins) has been established. But the route of administration makes a substantial difference—*if you give estrogen orally, you can end up increasing the risk of cardiovascular disease*. In the WHI study, both Premarin and Provera were administered orally, through a pill. In fact, most of the studies on combined HRT have used this method of administration.

Administering estrogen orally makes a big difference in its effect on the cardiovascular system because of the way it is processed in the liver. Had the WHI study been conducted with some type of transdermal estradiol, odds are strong that the effects on cardiovascular health would have been different. And, in their concluding words, the authors of the report stated this clearly.

Here's the problem. Once swallowed, oral estrogen is broken down in the gut and absorbed. From there, it is sent through the liver, the organ responsible for detoxifying whatever is consumed before it is distributed throughout the body in the circulatory system. There, in the liver, the estrogens stimulate the production of both an inflammation factor called *C-reactive protein* (CRP) and clotting factors that cause blood to clot more easily. And both CRP and clotting factors reflect a rise in the risks of heart attacks and strokes—currently, elevated CRP is believed to be as important a risk factor in this regard as high LDL and low HDL cholesterol.

Investigators at the University of Texas' Southwestern Medical Center mounted a study to determine whether transdermal estradiol would raise CRP levels the way that oral estrogens do. They enrolled twenty-one postmenopausal women—some got transdermal estradiol (100 micrograms), some got oral estrogens (0.625 mg, a much higher dose, necessary because the first-pass effect—the way in which the hormone is altered as it is processed by the liver—alters a large proportion of each dose before it can have its intended actions in the body), and some got a placebo. The women on transdermal estradiol had no change in their CRP levels; those on oral estrogens had a more than twofold increase in the levels of this inflammation marker. Levels of *insulin-like growth factor-1,* IGF-1, were also measured in this study; IGF-1 is a growth factor that counters harmful inflammation. Transdermal estrogens did not affect it, but oral estrogens caused IGF-1 to fall significantly. Two additional studies, to be completed in 2009 and 2010, are underway to demonstrate this important difference between oral and transdermal estrogen replacement therapy. Bottom line: transdermal estrogens, delivered through the skin, do not increase CRP.

Delivery of estrogens through or beneath the skin bypasses the liver, just as the body's naturally produced hormones do. *A woman's ovary* ***never*** *secretes estrogen into the stomach*; it is secreted into the bloodstream, just as it is with transdermal estrogen replacement.

Today, transdermal estrogens are increasingly popular, and ongoing studies of these estrogen-delivery systems will likely find they do not increase the risk of heart disease.

Flaw Three—It's the Progestins, Stupid

Now, let's harken back to the Third Tenet of women's HRT. *Progestins, the synthetic version of progesterone that is found in Prempro, significantly increase cardiovascular risk and the risk of breast cancer. Progesterone, the hormone that is made in the body and that is found in bio-identical hormone replacement therapy, does not increase the risk of either. It may even decrease the risk of both.*

Before the WHI study came out in 2002, it was just about

impossible to find any kind of consensus statement from the experts as to whether any of the benefits that had been clearly established for postmenopausal *estrogen* replacement therapy (ERT) (which, let's remember, is only safe for women who have had a hysterectomy) still apply *once progestins are added to the mix.*

It is generally felt that a woman with a uterus cannot safely use ERT alone, and most menopausal women have uteruses. The question of whether progestins were harmful to the heart (and breasts) needed to be answered in order to determine the safety of progestin + estrogen HRT. But this issue of whether adding progestin to ERT was safe for the heart (and breasts) failed to be clarified *before* it was prescribed to millions of women, and once this drug had been unleashed on the unsuspecting public, the drug companies became very reluctant to address this issue directly. Without progestins, most of their multi-billion dollar market for HRT would disappear.

Also, consider that oral contraceptives, a huge source of revenue for drug makers, contain progestins. Some women take these drugs for years, or even for the majority of their reproductive lives. To admit that progestins are dangerous would put drug companies at major risk of huge liabilities. They weren't in any hurry to explore this issue, but, parenthetically, research does show that long-term use of oral contraceptives raises the risk of liver and breast cancers. In 2006, findings from the WHI revealed that women who had used oral contraceptives had an increase in breast cancer risk. But this is not something you'll hear discussed in the media, because oral contraceptives are such an important birth-control measure.

So, progestins have been promoted as the primary option for postmenopausal HRT in any woman with an intact uterus. Physicians and the media talk about progestins as though they are progesterone, which they decidedly are *not.*

As of now, the media has yet to provide any clarity about whether the progestins are the real issue. Only if you read carefully between the lines will you come to the conclusion that progestins are the evil stepsister to bio-identical estrogens and progesterone.

Oral estrogens are associated with a two- to three-fold increased risk of *thromboembolism*—where blood thickens and clots, potentially lodging in a vein (deep vein thrombosis) and causing major problems. It also appears that progestins may make a significant contribution to this side effect of Premarin-plus-progestin HRT: In a study published in the *Archives of Internal Medicine* in 2006, the effect of oral estrogens plus progestins on clotting were evaluated in women who had had their uteruses removed. The investigators found a much higher risk of thromboembolism and deep vein thrombosis in women who were on oral estrogens plus progestin than in women who used only oral estrogen.

I'm not sure how it could get much clearer.

Estrogen, Progestins, and the Heart in a Nutshell

Positive (+): Estrogens reduce bad LDL cholesterol and fibrinogen (a clotting factor that can make blood excessively sticky).

Negative (-): Progestins oppose estrogens' reduction of LDL and the anti-clotting effect.

Negative (-): The first-pass effect in the liver increases C-reactive protein (CRP) and clotting factors.

(-1) + (-1) + (+1) = (-1), the result, as learned in elementary school.

When estrogens are administered through routes that bypass the liver (through the skin, intravaginally, by injection, or subcutaneously), *you remove one of the negatives*. You then have zero: neither a benefit nor a detriment to the cardiovascular system. If you then remove the progestins and add in natural progesterone (which is believed to benefit the heart—more on this later), along with non-oral, bio-identical estrogen, you end up with two positives in favor of HRT for heart health.

Flaw Four—They Didn't Start 'Em Young

The average age of the women enrolled in the WHI study was sixty-two. Most of them had been menopausal for ten or more years, with none of the potential heart-health benefits of HRT, those same benefits that had been demonstrated in most studies for decades before the ax fell.

Many changes in blood-vessel health, including silent inflammation, rising blood lipids (total and LDL cholesterol), and thickened blood-vessel walls, had silently progressed during the ten-year gap these WHI subjects had between menopause and starting on HRT in the study.

How Old is Too Old for BHRT?

The WHI enrolled women who were already in their sixties. This leads to the question: Can a woman in her sixties, or beyond, benefit from bio-identical HRT?

Women ten years or more past menopause should probably stay away from oral estrogens. But with non-oral estrogens, no increase in cardiovascular risk has been found, even in older women. I have patients over eighty, male and female, who are doing wonderfully on bio-identical hormone replacement.

Because of the enormous cost, there will probably never be another study of WHI's magnitude. To assume, however, because of those findings, that *all* forms of estrogen increase cardiovascular disease, breast cancer risk, and the risk of dementia, is a terrible travesty. Unfortunately, that's the message a large number of physicians and their patients have heard loud and clear, and that's the message they're left with.

Bio-identical hormone therapy, appropriately used, will keep you young longer. It will protect you against the painful, debilitating, and deadly diseases that affect many as they age. Do *you* want to wait five to ten years for someone to get the funds together to perform that BHRT study, and another five to ten years to get the results?

I don't want you to, either. Read on.

5

Mighty, Menopausal, and Marvelous

Estrogen Replacement for Women

A note to readers: This chapter and the next three are devoted to female HRT; the two chapters after that, to male HRT. Some women might want to read about male HRT to help a male friend, family member, or companion; some men might want to read about female HRT to do the same for a loved one or friend. But keep in mind that you don't have to read the chapters for the other gender; the sections for each gender stand on their own.

Vera's Power Surges

In the summertime, we keep my patient consultation room around 70–72 degrees, and cooler than that in the wintertime. It's not because I like paying for air conditioning, or even because I like to wear extra clothing. It's because of the most common adverse symptom of estrogen deficiency: vasomotor instability, more commonly known as hot flashes.

Vasomotor

Relating to the nerves and muscles that cause blood vessels to constrict or dilate. Vasomotor symptoms in menopause—hot flashes and night sweats—are caused by hormonal changes that affect vasomotor function.

Vera is a fifty-one-year-old power company executive who had been experiencing hot flashes, mood changes, and night sweats off and on for about two years when I first saw her. On three or four occasions during our thirty-minute new-patient consultation, she pulled some papers from her pocketbook and fanned herself for a few minutes. She said she had finally decided it was imperative to do something about the hot-flash problem when she was making a presentation at work to a group of high-ranking executives. During her forty-five-minute presentation, she had five episodes of feeling as though her face was on fire and sweating through her clothes, in spite of it being a cold winter day.

She had also been losing sleep for several months because every night she would awaken hot and soaking wet, and changing her nightgown at 3:00 AM every night was getting old. When I questioned Vera further, I found she also had a majority of the other symptoms of hormone deficiency, including brain fog, decreased libido, difficulty reaching orgasm, irritability, moodiness, vaginal dryness, and weight gain.

When her hormone assays revealed low levels of estrogen, progesterone, and testosterone, I started her on a regimen of balanced hormone replacement therapy. Within thirty-six hours, her hot flashes, irritability, and night sweats were gone. Vera relates that she and her husband are more sexually active and happier together now than in many years. She was recently given a big promotion at work, and I dare say she's a whole lot cooler during presentations.

In my practice, I consistently find that, as with Vera, women on BHRT experience better sleep, positive changes in hair and skin, more stable mood, improved cognition (memory and concentration), disappearance of brain fog, and more capable decision-making. Every day at work, I hear women on balanced hormone replacement therapy telling me, "I have not slept this well in twenty years," or, "I have never felt better in my life that I can remember."

Although progesterone plays a major role in this improved well-being, estrogens have the most research and practical use behind them as a mainstay of female HRT after menopause.

Before getting into the details of how bio-identical estrogen replacement can help you thrive through and beyond menopause, I want to talk about the workings of your reproductive hormones in your childbearing years, during which you are most likely to enjoy good health and protection against age-related conditions. Consider this is our instruction book for using BHRT to create *The Youth Effect* during and after menopause.

Your Hormones Before Menopause

Within the ovaries of a grown woman sit some several thousand immature eggs, known as follicles, which have been there since only a few short months after she herself was conceived. There are two types of cells in these follicles—*granulosa cells* and *theca cells*—both of which produce hormones in response to stimulation by the follicle-stimulating hormone (FSH).

Early in the menstrual cycle, during the *follicular* phase, FSH increases, leading to greater production of estradiol by the ovary. Estradiol promotes the preparation of the thick uterine lining for the possible implantation of an embryo, and alters cervical mucus in a way that optimizes chances for fertilization.

Luteinizing hormone (LH) stimulates theca cells to produce the *androgens* androstenedione *(an-dro-steen-die-ohn)* and testosterone. Although scientific consensus has yet to be reached about the role of androgens in the menstrual cycle, it is probable that they help reproduction along by enhancing the woman's libido, and they are converted into estrogens by enzymes, helping to further prepare the uterus for possible conception.

In this phase, one follicle is transformed into a mature *oocyte* (egg cell). In the middle of the cycle, a surge in LH causes this ripened follicle to rupture, beginning the luteal phase of the cycle. This is the part of the cycle where progesterone levels are high. Usually, this phase of the cycle is accompanied by a surge in a woman's libido and overall mood.

When the follicle ruptures at ovulation, the egg is released into the fallopian tube, the end of which has been pulled just a little closer to the ovary by a specialized muscle. Nature's goal is to first get that egg through the end of that tube, and then for the egg to drift down towards the uterus while awaiting the arrival of a few million gamely swimming sperm. After ovulation, the empty follicle then becomes the corpus luteum. This tiny remnant of ovulation is responsible for producing progesterone while that egg makes its way to the uterus.

Corpus Luteum

This is the empty ovarian follicle that has just released an egg into the fallopian tube—and the magical spot where ovarian progesterone is made.

If one of those little swimmers hits the fertilization jackpot, the corpus luteum will continue to mature and produce progesterone through the first three or so months of the pregnancy, at which point the placenta takes over the job, producing many times more progesterone than is ever produced by a woman's body in a non-pregnant state. If pregnancy occurs but the corpus luteum fails to make enough progesterone to maintain the pregnancy, this *luteal failure* is likely to lead to a miscarriage.

If pregnancy does not occur, the corpus luteum degenerates, leading to declining levels of progesterone. Once progesterone drops below a specific threshold, the menstrual period begins, and estrogen, progesterone, and androgens are at their lowest ebb—then the cycle starts again. A normal cycle can last anywhere from twenty-five to thirty-four days.

Perimenopause and Menopause

As menopause approaches, these cyclic changes in FSH and

LH continue, just as they have since *menarche* (a woman's first menstrual period). But during the menopausal transition, the ovaries fail to respond to the FSH/LH signals. They stop producing adequate amounts of estradiol for follicular development. In essence, the thermostat keeps telling the heat pump to do its thing, but the connection is lost, the feedback loop is broken. The FSH/LH thermostat keeps cranking away, amping up its message to the ovaries: "Come on, you can do it. Get cracking on those hormones. The rest of the body is counting on you." This increasingly desperate shout-out and the ovaries' failure to respond are the factors believed to cause hot flashes and night sweats.

FSH/LH levels can become quite high during the years preceding menopause as the hypothalamus and pituitary continue to try to cajole the ovary into producing the reproductive hormones. To some degree, a measurement of FSH levels can be used to determine where a woman is in the menopausal transition, and to see how well replacing her hormones during that transitional phase, when FSH and LH rise higher and higher, is going. FSH and LH can fluctuate fairly widely from one cycle to another during the transition.

In the several years before your periods cease altogether, you may experience something commonly known as *perimenopause*. During perimenopause, ovarian function is winding down, and symptoms usually arise as hormone levels wane or fluctuate wildly. You may find yourself feeling downright rotten a lot of the time; if you are, your body is sending you a message that something is out of balance, and that thing is most likely your hormones. For several years prior to menopause, some women's periods may be quite irregular and may become extremely heavy and uncomfortable.

If you are still in your mid-to-late thirties or early forties, the years well before your periods are likely to stop, you may be wondering what on earth is happening to your body. There is weight gain, bloating, heavy periods, maybe fibroids or worsening cramps, menstrual migraines, skin aging fast, no libido...aren't you too young to have to start thinking about menopause? Maybe not. Maybe the changes you are experiencing *are* due to hormone imbalances, but not the same imbalances experienced by a woman who has not menstruated for a year and is officially menopausal.

By definition, menopause is the complete cessation of periods for one year. Once you have reached that point, your body's production of progesterone is almost zero, and your body's production of the estrogens, which can still be made in fat cells, is well below its levels in the premenopausal years. Again, this is a totally natural transition, but it can spur some undesirable changes in your health. Replacing these estrogens can help prevent or delay those changes.

Perimenopausal Women May Not Need ERT, But They Often Need Progesterone

A woman who is in perimenopause, which can begin as her fertility wanes in her thirties and her hormone balance changes, is less likely to have low estrogen levels unless she has had an oophorectomy (removal of the ovaries only). Many perimenopausal women have anovulatory cycles, where plenty of estrogen is produced and a nice thick endometrial lining is built up, but no ovulation takes place and no progesterone is produced. These women will definitely *not* benefit from additional estrogens; what they need is progesterone (*see* Chapter 6).

Heather's Happy Family

When she turned up in my office, Heather was thirty-five and a busy mother of three boys (two of them were five-year-old twins). Her mother, a menopausal patient of mine, felt that Heather had some sort of hormonal imbalance, which had led her to being quite depressed and, at times, irrational, and encouraged her to come and see me.

Prior to having children, Heather had been a successful lawyer who seemed able to juggle all of her responsibilities with ease. After having children, she stopped working at her law firm and gradually seemed to lose her edge. She believed she had everything she wanted, but couldn't shake a growing sense of unhappiness with her life and with the people around her.

Her distress was serious enough to persuade her to seek psychological counseling. By the time she came to see me, she had been put on three different antidepressants. While they all seemed to help to some degree for a period of time, she never seemed to be the happy, "with-it" person everyone knew before. When I first saw Heather, she was on Lexapro and taking Ambien to help her sleep at night. Her libido had bottomed out completely; she had gained forty pounds since her pre-pregnancy days; and her periods were longer, heavier, and not as regular. The antidepressants were, in all likelihood, worsening her symptoms—particularly, her decreased libido.

Her lab work revealed that she had low levels of both progesterone and testosterone. This combination is not unusual in women her age with her constellation of symptoms. I decided to try Heather on a progesterone cream, which she used twice a day for fifteen days of each month, plus a low dose of sublingual testosterone. Six weeks later, after re-checking blood levels of her hormones and determining that her progesterone and testosterone levels were optimal, I started weaning her off the Lexapro and Ambien.

Heather now takes no antidepressants or sleep medications. She's feeling more like her old self, and her periods are lighter and more predictable. Thanks to the combination of bio-identical HRT, renewed self-esteem, and improved diet, she is twenty pounds into losing that forty pounds she wants to shed. Her libido has returned and her sex life is back on track.

I can't tell you that every depressed, moody mother in her mid-thirties is going to benefit from hormone supplementation. I can tell you that it's worth looking into the possibility. Just ask Heather and her happy family.

An Introduction to Estrogen Replacement Therapy (ERT)

As mentioned earlier, estrogen replacement has been around for sixty-plus years. Originally, estrogen replacement therapy's main reason for existence was to relieve vasomotor symptoms (hot flashes, night sweats). Subsequently, the other benefits of ERT were discovered and touted by the therapy's proponents.

Unquestionably, ERT (including Premarin) relieves vasomotor symptoms. This is its primary indication in most medical practices. Adding estrogens back in causes the pituitary's FSH/LH shouts to the ovary to die down, dramatically reducing or eliminating hot flashes and night sweats. The lower your FSH, the less your chance of symptoms. In fact, perhaps the most reliable laboratory test for following the effectiveness of HRT is the FSH level. This level shows us that the feedback loop is back in gear—a great indicator that hormone balance has been achieved.

Although estrogens are essential for fertility and successful pregnancy, the many other roles of estrogen become apparent to women when they become deficient in the hormone at menopause. Most scientific information about estrogen's role in cellular metabolism comes from studies on the changes that occur at that time, and how estrogen replacement can reverse those changes.

Highly reliable studies on the use of estrogen replacement in menopause show that women who use this hormone appropriately live longer, live independently for more of their lives, have better sex and stronger libido, and have better urinary and bowel control.

A premenopausal woman's body makes about 100–200 *micrograms* of estrogen per day, and that amount usually declines by 50–60 percent after menopause.

Benefits of Estrogen Replacement Therapy (ERT)

Overall, life expectancy is an average 3.5 years longer compared with a woman who does not use ERT. In addition, ERT provides the following:

1. Prevention of atrophy in the urogenital tract
2. Relief of vasomotor symptoms
3. Risk for Alzheimer's disease reduced 50 percent
4. Risk for colon cancer reduced 50 percent
5. Risk for coronary heart disease reduced 50 percent
6. Risk for osteoporosis reduced 80 percent
7. Small reduction in risk for arthritis

In my own clinical experience, estrogen's benefits in menopausal women also include better sleep, positive changes in hair and skin, more stable mood, improved thinking ability, memory, and concentration, disappearance of brain fog, more capable decision-making, an end to vaginal dryness and discomfort with intercourse, and a decrease in bladder problems. Loved ones tell me, "She's a *different person,*" or "She's back to being her old self." And, as I stated in the First Tenet of women's HRT, most of these benefits are seen *even with conventional Premarin therapy.*

The Three Graces: Estradiol, Estrone, and Estriol

Three estrogens are produced in the human body:

1. **Estradiol**, the dominant form of this hormone in premenopausal women, produced primarily by the ovary;
2. **Estriol**, generally a bit player, except during pregnancy, when it is the dominant estrogen produced by the placenta; and
3. **Estrone**, the estrogen that becomes dominant following menopause, is made mostly in fat cells through conversion of testosterone (most postmenopausal women do not need additional estrone).

Estradiol is the major player, the most abundant estrogen in the years when a woman is in her physical prime. Generally, a direct correlation exists between a woman's physical well-being and her estradiol levels. In other words, low estradiol usually shows up in a woman who is not in the best of health, and a woman in good or great health is more likely to have estradiol levels within ideal limits.

Hot flashes, night sweats, vaginal dryness, sleep disturbance, weight gain, and mood changes that crop up during the menopausal transition and soon after are a direct result of reduced estradiol activity in the body.

Since almost every cell in your body has receptors for estrogen, progesterone, and testosterone, it's reasonable to expect that a lack of any of these hormones would have some effect on every cell.

Table 5.1

Estrogen Effects in Women

What Doctors Say	Plain English Translation
Proliferation of endometrium	Thickened lining of the uterus
Proliferation of breast cells	Causes breast cells to grow and multiply
Lowers LDL cholesterol	Reduces bad form of cholesterol most strongly linked with heart disease
Reduces intimal thickness of coronary arteries	Helps keep arteries that feed the heart muscle clear
Decreases fibrinogen	Makes blood less sticky and less likely to clot
Positive effect on hair follicles	Lustrous locks less prone to thinning
Positive effect on skin	Reduces wrinkling and other signs of skin aging
Positive effect on colon mucosa	Helps reduce changes in colon lining that are linked with increased colon-cancer risk
Decreased inflammation in brain	Inflammation in the brain is a risk factor for dementia – Alzheimer's and others – so this should decrease your risk of losing mental function with aging
Thickening of vaginal lining	Better sex with less pain

Increase in cervical mucus	Ditto; also supports conception in premenopausal women
Decreased bone loss	Helps bones hang on to minerals that maintain their hardness; helps prevent osteoporosis
Increased tear secretion	Fewer dry-eye complaints
Stabilized vasoconstrictive activity	Helps reduce over-constriction of blood vessels that can occur with stress or other factors; improves blood flow
Stabilizes neurotransmitters in the brain	Reduces mood swings, depression, and anxiety common with menopausal transition
At puberty, development of secondary sex characteristics	Causes growth of pubic hair, breast budding, and uterine development in girls entering puberty
Can increase secretion of other hormones, including thyroid-binding globulin, aldosterone, and prolactin	Promotes balanced production of other important hormones
Driving force behind maturation of egg cells and corpus luteum in ovaries	Helps mature egg cell for ovulation; stimulates the ovaries to make follicles

Estrogen and the Heart

Prior to menopause, women have a significantly lower incidence of heart disease than men at the same age. Within five years after the menopause, women not on HRT have the same incidence of heart disease as men at the same age. What happens at and after menopause that causes this increase?

We know for sure that estradiol, progesterone, and testosterone levels plummet during that time, but, as they say in the world of scientific research, *correlation does not prove causality.*

Two things happening at the same time does not prove that one causes the other.

When it sees a correlation, however, science can investigate further to make a strong case for causality. And scientific studies that directly evaluate the blood vessels and hearts of experimental animals and people, both under the influence of estrogens and without their influence, do show that estrogen has substantial benefits for the cardiovascular system—benefits that help keep heart attacks and other kinds of cardiovascular disease at bay.

For about twenty years, from 1980 to 2000, numerous studies revealed a decreased risk of cardiovascular events with post-menopausal estrogen replacement: heart attacks and strokes, The WHI study did not refute this. In fact, a follow-up analysis of the estrogen-only arm of the study (WHI-2) found that even Premarin provides some significant benefits to the heart. Only in the last three years has doubt been cast on the cardiovascular benefits of ERT.

As discussed in Chapter 4, if estrogen is given orally, it can increase the risk of deep vein thrombosis (clotting); and if progestin is added, it cancels out some important cardiovascular protections offered by estrogens. Using pellets, creams, lozenges, or patches cancels out this risk by putting the estrogens directly into your circulation without their having to be processed by the liver. Using natural progesterone instead of progestins will allow those heart-healthy effects of estrogens to shine through.

How Estrogens Protect the Heart

Estrogens Lower Bad Cholesterol and Raise Good Cholesterol

By now, people have heard this said about many therapies and treatments, but it is still true that adequate estrogen levels lower LDL cholesterol and increase HDL cholesterol. Estrogen has positive effects on the cells that line blood-vessel walls—cells that, when damaged, start a chain reaction that leads to the formation of a *plaque.* Because the vessels that feed the heart muscle have lots of twists and turns, and because the muscle they lie on is in constant motion, they are vulnerable to damage from sheer stress as blood constantly races past them. Those vessels are more likely than others to be damaged and develop plaques.

Estrogen Relaxes and Opens Arteries

Blood vessels also have muscular walls beneath the innermost lining. Those walls contract to raise blood pressure and relax to lower it. Agents that relax blood-vessel walls are good for the heart and cardiovascular system, and estrogen promotes this kind of relaxation. It does so by enhancing *nitric-oxide* production—a substance that has distinct relaxant effects on smooth muscle—in the blood-vessel walls.

Estrogen Improves Blood-Sugar and Insulin Regulation

Increases in both blood sugar and insulin, both characteristic of type 2 diabetes, prediabetes, and (to a lesser extent) aging, wreak havoc on the cardiovascular system.

Prediabetes

This condition is usually linked with overweight or obesity. Body cells become resistant to insulin—the hormone that guides sugars from the bloodstream into the cells—and blood sugar rises. Insulin secretion increases to try and override the resistance. Left untreated (through changes in diet and exercise), this physiological state is likely to lead to diabetes.

Many studies find that HRT has positive effects on insulin and carbohydrate metabolism. Specifically, estrogen replacement therapy decreases fasting insulin and blood-sugar levels. Some studies suggest that certain synthetic estrogens (ethinyl estradiol and mestranol) have the opposite effect of bio-identical estrogens when it comes to blood sugar and insulin levels, possibly increasing the risk of prediabetes and ultimately diabetes.

The mountain of evidence supporting the benefit of pharmaceutical HRT to the cardiovascular system led the American Medical Association, the American Heart Association, the American College of OB/GYN, and other highly respected organizations to wholeheartedly endorse it for the prevention of cardiovascular disease in postmenopausal women. However, in 2001, this support fell apart when the HERS trial found that women who started HRT after having a heart attack had a twofold increased risk over non-users of having a second heart attack within one year. No one was talking about the fact that the *oral* estrogens (and progestins) were probably to blame. Instead, estrogen's benefits were called into serious question.

Inflammation Conflagration

You've probably heard a good deal about inflammation lately if you follow health news. And if you're really well-versed on the subject, you know that C-reactive protein (CRP) is used to measure a type of inflammation that is a threat to heart health. The most up-to-date cardiac profiles now use this measurement, which is considered every bit as accurate a predictor of heart disease as cholesterol levels. And oral estrogens cause CRP to rise.

Inflammation is, most simply, a way in which the immune system works to drive out unwanted agents and set the stage for healing damaged tissues. When you smack your shin bone on the coffee table, it swells, becomes red, and hurts—all these are hallmarks of inflammation. Fluids and blood are attracted to the area by specialized immune cells, which then go to work breaking down tissues damaged in the accident and making way for the rebuilding of new, healthy tissues. An infection in your body has the same effect, whether it's on the surface where you can see it, or inside where it's invisible. A fever is a form of inflammatory response.

Current evidence shows that cardiovascular disease, which includes heart attacks and strokes, is also caused, at least in part, by accelerated inflammation in blood-vessel walls. That inflammation can be measured by an inexpensive, easy-to-perform CRP test. This test is likely to become a standard part of preventive health exams in the near future.

Avoiding agents that cause CRP to rise, including oral estrogens, will help prevent artery inflammation that can predispose you to heart attacks and strokes.

Your Brain...On Estrogen

"Doctor, if I could just get rid of this brain fogginess, I would be forever grateful."

"I just can't remember anything anymore!"

"I'm not as sharp as I used to be."

I hear comments like these every day. They are almost universal among perimenopausal and menopausal women. Really, it's no surprise. From what is known about the positive cognitive effect of estrogens, it makes perfect sense that a decreased hormone effect would cause brain fog to descend.

HRT can help. In fact, most of the helpful effect that HRT has on cognitive function seems to be mediated through estrogen. Testosterone and progesterone seem to have a role as well, which I'll discuss later.

Estrogens are known to increase blood flow in the cerebrum, the thinking part of the brain. They stimulate the growth of connections between brain cells, inhibit the breakdown of neurotransmitters that affect mood and cognitive function (serotonin, dopamine, and norepinephrine), and increase the production of an enzyme in the brain that affects perception and memory.

Numerous studies indicate that estrogen replacement therapy reduces the risk of developing Alzheimer's disease, and that it may also be helpful for improving the mental status of female

Alzheimer's patients. The research suggests that these Alzheimer's-preventive effects are most likely to be achieved in women who start using BHRT right around the time of the menopause—waiting until a person reaches her sixties may reduce these benefits. Other important research that looked at Alzheimer's risk in women found that those women whose brain health seemed to benefit from ERT were the ones who started the therapy well before their sixties.

The Women's Health Initiative Memory Study (WHIMS)

Cognitive-function effects of Premarin and progestin were found in a subgroup of the women who participated in the WHI. Estrogen and estrogen plus progestin seemed to slightly *increase* women's risk of dementia. This didn't make sense in light of many past studies that had shown benefits of estrogen for women's brain function. Here are several relevant points to keep in mind as you consider the risks and benefits of *bio-identical, physiological* HRT on brain function as you age.

1. The women enrolled in WHIMS were sixty-five and up when they started taking HRT. Again, this may be a matter of too little, too late. As people age, blood vessels in the brain can become clogged just like those of the heart, and once this process has begun, there is some danger in adding oral estrogens to the mix.
2. Studies of *endogenous* (made in the body) estrogen levels in aging women find that higher estrogen = better brain function. Introducing bio-identical estrogens into the body of a postmenopausal woman mimics naturally higher levels. This tack is more likely to be beneficial to brain function and protective against dementia than Prempro.

Studies involving both animal and human subjects provide ample evidence that ovarian hormones have a role in brain function. Processes central to the function of the nervous system are affected by the addition of estrogen. Although there are no specific indications for the use of estrogens in the treatment of any neurological disease, there are data indicating estrogen's role in the mediation of such problems as cognitive function, dementia, depression, epilepsy, pain syndromes, Parkinson's disease, and premenstrual syndrome (PMS).

Lifelong Mental Sharpness and Quality of Life

Research from Stanford University and elsewhere has found that postmenopausal hormone therapy can improve a woman's quality of life. In the end, this may be just as worthwhile a consideration as a long-term risk for a disease. Unfortunately, at this juncture, the scientific results are mixed; the WHI study results found no effect on quality of life in either the Prempro or the Premarin-only group.

My personal experience with bio-identical ERT in my own patients has convinced me that a large-scale study would show great improvement in quality of life for women who need and get help with hormonal replacement after menopause.

Research into pharmaceutical HRT with progestins is not a good barometer of the effect of hormone replacement on the quality of life. Although the natural hormone progesterone is known to be neuroprotective (protective of brain cells, also called neurons), the manufactured progestin Provera does not have this effect.

Neuroscientists have, in fact, found that Provera is not benign in this regard—it actually *antagonizes* the neuroprotective, neuron-building effects of bio-identical estradiol. Medroxyprogesterone acetate (the generic name of Provera) was found to accelerate the death of neurons exposed to glutamate, an amino acid that can literally excite neurons to death. This is definitely not a substance that is going to improve your mental sharpness or quality of life.

Loss of hearing is a major complaint in aging people—it is a problem linked to age-related deterioration of brain cells. In September 2006, researchers released the results of a study designed to see whether Premarin would have positive effects on hearing in aging women. To their surprise, they found no benefit to hearing (measured by a detailed battery of hearing tests) in women on Premarin alone, but also found that hearing was not adversely affected, either.

In women on Premarin plus progestin, however, they found a hearing *loss*. The progestins appeared to significantly accelerate hearing loss—women on Premarin plus progestin had the hearing of women five to ten years older. The portions of the brain used for hearing were found to be negatively affected by progestins.

Your Bones on Estrogens—Kathy's Case

By the time Kathy reached fifty-two, she had been on Prempro for the previous two years, and was feeling okay. Her pelvic exam on her annual visit to her gynecologist yielded normal results. She also had some routine blood work done, and was sent for a mammogram and a DEXA scan—a test used to measure bone density in the hip and spine. Two weeks later, her gynecologist called to report that her scan showed evidence of bone loss and he put her on a drug called Fosamax (generic name, alendronate, in a class of drugs called bisphosphonates).

Despite following the instructions from her pharmacist, Kathy immediately had a very common side effect of this drug—severe pain caused by esophagitis (inflammation of the esophagus). Although the research claims that the risk of esophagitis is low to nonexistent as long as patients take the medication according to directions, I'd estimate that this side effect appears in at least 25 percent of the patients I've seen who have taken any bisphosphonate drug.

Drugs for Osteoporosis Are Poor Substitutes for Bio-Identical HRT

As soon as women began to question the safety of HRT on a large scale, other drugs began to be introduced as substitutes for the prevention and treatment of maladies previously treated or prevented by HRT. For example, bisphosphonates (alendronate, sold as Fosamax; etidronate, sold as Didrocal; and risedronate, sold as Actonel) and selective estrogen receptor modulators (SERMs, including raloxifene, sold as Evista) are increasingly used to prevent osteoporosis in place of drugs like Prempro. These drugs are risky and don't provide as much benefit as bio-identical HRT.

Bisphosphonates slow bone loss by suppressing the effect of *osteoclasts* that break down bone. The drug is taken once a week on an empty stomach. You can't lie down or eat anything for an hour after taking it. Possible side effects include irritation of the esophagus, stomach upset, constipation, and muscle or bone pain. Multiple studies find that side effects involving the esophagus occur in 11–47 percent of those who take bisphosphonate drugs.

A new, very rare, and potentially serious side effect of bisphosphonates—*osteonecrosis* of the jaw—has been identified. Bone tissue in the jaw dies off, usually after women who are taking these medicines have dental work done.

Newer bisphosphonates are taken once a month (that's Boniva, generic name ibandronate) or intravenously (Aredia, generic name pamidronate sodium; or Zometa, generic name zoledronic acid). Their effectiveness is comparable to that of estrogen HRT, with an average increase in bone-mineral density (BMD) of 2.5 percent seen, and a 62-percent drop in the risk for spinal fracture over two years.

Selective estrogen receptor modulators (SERMs), such as Evista (raloxifene), work by both activating and blocking estrogen receptors. The breast cancer drug tamoxifen is also a SERM. These are not suitable for postmenopausal HRT, because they have estrogen effects only in certain tissues, including bone. The main side-effect concern with SERMs is blood clots in the legs and pelvis. SERMs are less effective than bisphosphonates, only increasing bone-mineral density by 1–2 percent over a four-year period, and reducing the risk for spinal fracture by about 30 percent.

Calcitonin and parathyroid hormones are other options for protecting against osteoporosis. Both these therapies are costly and inconvenient.The bottom line is that none of these medicines are as safe or effective at building and maintaining bone as properly administered bio-identical estrogen plus progesterone and testosterone. HRT is the gold-standard preventive and treatment against osteoporosis; other options are offered only because of the supposed risks of long-term HRT, which, as you are learning, are not a concern with BHRT.

Kathy was advised to discontinue Fosamax and was switched to Actonel, another bisphosphonate, which she started taking the following week. She again had stomach pain, but it wasn't as severe as the pain from the first drug. Despite the pain, Kathy was advised to continue taking Actonel; she was told it might be unrelated to the drug, and it would probably resolve. It didn't. Finally, after four doses over the course of a month, she stopped it on her own because the pain had worsened, and didn't totally diminish until six weeks after she stopped the Actonel.

Shortly after that, she came to see me for BHRT. I got her off Prempro and onto a BHRT regimen consisting of estradiol and testosterone subcutaneous pellets and oral progesterone. She's been on this regimen for three years now and feels great.

Interestingly, she saw her family doctor, an internist, about three months after we put her on BHRT. Kathy's doctor advised that she didn't "much believe in those bio-identical hormones," and tried to put her on a new drug, Forteo (generic name, teriparatide), that the drug rep had just pitched to her. At the time, Forteo had just been approved to treat advanced osteoporosis, or to be used when other drug therapy for osteoporosis fails. It is a daily, self-administered injection that jacks up calcium levels in the tissues. Common side effects include gallstones and kidney stones, and the drug costs $7200 a year. And guess what? It's a high (non-physiologic) dose of bio-identical parathyroid hormone. (The side effects of a high, non-physiologic dose of parathyroid hormone would be just as serious as those of a high, non-physiologic dose of estrogen, progesterone, or testosterone.)

Bone-Building Help

The parathyroid hormone, produced in the parathyroid gland, helps the body use calcium to build bone.

Kathy came by the next day to get my opinion on whether the Forteo was necessary. I told her, "Your internist doesn't realize that BHRT will treat the problem underlying bone loss—a deficiency of estrogen, testosterone, and progesterone." These hormones all have a positive effect on bone metabolism.

Kathy never had a deficiency of Fosamax, Actonel, or parathyroid hormone. She never took the Forteo. She did continue her subcutaneous pellet therapy, and a DEXA scan done eighteen months after the first one revealed a significant *increase* in bone density in her hip and spine. I'm happy to report she's feeling great and doing well without any esophagitis or having to give herself a shot every day. I'm equally happy that we are saving her and our healthcare system $7200 a year.

Osteoporosis—A Major Women's Health Problem

Over the last ten years, the cost of diagnosing and treating osteoporosis has made a major contribution to overall healthcare costs. Much of the excitement that bubbled over about pharmaceutical HRT had to do with its support for maintaining better bone mass after menopause.

As pharmaceutical HRT has fallen out of favor for long-term use, the treatment and prevention of this illness has been a very expensive, slippery slope greased with drug-company money. The faster healthcare barrels down that slope, the more distance it travels from actually treating the underlying problem: a change in the balance of specific hormones that occurs with age, the very hormones responsible for maintaining existing bone and building new bone.

The increasingly widespread use of bone-density testing with the DEXA scan has led to more women being diagnosed with osteoporosis and osteopenia. As more drugs and more tests are developed for this disease, the number of people being diagnosed and treated is skyrocketing. In the past ten or so years, at least five drugs have been specifically marketed solely for the treatment and/or prevention of osteoporosis. And, there are at least that many in the pipeline now. What you won't hear from any drug rep, or read in any direct-to-consumer ad for these drugs, is that *no drug formulated for the prevention or treatment of osteoporosis has been shown to be more effective than balanced hormone replacement therapy.*

The drugs being used to treat and prevent osteoporosis are akin to applying a tourniquet on a bleeding vessel rather than avoiding a cut in the first place. Doesn't it make more sense to treat the underlying cause of a problem than to treat the result of the problem?

The cause of bone loss in women is loss of adequate hormone effect. There is absolutely no question about this. Maximum bone density is achieved in most women around the age of thirty-five to forty; there is generally some loss of bone from forty to fifty, or at the time of menopause, and then there is a more rapid loss of bone density after menopause. Over time, there is a direct correlation between the course of bone loss and the course of decline in estrogen, progesterone, and testosterone in the ovaries. All three of these hormones have receptors on bone—and *they are there for a reason.* They have a direct bearing on bone metabolism.

Estrogen does not build bone, but it prevents *loss* of bone. Progesterone and testosterone are the primary stimulants of *osteoblasts*, which are the bone cells that make new bone. At the same time in a woman's life that progesterone and testosterone levels begin to decline (late thirties, early forties), there is a leveling-off, or the beginnings of a decrease, in bone density. Then, in menopause, estradiol, progesterone, and testosterone levels drop precipitously, which leads to more rapid bone loss.

Giving back a woman's own natural hormones works better than anything else to preserve bone mass. Using bio-identical hormones to prevent osteoporosis has many other advantages, including that it is less expensive than such drugs as Actonel and Forteo, and essentially has no side effects.

One of the positive outcomes of the WHI study was that, in all phases of the study, estrogen therapy showed a significant increase in bone density—even without the added benefit of testosterone.

Unfortunately, many physicians have been unreasonably spooked about HRT. Most of them go the route the makers of osteoporosis drugs have laid out for them. Unbalanced, high-dose bio-identical parathyroid hormone actually stimulates new bone formation, and so far, there's no information to substantiate that it is a better choice than balanced bio-identical hormone replacement therapy when it comes to increasing bone density.

Ultra Low-Dose ERT and Bone Health

In 2004, researchers at Harvard University published the results of a study on bio-identical estradiol in the journal *Obstetrics and Gynecology*. For two years, they gave women between the ages of sixty and eighty an ultra-low-dose bio-identical estradiol patch—delivering a fourth the usual HRT dose—or a placebo. No progestin or progesterone was given. All the women also got calcium and vitamin-D supplements for the duration of the study.

Women on estradiol had an average fourfold increase in bone-mineral density in their lumbar spine compared with the placebo group. Hip BMD decreased significantly in the placebo patients and increased in estradiol users. One woman in the estradiol group developed endometrial hyperplasia (a precancerous condition), which cleared up quickly with a short course of progestin.

HRT and Colon Cancer

Colon cancer is the third leading cancer killer in women. There is no controversy regarding the protective effects of supplemental estrogen against colon cancer. The WHI study confirmed what has been shown in several previous studies, that estrogen replacement therapy reduces a woman's risk of colon cancer by about 50 percent. The mechanism is not well understood, but the effect of estrogens on the action of bile acids in the colon are one promising avenue of research on this.

A 2007 article on an analysis of 834 women who had participated in the Nurses' Health Study seems to further cement the connection between estrogen replacement and a reduced risk of dying from cancer of the colon or rectum. Between 1976 and 2000, this group of women had been diagnosed with colorectal cancer. Those who reported the use of estrogen HRT before their diagnosis turned out to have a 36-percent reduced risk of death from colon cancer—*and* a 26-percent reduced risk of death from any cause—for several years after diagnosis. Women who used estrogen within the five years before the cancer diagnosis were the most likely to enjoy this survival advantage. No such benefit was seen in women who started estrogens *after* diagnosis, or who used it prior to five years before diagnosis.

Estrogen and Osteoarthritis

Although not generally life-threatening, osteoarthritis (OA) can be debilitating and can cause enormous amounts of pain. Some cases require surgical intervention or long-term treatment with drugs that can cause bleeding ulcers or other gastrointestinal upsets.

Moderate exercise and the maintenance of ideal weight, flexibility, and strength are the foundations of osteoarthritis prevention. A diet low in bad fats, sugars, and refined carbohydrates, and rich in good fats and plant foods is important, too, as this type of diet lowers the levels of inflammation, which is bad for your joints and can make existing arthritis worse throughout your body. (More on bad fats, good fats, and other issues of dietary concern in Chapter 11.) It appears that hormone balance could help with this, too.

In a study performed at the University of Michigan, Mary Fran Sowers, Ph.D. and her colleagues found that women in perimenopause who had the lowest circulating levels of estradiol were almost twice as likely to develop knee osteoarthritis over a three-year period, compared to women with higher estradiol levels. Women who had the lowest levels of 2-hydroxyestrone, which is produced in the body when estrogen is broken down and can be measured in urine, had an almost threefold risk of developing OA of the knee.

Studies of older women find that those who use estrogen HRT have a significantly reduced risk of developing osteoarthritis. Data from the Study of Osteoporosis Fractures Research Group, reported at the 1999 Meeting of the American College of Rheumatology in Boston, Massachusetts, found a 50-percent decreased risk of narrowing joint space (a measurement of arthritis damage) in women who used estrogen replacement therapy over an average period of eight years. Other research reveals that HRT with estrogens (with and without progestin) reduces the risk of knee osteoarthritis, but this risk reduction is lost once the hormone replacement therapy stops.

More recently, a follow-up of the 26,000-plus subjects in the Women's Health Initiative contributed to the case for estrogens as a method of preventing osteoarthritis. Investigators found that the 10,049 women who had used estrogen-only HRT (following hysterectomy) had a significantly lower incidence of joint-replacement surgeries, which are almost always performed because of osteoarthritis. The protective effect appeared strongest for hip replacements.

Estrogens and Urogenital Atrophy

Menopause can cause distinctive changes in the female *urogenital* tract—the vagina, bladder, and urethra (the tube that moves urine out of the body from the bladder). The close proximity of these organs (the bladder sits on top of the vagina) means that problems for one usually coincide with problems for the other.

Postmenopausal women eventually experience vaginal dryness and discomfort. Many also contract more urinary tract infections than they did before menopause, and they tend to lose urine involuntarily during a sneeze, a coughing fit, or a belly laugh, a phenomenon known as *stress urinary incontinence.* All these problems are related to a decreased estrogen effect, and they can almost always be resolved with ERT. As I will discuss later, testosterone also has a role in urinary continence, helping to tone the muscles that support the vagina and bladder.

Vaginal dryness is one of the three most common symptoms of deficient estrogen in menopausal women. In my experience, it is almost always eliminated with subcutaneous estradiol pellets, the only treatment for this troublesome issue that I have used with near-total success. For years, the only options were messy creams and suppositories. Now, women who would rather use topical vaginal estrogen, as opposed to systemic estrogen, also have a vaginal ring that gets changed every three months available to them, or a vaginal tablet used twice a week. Both contain pure estradiol.

Choosing the Right ERT for You

If you were to walk into my office looking for advice on whether you are a good candidate for ERT, here's what you could expect.

First, I'd order blood tests of your hormone levels. Once those came back, we'd get together again and talk about any symptoms you're experiencing. I'd consider your weight and your age to figure out your starting dose, and I'd start on the low end and work up to a higher dose if your symptoms aren't alleviated.

I would give you a handout that details all of your options, and together we would go over it and decide which delivery method and which hormone works best for you. We would talk about which methods your insurance would be most likely to cover, and the overall cost. My preference is usually estradiol in transdermal or subcutaneous pellet form. One to two months following the onset of treatment, I would re-test you and clinically evaluate you to see whether I'd gotten the dose right.

With all my patients, I get to know their baseline hormone levels and their usual signs of hormone deficiency, so there's no need to test every time they come in. I try to get blood work on every patient every year to ensure they are all still in their optimal ranges.

Here are more details about the different delivery methods used for bio-identical estrogens.

Pellets

Compounding pharmacies make bio-identical pellets of estradiol in specific dosages recommended by the prescribing physician.

The pellets can be as small as a saccharine tablet but are never larger than a grain of rice. They are inserted in the body through a one-eighth-inch incision (the area is numbed first) that heals without stitches—a small bandage is all that's required. The most common site of incision is the hip, although some practitioners prefer the abdomen.

The first pellet lasts three to four months, slowly and steadily dissolving and releasing small amounts of its hormone into the circulation. After that, each pellet typically lasts four to six months, though, in rare instances, they may last up to a year. I usually tell my patients to come back for another pellet when they start having symptoms again. Those symptoms are usually mood-related. Irritability and less restful sleep are common indicators that tell women a new pellet is needed, but some come back when hot flashes or night sweats begin again.

I do my best to give as low a dose as possible while still offering the patient's body enough hormone to move it back towards a youthful balance. Usually, the best way to determine just the right amount for each patient is the presence or absence of symptoms, although lab tests also help me find it.

Patches

Transdermal estrogen—whether delivered in patch, lotion, cream, or gel—has been found, in many studies, to be an effective treatment for those pesky hot flashes, with a safety profile that oral estrogens can't touch. You don't have to swallow estrogens to get relief. Properly prescribed transdermal estrogens have been found to maintain estradiol levels right around typical premenopausal concentrations in menopausal women.

The estradiol patch, a thin piece of soft plastic impregnated with the hormone, was first introduced in 1984 as **Estraderm**. It is bio-identical estradiol delivered transdermally (across the skin) and into the bloodstream. Today's patches, including **Alora**, **Climara, Esclim, Vivelle**, and **Vivelle-Dot**, can be as small as a postage stamp or as large as a silver dollar. They are worn on the lower abdomen, hip, low back, or buttocks, and changed, on average, every three to four days. (Some patches last up to seven days.)

Estradiol is released from the patch in a fairly steady manner and is absorbed through the skin and into the bloodstream. Similar to pellets and other non-oral preparations, this transdermal route avoids first-pass effect, making it safer from a cardiovascular standpoint. The estrogen patch delivers a steady level of the hormone, generally making it a more physiological method than creams or pills. With them, you can swim, shower, or hot-tub without being concerned that these activities will interfere with the delivery of the hormone.

Currently, estradiol is the only hormone available in patch form. Although an estradiol plus progestin patch is available, I don't recommend it, and by now you know why. On down the line, however, I am hopeful that a progesterone patch and a combination estradiol/progesterone patch will be developed.

Topical Lotions, Creams, and Gels

Some physicians who prescribe bio-identical HRT use combinations of estradiol, estriol, and estrone. These products are made to order by compounding pharmacies, and can be used orally, sublingually, or topically, as gels or creams. They can also be made into vaginal creams, which may work to directly address urinary incontinence and vaginal atrophy.

Some over-the-counter transdermal products advertise themselves as "estrogen creams" when they contain herbs that can serve as precursors to estrogens. Wild yam, soy, and other estrogenic substances, delivered transdermally, have not been shown to convert to forms of estrogen that can soak into the skin and be active in the body. Don't waste your money on products like these; stick with the real thing – bio-identical estradiol, which is only available by prescription.

Two options for estradiol replacement are, as yet, niche players in the market—**Estrogel**, a quick-drying gel applied to one arm, and **Estrasorb**, a lotion applied daily to both legs. Both are good, commercially available, effective products, but are mostly for women who do not want to use pellets and don't tolerate the patch. I do have a handful of patients on each who are doing well and are happy with them.

There are currently two other non-oral estradiol products available: **Femring**, a plastic vaginal ring, and **Depoestradiol**, a monthly intramuscular injection.

Estrogen Recommendations	
Delivery Method	**Frequency Used**
Subcutaneous pellets	Every 4-6 months, or with return of symptoms
Patches	Change every 3-7 days, depending on type and dosage
Lotions and creams (Estrosorb and others)	Once to twice daily, on skin or intravaginally
Gel (Estrogel)	Once to twice daily

The Return of "Aunt Mary"

With the replacement of estradiol and the intermittent use of progesterone, which mimics a premenopausal woman's hormone cycle, you may start to have a monthly menstruation again.

According to many of my patients, having periods following menopause is the most difficult aspect of bio-identical HRT. During follow-up visits with my patients, I spend a great deal of time talking about this issue. In the end, some women choose to stop taking estrogen because their postmenopausal menstrual periods are either too heavy or too bothersome. Since I don't have to contend with menstruation, I certainly can't tell them they're being unreasonable, but I do have thoughts on this subject.

The first thing to keep in mind is that your overall health and sense of well-being is better off having an adequate estrogen effect, which is demonstrated by a monthly period, than having an inadequate estrogen effect and no period. Also keep in mind that more days per month of progesterone—for example, twenty-five days to a full month of progesterone each month instead of twelve to fifteen—is more likely to prevent monthly periods. (*See* Chapter 6 for further details.)

But if a patient of mine does not want to use estrogens at all, I can still set them up on progesterone, and on testosterone, if needed. I have done this with several patients who had breast cancer in the past and would not touch estrogens under any circumstances. (Do all women with a history of breast cancer have to avoid estrogens? Not necessarily. I'll address this topic in detail in Chapter 8.)

How Long Should Women Use Estrogens and Other Bioidentical Hormones?

I probably get this question two or three times a day. My answer and my belief is that BHRT is worth staying on for a lifetime. Your gonads aren't going to kick back in. A person who is deficient in thyroid hormone or insulin takes replacement hormones for the rest of her/his life. The sex hormones will provide their greatest benefit when you integrate them into your life for good, just as you integrate a healthful diet, nutritional supplements, and a regular exercise program.

6

No Estrogen Without Progesterone

No discussion of progesterone could possibly be complete without mention of the late Dr. John Lee. I never had the pleasure of meeting Dr. Lee, but over the last ten years his books, tapes, and lectures have influenced the way many of my patients feel about hormone replacement therapy. Along the way, these patients helped convince me of the value of Dr. Lee's work, and the message about progesterone that he began to share back in 1979.

While I can't say I agree with all Dr. Lee's dictums—and had he not passed away in 2003 before we had a chance to meet—he certainly would not have agreed with all of mine. He was a courageous pioneer who dared to question the synthetic-HRT status quo *years* before the WHI study made the world snap to attention. His writings have impacted my own philosophy and approach to hormone replacement therapy. His work, and the assistance of writers Virginia Hopkins and Melissa Block, who helped make his message more accessible, has made a difference in the lives of millions of women, inspiring them to become educated about the balance of female hormones and how they could be used wisely to promote good health in the years just before, during, and following menopause.

Dr. Lee's biggest contribution was to let women know that natural progesterone was a great balancer and protector, useful for women from perimenopause through menopause. His work inspired research by Helene Leonetti, MD, and others, demonstrating that bio-identical transdermal progesterone protects the endometrium in women on estrogen and doesn't increase their risk of breast cancer. Indeed, Dr. Lee and many others have found that progesterone in its natural form is protective against this dreaded disease.

Progesterone is produced almost exclusively by the corpus luteum, a remnant of ovulation, during the luteal phase of the menstrual cycle. When a pregnancy ensues, progesterone is then made in large amounts by the placenta. If a woman does not ovulate or is not pregnant, very little, if any, progesterone is produced. Dr. Lee's books pointed out that many women in perimenopause do not ovulate with each menstrual cycle, and since these women are still making plenty of estrogen, they become *estrogen dominant* until menopause, when estrogen levels also drop. Estrogen dominance (a phrase coined by Dr. Lee) is an issue that can be—and often has been—made much worse by the wrong kind of HRT. And Dr. Lee was the first medical authority to speak out about my Third Tenet of women's HRT: Progestins, when combined with estrogens, significantly increase cardiovascular risk and the risk of breast cancer. Or, as I said it in Chapter 4, *it's the progestins, stupid.*

Progesterone 101

The role of progesterone in the non-pregnant woman is pretty clear-cut—it moderates and matures the effect of estrogen. Technically, it *down-regulates estrogen receptors.* In other words, it decreases the proliferative effect of estrogen, allowing the cells that are stimulated by estrogen to achieve their full potential and then die a natural death, as all normal cells do. This balancing effect is key to the normal hormone effect in the body, and key to effective, safe hormone replacement therapy. Progesterone is especially important in the breasts, where it down-regulates estrogen receptors in a way that suppresses the proliferation of *estrogen-induced mammary epithelial tissues.* This proliferation is the initial change that may lead to cancer when estrogen stimulation is too great.

Progesterone, a word that means *in favor of pregnancy*, is, without question, the most important hormone in pregnancy. Without adequate levels of progesterone throughout, a pregnancy will abort. And without the calming effects of having many times the non-pregnant concentrations of this hormone in her body, the mom-to-be would find those last weeks of pregnancy a lot harder to endure.

One of the properties of progesterone is to relax smooth muscle fibers. Since the uterine wall, which expands from the size of a woman's fist to being larger than a watermelon, is composed of nothing but smooth-muscle fibers, it is imperative that adequate progesterone be present to keep these muscle fibers from contracting and putting a pregnant woman into labor prior to full term. Thirty years ago, progesterone injections were used to treat pre-term labor, and after a long hiatus, progesterone is once again being used to help prevent women from giving birth too soon.

In fact, women with a history of pre-term labor are usually given weekly injections of progesterone from about the seventh month of pregnancy on—sooner, if needed—up until the pregnancy is far enough along for the baby to be born without problems. In couples with infertility who get pregnant with *in vitro* fertilization, progesterone therapy is an important part of helping an embryo take hold once it's implanted. Usually, the mother-to-be is given progesterone for at least the first twelve weeks, until the placenta is ready to supply the body's needs for progesterone.

Using progestins for either of these purposes would be a disaster—they cause birth defects. What better evidence is there of the enormous difference between progesterone and progestins?

Figure 6.1
Effects of Progesterone vs Progestin

Molecular Structure of Natural Progesterone vs. Medroxyprogesterone

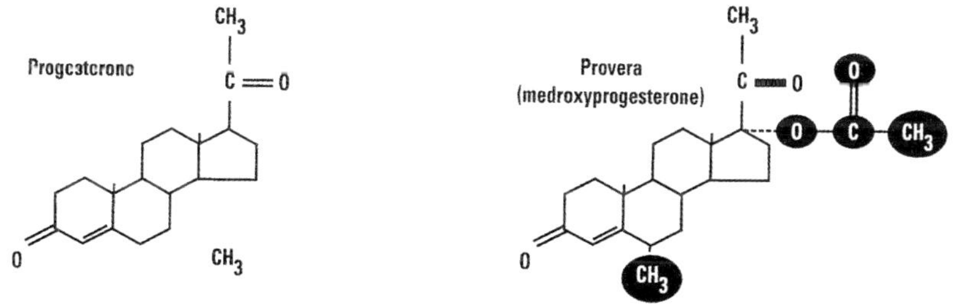

Progesterone

Provera (medroxyprogesterone)

Progesterone	**Medroxyprogesterone Acetate (a progestin)**
Cholesterol with O double-bonded	Cholesterol O – C – CH3 with O double-bonded plus CCH3
Progesterone Effects	**Progestin Effects**
Protects endometrium	Protects endometrium
Necessary for survival of embryo	Used in oral contraceptives and abortifascients (e.g. the morning-after pill) to prevent implantation; may cause birth defects
Matures estrogen effects on breast tissue	Blocks progesterone receptor; increases breast cancer risk
Stimulates new bone formation	No positive effect on bone formation
Prevents coronary artery spasm and (probably) prevents atherosclerotic plaques in heart vessels	Cancels out estrogen's positive effects on blood holesterol; has blood-vescsel-constricting effect

Progesterone, Puberty, and PMS

In many teenage girls who have only just begun to menstruate, the hormonal interaction between the hypothalamus, pituitary, and ovary have not developed or matured enough for a hormone balance to be achieved. This usually results in the ovary producing more-than-adequate estrogen *without the balancing effect of adequate progesterone.*

A young woman just starting to menstruate is often not ovulating. No ovulation means not enough progesterone to maintain a pregnancy, or to counteract the powerful effects of estrogens. This same young woman may develop ferocious PMS, heavy periods, and related symptoms, and she often ends up on the gynecologist's table, having been dragged in by her mother, who is at her wit's end. All too frequently, today's knee-jerk treatment for this is to start the young girl on oral contraceptives.

With girls maturing earlier than ever, these drugs may be

introduced in the very early teen years. Today it is known that, if a girl starts to take these drugs early in life, it may set her up for significant increases in a risk for breast cancer later on. Oral contraceptives block the natural action of progesterone (once ovulation begins to happen regularly); those progesterone receptor sites are taken up by the progestins in the oral contraceptives.

Fortunately, oral contraceptives aren't the only solution when your daughter transforms from sweet child to snarling, raging adolescent, in what seems to be the blink of an eye. In my experience, natural progesterone is a viable alternative. It is often effective at controlling, or at least reducing, the severity of some, if not all, the teen's distressing estrogen-dominant symptoms. Another big upside is that you avoid exposing the not-fully-developed young woman to the high doses of estrogen and progestin found in oral contraceptives.

Since a lack of progesterone is the cause of the problem to begin with, and since treatment with bio-identical progesterone has essentially no downside or adverse consequences, this seems to be a no-brainer. Oral micronized progesterone or progesterone cream can be used to help these young women regain hormone balance.

Estrogen Dominance in the Years Before Menopause

Premenopausal women frequently experience PMS and heavy periods as well. A woman passing through her reproductive life may also have to contend with endometriosis, fibrocystic breasts, fibroid tumors of the uterus, or menstrual migraines, and these phenomena all tend to be related to inadequate progesterone and too much estrogen.

Dr. Lee was the first to tell the world that women are vulnerable to anovulatory cycles, where ovulation doesn't happen and progesterone doesn't get made in sufficient amounts to counteract high-estrogen levels. Anovulatory cycles are more common in women as they near menopause, and they tend to create a situation where estrogen effects are dominant in the woman's body. Endometriosis, fibrocystic breasts, fibroid tumors of the uterus, heavy periods, menstrual migraines, and PMS, can all spring from this state of estrogen dominance.

Many anecdotal, observational studies have documented the positive effects of progesterone therapy on these female complaints, but lack of funding has, so far, precluded any well-controlled studies that could give us real answers. In my opinion, it is certainly reasonable to at least try progesterone therapy (without estrogens) in women with estrogen-dominance symptoms. Progesterone therapy is relatively inexpensive and has, essentially, no potential for harm.

Progesterone for the Perils of Perimenopause

Perimenopause is that transition phase around the menopause—the swan song of a woman's ovaries as they start to peter out. Characteristic changes in hormone output include decreased production of progesterone and testosterone, and fluctuating levels of estrogen. More often than not, the net effect is a decrease in the ratio of progesterone to estrogen—in other words, estrogen becomes more dominant. Perimenopause can feel like a flashback to the mood swings and heavy periods of adolescence.

It's also a flashback for conventional medicine, which likes to treat perimenopausal complaints—as it likes to treat similar complaints in barely pubescent girls—with oral contraceptives. This became common practice about fifteen years ago at the suggestion of ... guess who? A drug company that manufactures oral contraceptives, of course. And now, every maker of oral contraceptives has jumped on this bandwagon and is recommending these drugs as a treatment for symptoms of hormone imbalance in perimenopausal women. Most gynecological organizations and societies have followed suit.

From the standpoint of regulating the menstrual cycle, oral contraceptives are effective. But adverse side effects are almost universal with these drugs. The risks of blood clotting and heart problems engendered by the use of oral contraceptives in a woman over forty are much more significant than the risks in a woman under thirty-five. Frankly, I think the widespread use of oral contraceptives will be something we look back on in twenty years, scratching our heads and asking, "What the heck were we *thinking*?"

My personal philosophy for treating perimenopausal issues

is to identify the hormonal imbalance at its root. The most common hormonal issue during perimenopause is a decrease in progesterone. This decrease, often in conjunction with high levels of estrogen, causes most of the adverse symptoms of perimenopause. So, treating that deficiency by replacing progesterone is almost always the solution that works. Imagine that.

Progesterone therapy is not only effective at normalizing the menstrual cycle, it also ameliorates mood disorders, which are very common in the perimenopause period. Along with these obvious benefits, it is also probable that the balancing effect of progesterone simultaneously reduces the risk of too much unopposed estrogen, which can lead to endometrial and breast cancer.

You don't force-feed a hungry person with a liter of soda and twelve candy bars. You don't give a sleep-deprived, exhausted person a huge dose of sleeping pills. These responses might solve the immediate problems, but in the long run, the responses are inappropriate in both scale and quality to the very simple difficulties at hand, and more problems soon follow. The hungry person needs a well-balanced, moderate meal, and the sleep-deprived person needs a comfortable place for an uninterrupted night's sleep. Just so, a woman who is deficient in progesterone should not be given estrogen and progestins from oral contraceptives. Doing so is not only bad physiologically, but if there is already an overabundance of estrogen relative to progesterone, you're pouring gasoline on an open fire. She simply needs replacement of whatever is missing. Nothing more, nothing less.

Postmenopausal Protector

Once menopause is over and done with, a woman's body makes about one percent of the 20–25 milligrams of progesterone per day that it made during the second half of a normal menstrual cycle.

Progesterone's role in postmenopausal hormone replacement is really quite simple. It is purely to mature the effect of estrogen. In essence, it acts like an insurance policy against the potentially adverse effects of unbalanced estrogen—progesterone down-regulates estrogen receptors in the breast and endometrium. To ignore this fact is clearly a mistake that leads to unnecessary increases in the risk for breast cancer, whether a woman takes estrogen as replacement or not. Even when estrogen falls to low levels after menopause, a woman can still be in an estrogen-dominant state from her body's production of estrone—particularly if she is overweight or obese.

The only cases of endometrial cancer I have seen in the last twenty years have been in postmenopausal women who never took any form of hormone replacement therapy. Women who do not take any form of estrogen replacement or hormone replacement still have a well-documented increase in breast cancer risk following menopause, and this is likely due to the fact that they continue to produce some estrogen and essentially no progesterone.

Progesterone affects much more than the uterus. The bottom line here is—*even if a woman chooses not to take estrogen replacement, it is reasonable for her to take progesterone to protect her uterus and breasts.* A woman with a hysterectomy still needs progesterone, *especially* if she is going to take estrogens. I hope by this point you see that the logic of all women using progesterone is sound—and the risk of not doing so is too big to ignore.

More zealous progesterone proponents would argue there are other significant benefits to progesterone therapy separate from balancing the estrogen effect. These include prevention of bone loss by stimulating new bone formation and prevention of heart disease by decreasing plaque formation in coronary arteries. While there is some evidence that these benefits are available with progesterone, they are as yet unproven in comparison with the benefits of estrogen. There are certainly benefits to bone and heart with balanced hormone replacement therapy, but the exact role of each individual hormone and its benefit is still a bit difficult to characterize separately.

Here are some benefits you can expect with appropriate progesterone replacement after menopause.

Table 6.2

Progesterone Effects in Women

What Doctors Say	Plain English Translation
Blocks effects of aldosterone, which causes the body to retain water	Reduces water bloat, acts as natural diuretic
Attaches to receptors for GABA (a neurotransmitter)	Naturally enhances mood and decreases anxiety and depression
Down-regulates estrogen receptors, leading to proper maturation of cells and normal cell death	Helps tone down estrogen's proliferative effects, reducing risk of estrogen-linked cancers
Promotes and maintains a healthy pregnancy	Promotes and maintains a healthy pregnancy
Matures milk ducts in breasts during pregnancy	Prepares the breasts for breastfeeding and matures breast cells in ways that protect against breast cancer
Stimulates osteoblast activity	Stimulates bone growth, helping to prevent osteoporosis

Progesterone Treatment Options

If the idea is to create physiological levels of this hormone, a woman does not need progesterone more than fifteen days of each month, For at least twenty-five years, women have been treated with continuous, combined HRT regimens that include estrogen and progestin every day. It has been shown, however, that taking progestins daily without breaks may cause the receptors for progesterone to become desensitized to the hormone-like drug. Research has shown that five or six days off of progestin each month is adequate to up-regulate progesterone receptors. No one knows for sure if this pertains to bio-identical progesterone, but it's a sensible piece of evidence to apply to the use of this natural hormone. This is why I generally advise its use for twelve to twenty-five days of the month, and not continuously.

Some women do prefer to use progesterone every day. I've looked at this issue upside down, backwards, and all the way through, and here's my perspective: If you were my patient, I'd tell you that you *need* progesterone twelve days out of the month. Want to take it more often? Does it make you feel better in any way to take it every day? Then go for it.

What's the best timing for progesterone dosing? Here are a few points for you to consider.

1. Continuous dosing of progesterone may prevent a period from occurring in a postmenopausal woman who is also on estrogens. However, some women may still bleed, even with continuous progesterone, and this kind of breakthrough bleeding can be unpredictable. It often resolves within a few months of beginning HRT.
2. Some women:
   - Are going to have some bleeding, and timing the bleeding with the dosing of progesterone is sometimes worthwhile from a convenience standpoint; it ends up easier to create a predictable monthly period by withdrawing progesterone for a time each month than to have breakthrough bleeding at unpredictable times; with a woman who has a uterus and has bleeding, it is often necessary to work with the timing, dosing, and route of delivery that works best for that individual.
   - Feel better on a cyclic progesterone regimen than a continuous regimen, and the converse is true as well.
   - Find it easier to take progesterone every day, instead of starting and stopping.
   - Just plain feel better on days when they take progesterone than on days when they don't.
3. Using progestin instead of progesterone *in any regimen* involves more side effects, including bloating, depression, headaches, irritability, moodiness, and weight gain.
4. Women who sleep better with progesterone like to take it every day around bedtime for that very reason.

Pills or Creams?

The dose of progesterone needed to create replacement is relatively high compared to estradiol and testosterone. This precludes it being given as a subcutaneous pellet. Although a transdermal patch would be a convenient delivery form for a lot of women, no such thing is available now, and I am not presently aware of any drug company that is even thinking about a progesterone patch. It holds little promise as a moneymaker, because it couldn't be patented, and competitors could charge what they liked to compete with the drug giants.

Progesterone capsules and vaginal creams are available only by prescription. Transdermal progesterone, usually referred to as progesterone cream, is available both with and without a prescription.

Oral Progesterone Capsules (Prometrium)

Prometrium is micronized progesterone packaged in a capsule with peanut oil to aid absorption. Micronized progesterone is micro-encapsulated progesterone, which goes through a process whereby the progesterone molecule is surrounded by a fat-soluble substance that enables the hormone to be absorbed through the wall of the intestine. Without this micronizing effect, progesterone cannot be absorbed when taken orally, and so passes through the bowel with no effect.

Solvay, the drug company that makes Prometrium, is to be commended for developing and producing this drug in 1996. I am sure it was a gamble; in those days, they were up against many other drug companies who touted their proprietary, patented progestins, claiming that their products were the same thing as progesterone, only better.

I probably use progesterone capsules more than any other form. Most women prefer it to the other methods. It's easy—just take a single dose at bedtime. The hormone is well-tolerated and adequately absorbed, and often aids sleep. Prometrium has been my most common prescription for progesterone, and I've used a ton of it over the last ten years. It comes in two dosages, 100 and 200 mg, and is available at any pharmacy with a prescription.

Other sources of oral progesterone are now available from compounding pharmacies. The same micronizing process is used by these pharmacists, and the compounding pharmacy can make any dose that is ordered by a prescribing physician.

To get an adequate amount of the hormone absorbed into the body, we generally have to use a dose of oral micronized progesterone that is about five to ten times that which the ovary produced. The absorption process and the first pass through the liver will break down most of the progesterone, leaving just enough to create physiologic levels (amounts close to those naturally produced in the normal menstrual cycle of a healthy young woman) in the body.

Since I began using micronized progesterone, I have found that—in direct opposition to the case with oral estrogens—the first pass effect in the liver seems to have benefits. The progesterone is metabolized slowly and can exert an effect over a longer period of time, and the metabolites that form in the liver have sedative effects, which most of my patients like a whole lot, and which isn't as pronounced with transdermal progesterone.

Occasionally, a patient of mine gets a dose that is more than she can tolerate. This problem is easy to recognize and remedy—all I do is reduce the dose.

Transdermal Progesterone Cream

A close contender for my favorite progesterone-delivery method is transdermal cream, the replacement method recommended by John Lee, M.D.

Although many brands of progesterone cream are commercially available without a prescription, I recommend that you obtain yours with a prescription, from a compounding pharmacy. Although drug companies don't stand to profit from making and testing bio-identical progesterone creams, little guys who want to cash in on the latest health trends can make great money by putting random skin cream in a bottle with a label that says, "natural progesterone." One study that analyzed commercially available progesterone creams (most of which advertise the specific content of progesterone on their labels) found that *half* of them contained absolutely none. Buyer beware.

Over-the-counter progesterone creams can be purchased in health food stores and on the Internet. Dr. John Lee's website, <www.johnleemd.com> is still being maintained, and has a current list of quality progesterone products; or you can go to Ms. Hopkins' website <www.virginiahopkinstestkits.com> for similar resources. I have tested for progesterone levels in a number of postmenopausal women who use these recommended over-the-counter products, and they generally appear to have at least some progesterone present. Some of these are doubtless worthwhile products, and they are certainly easily accessible, but quite often they are more expensive than what you can get by prescription. And further, with a prescription medication, you know what you are getting (and what you are not getting).

Like all compounded prescriptions, progesterone can be made up in any dose needed and packaged in many different ways. My patients typically prefer it packaged in small syringes that are marked so they can get precise dosing. (This type of syringe has a hollow tube with a plunger and an opening at one end where the cream is dispensed as the plunger is pressed down.)

Progesterone cream, because it is rapidly absorbed and metabolized, is best used twice a day, usually in the morning after your shower or bath, and again at bedtime. There are many different options for the base cream in which the hormone can be mixed. Most compounding pharmacies use an odorless, non-greasy lipogel that is basically a vanishing cream. Many other options are available. Talk with your doctor and pharmacist to figure out what works best for you.

Some authorities believe that a twice-daily transdermal progesterone regimen is still not adequate to protect the endometrium. This belief has to do with the fact that transdermal progesterone cream has, in some studies, not been found to cause blood-progesterone levels to rise to levels believed necessary to protect the endometrium. Saliva levels, however, rise markedly, and studies do support the endometrial protection offered by this therapy, so blood progesterone levels may not be the most accurate indicators of progesterone activity in the body.

A 2003 study confirmed that the use of a progesterone cream twice daily did, indeed, have the same anti-proliferative effects on the uterine lining as bio-identical oral progesterone. (The same was found in a study of vaginal progesterone gel.) The investigators used endometrial biopsies before and after treatment—the same method that was used to determine whether progestins were protecting the endometrium. The use of this method makes these results pretty much impossible to dispute.

I have prescribed a lot of progesterone cream through the years, and to my knowledge have never had a patient develop atypical endometrial hyperplasia or cancer while on BHRT, including progesterone cream.

Progesterone cream can be applied to any skin surface. Recommended sites for applying progesterone cream include the face, neck, chest, inner arms, and thighs. Rotate the sites over the days you use the cream. Use enough cream to supply 15–20 mg of progesterone per day for twelve to twenty-five days of the month. This amount will vary depending on the concentration of progesterone in the cream you use.

No matter what the vehicle, progesterone needs to be used *at least* twelve to fifteen days out of every thirty to create the necessary balance in the body.

Six of One, A Half-Dozen of the Other

Studies have confirmed that both oral micronized progesterone and transdermal progesterone creams are absorbed in adequate amounts to protect the endometrium against proliferative changes due to estrogen effects. This protection is the gold standard for progesterone's effectiveness in hormone replacement therapy. You can choose whichever you prefer as a natural progesterone replacement. In addition, sublingual and vaginal progesterone get the hormone into the bloodstream in adequate amounts, so they can also protect the endometrium.

Vaginal Progesterone Cream

Crinone is the brand name of the one commercially effective brand of bio-identical progesterone gel designed for vaginal application. It's effective, but I have never prescribed it.

Some would argue that since it's made by a big drugmaker and FDA-approved, it must be better. Poppycock. I'd have a mass rebellion on my hands if I tried to prescribe Crinone to my patients. With so many other workable options, having little globules of gel leaking out of the body for half the month is a dealbreaker for most women. Crinone is also very expensive.

Women who are fighting infertility or trying to maintain a pregnancy may be given a choice by their medical team between painful intramuscular progesterone injections and Crinone, and these women will probably choose the vaginal progesterone. It's too bad some fertility doctors haven't caught on that a quality transdermal progesterone cream, or oral micronized progesterone could work just as well, with less expense, mess, and inconvenience.

Progesterone Drops and Troches

Sublingual drops (applied under the tongue) and sublingual troches (lozenges dissolved under the tongue) are also available. Some patients complain about the taste, and they can be cumbersome to use. There are not a whole lot of data to support the effectiveness of these methods, and they are generally not as convenient as the cream or capsule—they probably need to be used twice a day because there appears to be rapid absorption and clearance of both. I have colleagues who are big on both these delivery methods, and for some, they may be better options than other methods listed here.

Progesterone Options

Any progesterone option should be used on 12 to 25 days of each month. A break of five to 15 days helps to awaken and reactivate progesterone receptor sites.

Progesterone Options	
Delivery Method	**Frequency Used**
Oral micronized progesterone (Prometrium)	Once daily, at bedtime
Progesterone cream	Twice daily
Sublingual (under the tongue) drops or troches	Twice daily
Vaginal gel (Crinone)	Daily or every other day

Congratulations, You're Becoming an Educated Patient

An educated patient uses the best (safest, most effective) therapies to maintain excellent health and reverse the progression of disease, and understands *how and why those therapies work*. She is the patient who is the most able collaborator in the doctor-patient dynamic. She is the patient who is best able to explain to friends and family why, all of a sudden, she's looking so energized and vibrant, transformed from being constantly cranky and tired. This is the patient who can deftly explain why she doesn't have to use that expensive, side-effect-laden drug that was giving her so much grief before. And often, the educated patients are the most successful at helping their own doctors to see the light.

7

Lean, Libidinous, and Loving It

Testosterone Replacement for Women

From our point of view as sexologists, for a woman to live with inadequate levels of testosterone is no small matter. For many it means the complete inability to experience sexual desire, sexual fantasy, arousal, and/or orgasm. The fact is that female sexuality without testosterone is a house without a foundation. No matter how hard a woman might try to assemble the building blocks of healthy sexual functioning—the required amounts of other hormones, a loving partner, adequate stimulation, possibly a good sexual fantasy—it cannot work if she does not have the basic foundation of enough testosterone.

Barbara Bartlik, M.D., and Helen Singer Kaplan, M.D., Ph.D., in their foreword to Susan Rako, M.D.'s *The Hormone of Desire.*

In the early days of my medical practice, I didn't routinely discuss libido with my patients. As that topic of conversation became more acceptable between doctor and patient, I realized how many women's lives were negatively affected by the loss of sexual desire and all the pleasures that come with that desire and its fulfillment.

Cocaine-loving psychiatrist Sigmund Freud was the originator of the term *libido.* Freud defined libido as part of the *id,* the aspect of a person's being that drives his or her sensual appetites. Freud believed libido to be a powerful, instinct-driven force that often caused people to go against society's expectations for decent and moral behavior. Conflict between id-driven desires and society's expectations, said Dr. Freud, was the source of *neurosis,* or general mental and emotional distress. Back then, it was said that, in order to avoid neurosis, people had to *sublimate* their sexual desires into innocuous activities. In other words, if you want to have a romantic liaison with someone or otherwise indulge your desire for sexual pleasure, but society forbids it, you'd be better off painting a picture or composing a sonnet to express your feelings.

What does society forbid now? Not much. Sex is everywhere. Heightened consciousness of human sexual interplay and possibility is pretty much universal in Westernized nations. You can enjoy all kinds of books, videos, movies, classes, couples therapies, and other tools for enhancing and improving your sex life. Abundant scientific research on sexuality and aging has demonstrated that enjoying a good sex life as you age promotes better health and longevity.

Testosterone adequacy is essential for female libido. Today's definition of libido is, quite simply, *the urge to have sex.* It's mental and physical and, if you aren't internally conflicted about it, quite a pleasurable experience in and of itself. It's a strong wellspring of human life force and excitement, and a source of loving, pleasurable connections between people. A healthy libido can bring unparalleled pleasure and joy. Without it, you can still have sex with the help of pharmaceutical technology, space-age lubricants, and the like, but why would you want to?

You may have grasped by now that the big deal about testosterone replacement for postmenopausal women is its effect on the libido. Physiological replacement of this hormone can most definitely increase the libido in either gender.

In her book, *The Hormone of Desire,* Susan Rako, M.D. says

testosterone is the hormone she is talking about. Back in the mid-1990s, she made a powerful case that testosterone can be safely replaced in women who lack it, and this can be an empowering step for the woman who wonders where her spark has gone, and misses it. Since her book was published, not much has changed in the medical mainstream, but more and more women are asking about testosterone and how it can help them have the best sex of their lives.

Jean's Story—Sexual Connection Lost and Found

Jean is a high school math teacher. In her late forties, she had the usual menopausal symptoms, and her doctor started her on Prempro. Within a few weeks, she felt better. Each of her symptoms, including hot flashes, irritability, night sweats, and vaginal dryness, had diminished or disappeared.

Although she felt more comfortable on Prempro, she did gain weight, especially in her waist. She felt quite bloated as well, and felt that her weight gain had definitely accelerated after going on Prempro. She was reassured by her doctor this was coincidental, and that Premarin had nothing to do with her putting on weight.

One big complaint of hers was a total lack of libido. Her husband eventually got to the point where he assumed that sex was not going to be an option for the remainder of their marriage. Their relationship had become less loving than in the first twenty-five years of their union, during which sex had always been enjoyable for them both and nurturing to their relationship.

Jean heard about BHRT around the same time the WHI study's findings, which found unacceptable elevations in heart disease and breast cancer risk in women on Prempro, were released in 2002. She got the idea that better options than Prempro might be out there, and ended up coming to see me shortly thereafter.

As I told Jean, and as I have said many times, if Premarin or Prempro were the only HRT available, I would prescribe them, and take them myself if needed. But, happily, they're *not* the only thing available. I told her, as I've told many patients before and since, "Prempro is really hormone *substitution,* it's not true hormone *replacement*." I could see the lightbulb go off in Jean's mind, as it has with a lot of my patients when they grasp the difference between bio-identical hormones and the usual HRT prescriptions.

I was able to get Jean off Prempro and onto BHRT, administered in the form of subcutaneous pellets of estradiol and testosterone, and progesterone capsules. It was a smooth transition, during which she continued to have relief of her vasomotor symptoms—hot flashes, night sweats. Since she had become very testosterone-deficient while on Prempro, the testosterone pellet provided her with great boosts in energy and libido.

Jean has now been on BHRT pellets for almost four years...and she and her husband are enjoying life and each other as if they were newlyweds. She lost about fifteen pounds in the year after she switched to BHRT, and has kept the weight off.

Does testosterone increase every woman's libido? No. Libido involves much more than hormones, including both physical and psychological elements. Plus, each woman's body responds differently to the same level of testosterone—it appears that some women are more sensitive to the hormone and can make do with less. Still, a large percentage of women over forty have low testosterone. Increasing that level with bio-identical testosterone is a safe way to restore libido in these women if a lack of libido is a problem for them. The correlation between low testosterone in women and decreased libido is basically 100 percent.

Almost all postmenopausal women have low enough levels of testosterone to drag the libido down. Testosterone replacement won't turn every menopausal woman into a sex kitten, but when it works, it *really* works—and my patients and their partners are thrilled with the difference.

Grandma's Getting It On

Although media attention is largely focused on sex between twenty-somethings, people aged forty to ninety-plus are having a great time in the sack, too. Many report that their sex lives during the years after forty are better than ever. Concerns about pregnancy, and the loss of libido that comes with nursing and caring for young children, are past, and many women in this age bracket are more confident and financially secure than they were in their more youthful years. They're more willing to ask for what they want from partners. Women in this age range are ripe for sexual satisfaction.

A 2006 American Association of Retired Persons (AARP) survey of 1,682 adults surveyed nationwide over a period of several years show the following results.

1. Most adults older than forty strongly believe that sex is for people of every age, and people with or without spouses or partners.
2. The rate at which men are using potency-enhancing drugs, such as Viagra, has doubled since 1999. Contrary to the belief that Viagra-addled men are chasing down their weary, sex-averse wives, or younger women, the female counterparts of men who try Viagra are gaining a lot of pleasure in the bargain.
3. Well-known sex therapist and physician, Jennifer Berman, MD, says in the article, "[T]he idea that older women are just happy to be done with sex is based on cultural stereotypes that equate women's sexual desire and desirability with a youthful body."
4. Overall, women in middle age and up to their seventies feel that sex is an important aspect of the quality of life. Even women who are in and beyond their seventies continue to have satisfying sex lives—or don't have them, but want them.
5. While it's rumored that women always are more libidinous in their thirties than in their seventies, it turns out that women of every age can lose their libidos, and women of every age can enjoy naturally strong libidos and great sex.

I do not mean to suggest that a woman who happily chooses not to be sexually involved is in any way abnormal or suffering from any mental disorder or pathological dysfunction. The classification of this so-called dysfunction as a disease state is less an attempt to help than it is a great motivation for drugmakers to create and market some form of female Viagra. But, for a woman who used to love sex and now has waning desire and misses that aspect of her life, or for a woman who has never really felt able to enjoy sexual intimacy and wants to experience that joy for the first time, a drug is not the answer. Why give a drug to fix a problem that is almost certainly due to testosterone deficiency?

Testosterone Replacement and Hypoactive Sexual Desire Disorder

A woman who has no libido and is unhappy enough about it to feel her life and relationships are being disrupted is said to have *hypoactive sexual desire disorder*. A recent, very promising study showed that the testosterone patch had broad benefits for women who met the diagnostic criteria for this disorder.

Five hundred and forty-nine women who had gone through a natural menopause were given, along with oral estrogen alone (if post-hysterectomy) or estrogen plus progestin, either a 300-microgram-per-day testosterone patch or a placebo patch twice a week for twenty-four weeks. Investigators talked with the subjects to gain information about how much satisfying sexual activity they had during the twenty-first through the twenty-fourth weeks of the study. The increase in the number of positive episodes was significantly greater for the testosterone users than for the placebo-patch wearers. Testosterone also improved sexual desire and relieved what the researchers quaintly called personal distress in women who were fortunate enough to get it instead of the inactive placebo.

The Forgotten Female Hormone

Testosterone has been overlooked, underutilized, and basically ignored in female hormone replacement therapy by the overwhelming majority of practitioners in this country. This is a great shame. Women have been unnecessarily overlooked for a long time because doctors have been reluctant to prescribe a hormone that has always been considered male.

In its typically misogynistic fashion, mainstream medicine has offered women estrogens to tone up and plump up their vaginal tissues and help increase lubrication, but conventional HRT drugs, such as Prempro and other combinations of horse estrogens and progestins, are known to often *dampen* the libido, not enhance it. Any testosterone oomph she might still have may actually be reduced by conventional HRT.

Even bio-identical estrogens can reduce levels of free testosterone in the body by raising the blood levels of proteins, which actually bind testosterone and make it inactive. Estrogen-only or estrogen/progestin HRT might help a woman's ability to engage in intercourse, but this doesn't address the issue of her *wanting* to do so. That's libido, and testosterone is often the missing piece here.

The ovary produces testosterone throughout a woman's reproductive life, and usually begins to produce less of it in her early forties—sometimes much earlier. Natural levels of testosterone in a woman in her forties are usually about half that of a woman in her twenties. Nearly one in four women ends up losing her uterus and/or ovaries to a hysterectomy, or has them shut down by some sort of medical treatment before natural menopause, and this causes an abrupt loss of testosterone. (A woman who keeps her ovaries can often lose some ovarian function following a hysterectomy.) Even women who get to natural menopause without any surgery to remove their reproductive organs are generally testosterone-deficient and greatly benefit from testosterone replacement therapy.

I'll next discuss some of the known benefits of replacing testosterone. Adding testosterone to your BHRT regimen will require the help of a physician willing to test you appropriately and prescribe the proper dosage of testosterone to get you back in the saddle, as it were, if that's where you'd like to be.

Testosterone Essentials

Like all the youth-effect hormones, testosterone has more than one effect on the body. Its benefits to female physiology go well beyond having a sex drive. Testosterone receptors are highly concentrated in a woman's nipples, clitoris, and vagina, but they're also abundant in the bones and brain.

Beginning at puberty, testosterone is produced in a woman's ovarian theca cells, and to a lesser extent in her adrenal glands. Her body's production of this hormone amounts to about 3/10th

of a milligram per day (compared to about seven mg a day for a teenage boy or young man).

Ovarian production of this steroid hormone generally begins to decline somewhere between a woman's late thirties to early forties, and continues to drop until around her fiftieth year, with some continuing to be produced by most women's ovaries even after menopause has passed. Some women never seem to get too low on testosterone—their levels might fall, but their libidos may not, suggesting that some women's bodies are better able to utilize this hormone. This, however, is the exception rather than the rule. In almost all postmenopausal women, testosterone falls below physiological levels—levels that evidence shows are adequate for optimal health and physical function.

Testosterone, Mood, and Cognition

Estrogen enhances cognitive function, but evidence also supports a role for physiological replacement of testosterone in the maintenance of brain power.

When I began to treat my patients with bio-identical testosterone, I saw an increase in reasoning, and intuitive and perceptive function. Time after time, I found that men and women who were low in testosterone and got appropriate replacement were cognitively sharper. This increase in mental function is almost always noticeable, and has even been quite dramatic at times. However, although there have been many studies on lower animals, from rats to chimpanzees, that have found marked and reproducible improvements in cognitive skills with testosterone replacement, there have been very few human studies performed to evaluate this benefit.

Studies of the effects of androgens (the so-called male hormones, including testosterone) in monkeys reveal a potential *neurotrophic* (nerve-cell-building) effect, which helps maintain a more youthful density of nerve cells in parts of the brain. This includes the hippocampus, the area of the brain that is the first to deteriorate in Alzheimer's disease.

Results of studies on the effects of testosterone alone (as opposed to it being administered in conjunction with estrogen) on cognitive function in women are mixed. (In men, there's no debate on this issue—the benefits of testosterone replacement on a man's cognitive function are well-established.) In women, the effects of estrogen and testosterone appear to work in concert, and are difficult to look at individually.

A 2006 study from Harvard University, published in the *Journal of Clinical Endocrinology and Metabolism,* lends support to testosterone's cognition-supporting effects. The investigators gave fifty-one women, with severe androgen deficiency (caused by a poor function of the pituitary gland), physiological replacement of testosterone. Some of the women got a patch that delivered 300 micrograms of testosterone per day, and others got a placebo patch with no testosterone. The women on testosterone quickly reached normal, age-appropriate testosterone levels and showed significant improvements in mood, sexual function, and some measurements of bone density. Few adverse effects were reported, no serious ones.

Some very interesting research points to roles for testosterone in maintaining or increasing assertiveness and self-confidence. Women who match the career-woman stereotype tend to have higher testosterone levels than women who do not. When you win a competition, or an argument, or have higher social status, your testosterone levels are likely to be higher than when you've been defeated, or are low on the social pecking order. Testosterone has been shown to stimulate the activity of *dopamine,* the neurotransmitter that increases libido, facilitates orgasm, makes us more alert and energetic, and intensifies our ability to experience pleasure.

Testosterone For Strong Bones and Firm Muscles

Numerous studies have found a direct positive effect of testosterone on bone metabolism, the process by which bone is built and maintained. Science's first clues about this came from the discovery that *osteoblasts,* the bone cells that are responsible for making new bone, have testosterone receptors. Further evidence came from studies showing that osteoblast activity decreases in testosterone-deficiency states; and, finally, research showed that testosterone replacement therapy increased new bone formation—and did so better than any patented medication found on drugstore shelves.

Most researchers now understand that replacement of both estrogen and testosterone is the best treatment for bone loss. Unlike the usual prescriptions for osteoporosis prevention, this therapy is, in fact, reversing the very process that led to the bone loss in the first place—a lack of estrogen and testosterone.

Because testosterone is an *anabolic* hormone that promotes the buildup of muscle mass and strength, along with building new bone, it also helps build stronger muscles by increasing their protein content. (In proper replacement dosages, bio-identical testosterone does *not,* however, cause women to develop oversized, masculine muscles.)

Testosterone also decreases fat storage, which in turn decreases body-fat percentage. How much of that dreaded postmenopausal weight gain can be forestalled with appropriate BHRT? It's not known for sure at this point, but based on what is known, it should at least help you to stay slim and strong well into old age.

Testosterone and Breast Health

1. As of now, the risk of breast cancer in postmenopausal women from testosterone and its replacement is not well understood, but the strength of the evidence suggests there is a protective effect against the cancer.
2. Testosterone helps down-regulate estrogen receptors in the breast, making them less vulnerable to estrogen's growth-promoting effects.
3. Testosterone levels tend to go down at the same time of life (menopause) that the incidence of breast cancer goes up.
4. Men have only a fraction of the breast cancer risk that women do, in spite of having the same kind of breast tissue (just less of it) and very low progesterone. (*See* Chapter 8 for more on the relationship between testosterone and breast cancer.)

Testosterone and Cardiovascular Health in Women

A 2006 study from researchers at the University of Pennsylvania in Philadelphia measured testosterone levels in 344 women between the ages of sixty-five and ninety-eight, and found that those with the highest levels of testosterone had three times more likelihood of heart disease than those with lower levels.

Sound alarming? Wait, it turns out that women with the *lowest* levels of testosterone also had elevations in heart-disease risk. And when the investigators adjusted their analysis of the data to account for insulin resistance in these women, the association between high testosterone levels and heart disease was reduced significantly. In other words, a woman who is insulin resistant *and* has higher testosterone levels is going to be at an elevated risk for heart disease.

Central Obesity

Women who have this type of obesity—an apple body shape with excess weight in the midsection—are more likely to be insulin resistant, and they tend to have higher-than-normal testosterone levels, plus other hormonal imbalances. They are also more likely to have had PCOS (polycystic ovarian syndrome) during their childbearing years.

Insulin resistance and central obesity are both major risk factors for cardiovascular disease, regardless of hormone levels. And, again, testosterone replacement in women is only recommended if she's measurably low in the hormone.

Studies of testosterone replacement with oral methyl-testosterone (non-bio-identical) show increases in bad cholesterol and decreases in good cholesterol. This is due to the first-pass effect, and the fact that it is *not* bio-identical testosterone. I don't recommend oral testosterone for this reason.

There is good evidence that properly administered testosterone can decrease cholesterol in women and has other positive effects on the cardiovascular system. These investigators clearly state they don't know whether testosterone might contribute to heart disease, or whether higher, naturally-occurring levels of testosterone might be an effect of some other risk factor, such as insulin resistance. Insulin resistance is usually associated with *low* testosterone in men; in women, only the very high androgen levels seen in women with endocrine disorders have been linked to insulin resistance

> Symptoms of Testosterone Deficiency in Women
>
> Do you recognize one or more of these symptoms or circumstances that usually bring me to recommend testosterone to my female patients?
>
> 1. Difficulty becoming sexually aroused or reaching orgasm, when you are used to these pleasures being more or less within your reach
> 2. Hysterectomy (partial or total)
> 3. Lack of feelings of well-being
> 4. Lack of libido
> 5. Low energy
> 6. Reduced muscle strength
> 7. Substantially reduced sexual sensation in the nipples and clitoris
> 8. Thinning pubic hair
>
> If so, you may be a good candidate for testosterone replacement.

Unfounded Fears: 'Roid Rages, Musclebound Bearded Women

Testosterone is an anabolic steroid, a term that makes most people think of 'roid rages and musclebound bodybuilders. But the body's own natural testosterone is an anabolic steroid, too. All this means is, it is a steroid hormone that causes *anabolism,* or the growth and maintenance of muscle. Estrogen is anabolic, too. A woman taking physiologically dosed, bio-identical testosterone will not, contrary to incorrect rumors, grow facial hair, huge muscles, or an enlarged clitoris.

The testosterone produced in the body in the prime of life

does indeed increase muscle mass, decrease body fat, and boost energy—all results any athlete would appreciate. Endogenous testosterone also helps relieve aches and pains.

At puberty, testosterone is responsible for the growth of a woman's pubic and underarm hair. The sensitive areas of the nipples, vagina, and clitoris are all loaded with testosterone receptors.

Table 7.1

Testosterone Effects in Women

What Doctors Say	Plain English Translation
Development of pubic and axillary hair	Growth of armpit and pubic hair at puberty
Development of sensation in nipple, vagina, and clitoris; increases libido	For the joys of sexual arousal and orgasm…thank testosterone
Precursor to estrogen	This hormone can be made into estrogens in the body
Down-regulation of estrogen receptors in the breast	May protect against breast cancer
Increases lean body mass and decreases body fat	May help you to maintain or reach a healthy weight
Increased sense of well-being and energy	Good mood and plenty of vim and vigor (aside from all the good sex)
Stimulates formation of new bone	Helps stave off osteoporosis

Free and Bound—How Testosterone Levels are Measured

Measuring testosterone activity in the body can be a challenge. This is because it travels around inside you in both free (unbound) and bound forms. Bound testosterone is attached to a protein molecule (either sex-hormone-binding globulin or albumin), which renders it unable to bind to hormone receptors and exert its influence on cells. Estrogens are bound in the same manner. It's as though the hormone has its hands full already and so can't do anything but tote this big protein around. Unbound, free testosterone is free to do its business, binding to receptors and altering cellular activity in specific ways. In women, 97–99 percent of testosterone is bound at any given time.

Traditional blood tests for testosterone measure the total testosterone, or the amount of free plus bound testosterone. And this often gives a misleading picture of testosterone activity in the body, as it tells us nothing about how much of that hormone is doing its job and how much is floating around attached to the equivalent of a hormone Barcalounger. The answer? Measure *free* testosterone, which usually comprises a small percentage of the total hormone in the body.

Interestingly, even imaging techniques, such as Positron Emisson Tomography (PET scans) can impressively and noninvasively (requiring no poking with needles or cutting the person open) illustrate when a person has low or high testosterone levels. The drawback, however, is that PET scans are now far too expensive to be routinely used for evaluating testosterone status.

But I have found a solution to this, namely that a woman's symptoms are just as informative to me, if not more so, as scans and lab tests when I'm trying to figure out the right dosage of testosterone. Because of the variations in each woman's sensitivity to the hormone, the symptoms of low testosterone are easy to spot, with a lack of libido usually at the top of the list.

Testosterone Options

There are a variety of delivery methods available for bio-identical testosterone.

Oral Testosterone

For most of my career, until I discovered compounded hormones, the only testosterone available for women was oral methyl-testosterone. When taken orally, to be absorbed, testosterone has to be chemically altered—a change that greatly enhances a woman's likelihood of unwanted side effects, such as acne, irritability, loss of pubic hair, moodiness, and scalp hair loss. It's no wonder that physicians hesitated to prescribe testosterone to women when this drug was their main option.

Testosterone Patch

A patch is now in the works. **Intrinsa**, Proctor & Gamble's testosterone patch for women, was sent to the FDA in 2005 for approval. Studies showed it effectively increased libido, the only indication for which the drug company had applied.

The FDA advisory panel reviewed the drug company's studies and recommended that the FDA not approve the patch for commercial use. They claimed that "the indication of increasing a woman's libido is not enough of a medical reason to warrant the approval of this potentially risky drug." They sent it back to Proctor & Gamble for five more years of safety testing.

Keep in mind that the potentially risky drug the FDA panel referred to is not a drug, it's a *hormone* that has been circulating in every human's blood since Adam and Eve. There is no reason whatsoever to believe that testosterone, or any other bio-identical hormone, when given in appropriate doses, does anything but good in the body. If and when the testosterone patch passes muster with the FDA, I'll welcome it as a valuable addition to options for female testosterone replacement.

Testosterone in Transdermal Cream, Sublingual, or Subcutaneous Pellet Form

Other non-oral, bio-identical, and very effective alternatives are already available. They all require a prescription, and are made by compounding pharmacists. With the people I treat, I've seen nothing that even comes close to the effectiveness of testosterone in pellet form—and no delivery method with fewer adverse side effects.

Transdermal testosterone cream has been around for some time, and it has a lot of devoted fans. Some physicians suggest putting the cream directly onto the clitoris or vulva, or inside the vagina, to help stimulate the testosterone receptors concentrated in these areas.

The Vulva

The vulva is the term for the external female genitalia. It is often referred to as the vagina, but you can't see the actual vagina, as it is the internal passageway from the cervix to the vulva.

No studies have confirmed this transdermal method's benefits, and my own professional experience with my patients using topical testosterone on the vulva has not been especially positive.

This cream is more effective, in my experience, when applied to the skin of the neck, inner arms, or inner thighs, but there is one small caveat with any transdermal testosterone—hair can grow at the application site, so rotating the sites is advised. Also, be aware that rapid absorption and clearance leads to peaks and valleys of blood levels—the proverbial roller-coaster effect. For best results, testosterone cream probably needs to be used twice daily.

Similarly, sublingual drops or troches of testosterone are rapidly absorbed, and have a short half-life in the body before they are eliminated. Of the sublingual forms, I like the troche. For my patients who prefer it, I generally advise them to use it twice daily for the smoothest effect.

Testosterone injections are also available. You can choose from various options, such as depo-testosterone, testosterone decanoate, and testosterone enanthate. They are all injected into the muscle of the buttocks, and they last from three to four weeks. The molecules of testosterone found in these injectable forms have been altered slightly, so are not technically bio-identical, but they are a close enough match in structure and function to be categorized as bio-identical by most BHRT experts, and used accordingly.

Injections provide a relatively good testosterone effect for a varied length of time, but with this delivery method, you're still in for a rapid cessation of the hormone's effect, and can end up on that roller coaster.

Pellets, my preferred method, are inserted every three to six months, and studies have demonstrated they provide a smooth, consistent level of hormone for a longer period of time. Because of their more physiological delivery of the hormone to tissues, I strongly believe that subcutaneous pellets are the treatment of choice for most women who are testosterone-deficient.

Testosterone Options for Women	
Delivery Method	**Frequency Used**
Subcutaneous pellet	Replaced every 3-6 months
Testosterone cream	1-2 times daily
Intramuscular (injected) testosterone	Once every 2-3 weeks
Oral methyltestosterone	Daily
Sublingual (under the tongue) testosterone	1-2 times daily
Testosterone patch	N/A (not yet available for women at this writing)

8

Hormones and Breast Cancer Prevention

Data from the National Cancer Institute for the years 2002–2003 showed a significant drop in breast cancer cases in the aftermath of the WHI. After a steady climb of 1 percent per year in breast cancer rates between 1999 and 2002, and a climb of 1.7 percent per year in the decade or so before that, there was a 7-percent drop in breast cancer diagnoses. The drop in estrogen-receptor-positive breast cancer diagnoses was even greater—about 14 percent. Data from 2004 showed a continuation of this trend, with an additional 7-percent drop in breast cancer diagnoses.

It's a little startling to see such a large drop in breast cancer incidence in such a short period of time, since a new case of breast cancer can't be diagnosed by any means until several years after it begins to grow. Several factors probably led to this relatively large decrease:

1. **Since the mid-1990s, a leveling-off or decrease in the number of breast cancers diagnosed has been expected to occur at about this time**. This is due to the surge of new breast cancers being diagnosed earlier because of better early diagnostic techniques, including mammography and ultrasound. As these techniques have become more widely utilized, diagnosis has been made earlier and earlier. We have now reached a point where there are diminishing returns; thus, we have a leveling-

off effect that results in fewer cancers being detected.

2. **The decrease in women taking HRT would result in a short-term delay in the diagnosis in women who have breast cancer.** Women on estrogen may be diagnosed earlier because their tumors tend to be easier to see on ultrasound or mammography images.
3. **Hundreds of thousands of women have switched from traditional HRT (Prempro) to bio-identical hormone replacement therapy (BHRT) in the past five years.** Based on both laboratory studies and a few clinical studies, it is also likely that the decrease in breast cancer incidence is due to increasing use of BHRT. This is because there are two factors at work to reduce the incidence: Decreasing use of a carcinogen (Prempro and other pharmaceutical HRT), and switching to the use of BHRT, which may *reduce* the risk of breast cancer. Of course, these factors are not going to be publicized by the press or any drug company.

The leap from "Prempro causes breast cancer" to "all hormone replacement causes breast cancer" is not based on sound logic or the available scientific information. Those who would have you believe that oral Premarin acts the same way in the body as transdermal estradiol (BHRT) are uninformed or ignorant of the facts. As far as breast cancer is concerned, the bad guys are obviously progestins—all of them. But the press and most doctors ignore the crucial difference between the bioactivity of progestins and progesterone (BHRT).

The fear of breast cancer is, without question, the biggest reason why women are afraid to take hormone replacement therapy. With all the information and misinformation that's been published in the press the past several years, it's no wonder.

Recall that the WHI study on Prempro was discontinued in July 2002 because of a 26-percent increase in breast cancer risk after an average 5.2 years taking Prempro compared with women on placebo. I've heard physicians downplay that statistic as not really meaningful, and in terms of pure numbers, it means only a handful of extra breast cancer diagnoses per 100,000 women. But if you are one of that 26 percent, it's 100 percent for you.

Those who downplay the significance of that 26-percent boost in breast cancer risk found in the WHI are also overlooking numerous other studies showing an even more pronounced increase in breast cancer risk with Premarin plus progestin HRT. The reduction in breast cancer risk seen with the WHI-2 study actually persisted for the nearly seven years of that study. The only difference in the two studies? The group that had the increased incidence of breast cancer was on estrogen plus progestin; the group that had the decrease in breast cancer occurrence was on estrogen only.

From 1995 to 2000, at least six large epidemiologic studies revealed exactly the same finding—a greater risk of breast cancer in women on combined estrogen plus progestin than on estrogen alone.

Epidemiologic Study

This type of study examines factors that influence health and disease in a population. For example, take a group of 10,000 menopausal women, and determine, through interviews and medical records, whether they are using, or have ever used, bio-identical hormones. The group then gets tracked over the years with periodic questionnaires and medical exams, and any illnesses or deaths are carefully recorded. At the end of the study, you could then use statistical analysis to see whether or not those who used BHRT extended their lives and put more life in their years.

In large numbers of women, two of these studies revealed a 53-percent and 41-percent increased risk, respectively, after more than five years of estrogen plus progestin. In a review of forty-five different studies dating back more than thirty years, another group of researchers concluded there was no reason to believe that treatment with estrogen alone—without progestin—increased a woman's risk of developing breast cancer.

Bottom line, as stated in my Third Tenet of women's HRT:

The progestin is the part of the equation that seems to increase the risk of breast cancer.

I've had many patients come to me distressed because another physician told them that progesterone causes breast cancer. These doctors have confused progestins with progesterone. They're different creatures, and the differences between them are the reason why one protects pregnancy, promotes health, and helps prevent cancer, while the other increases risk of cancer, heart attacks, and strokes.

Progestins, Progesterone, and Your Breasts

The primary function of progesterone is to balance the effect of estrogen. This reins in the growth of cells so they do not grow out of control. Numerous studies performed on both normal breast cells and breast cancer cells show that progesterone decreases both their growth rate and the multiplication of cells—the direct opposite of estrogen's action on those cells.

One researcher, K.L. Chang, did a fascinating study on this subject. He enrolled forty premenopausal women, ages eighteen to forty-five, all of whom were scheduled for lumpectomy surgery around the twelfth day of their menstrual cycles. Starting on the first day of each woman's menstrual cycle, she applied a placebo gel or one of three gels containing hormones to the affected breast: a gel delivering 25 mg per day of bio-identical progesterone, a gel delivering 1.5 mg daily of estradiol, or a gel containing a combination of progesterone plus estradiol. The women were randomly assigned to these various treatments and did not know which they were using. During the lumpectomy, tissue samples were taken to evaluate proliferation—the rate at which cells were multiplying. The higher the proliferation rate, the more danger of cancer growth.

The study concluded that "[i]ncreased E2 [estradiol] concentration increases the number of cycling epithelial cells [i.e. the rate of proliferation in the breast]. Increased P [bio-identical progesterone] concentration significantly decreases the number of cycling epithelial cells...exposure to P for 10–13 days reduces E2-induced proliferation of normal breast epithelial cells in vivo." The women who used the progesterone-plus-estradiol gel had the same proliferation rate as those who used the placebo gel. In other words, the right balance of topical estradiol plus progesterone does not reduce proliferation, but it also doesn't accelerate it.

Several laboratory studies have shown that progestins not only do not inhibit the estrogen-stimulated growth of breast cells, they also block the progesterone receptors on those cells. Whatever progesterone is available cannot get to the receptor to down-regulate the growth stimulation from estrogens.

I don't know how this could be any more clear cut. For those who require further convincing, I'll give you even more information to demonstrate that progesterone, and, to some degree, testosterone, are the key HRT players that may well reduce the risk of breast cancer.

Lifetime Hormone Exposure and Breast Cancer Risk

A woman's childbearing and breastfeeding histories have a powerful influence on her risk of breast cancer. The more babies a woman has, and the longer she breastfeeds them, the lower her risk of this disease.

A woman who has children before she's thirty has a much better chance of avoiding breast cancer. A woman who has a child prior to the age of twenty-four has half the breast cancer risk of a woman who has her first child after age thirty-five. Having a child by age eighteen decreases her risk to one-third the risk of the woman who puts off childbearing until age thirty-five. In fact, if you've had your first child by age twenty, you have virtually no risk at all of ever having breast cancer. Women who never have a child stand at greatest risk of breast cancer. Nuns, as a group, have the highest vulnerability to this disease.

It would seem that while women have rightfully gained the freedom to live lives that aren't mired in mothering and parenting responsibilities until they're good and ready, in exchange, they are presented with a substantially increased risk of being diagnosed with breast cancer.

The theory generally used to explain the breast-protective effect of early, full-term pregnancy is that the high concentrations of progesterone during pregnancy serve to mature the breast tissue. In terms of this protective effect, one pregnancy is good, two is better, and three is better still—it seems that breast tissue continues to mature through the first two or three times a woman carries a baby to term. The more mature the breast tissue, the less likely those breast cells will grow abnormally in ways that could lead to cancer. Early pregnancy matures breast tissue earlier in a woman's life, further reducing the chances of carcinogenic changes taking root.

A woman's lifetime exposure to reproductive hormones—particularly the progesterone bath she gets during each pregnancy and the unique hormonal situation she enters into during the first months or year of breastfeeding—gives her long-term protection against breast cancer.

I think it's safe to assume, if you are reading these words, it's a little late for you to try and have children before turning thirty, and you're probably done with breastfeeding for good. You may have been one of the millions of mothers who was told that formula was better for your children than your own milk. And it's a safe bet that no one suggested not using your breasts for the purpose they were intended could have consequences.

It appears that the body of a woman who hasn't had lots of children that all got breastfed for two or three years can, in a way, be fooled by bio-identical HRT into aging more gracefully and warding off breast cancer.

Unfounded Fears about Estrogens and Breast Cancer

If a woman has any family history of breast cancer, she gets the unequivocal message from most doctors that estrogen is the worst possible thing she could put into her body. Women are given the impression that estrogen always fans the flames of breast cancer. But there's more to this picture.

Two types of breast cancer exist. There is hormone-receptor positive (ER/PR+) and hormone-receptor negative (ER/PR-). Receptor-positive cancers need estrogens and progesterone to grow; the other type doesn't, and is, overall, much harder to treat. Fortunately, about 75 percent of breast cancers are the easier-to-treat ER/PR+. In a study performed at the Fred Hutchinson Cancer Center in Washington State and funded by the National Cancer Institute, investigators looked at the long-term effects of estrogen-only and combined (estrogen plus progestin) HRT on breast cancer risk in 2000 women, ages sixty-five to seventy-nine. They found that *only* combined HRT increased the risk of ER/PR+ tumors. The estrogen regimen by itself did not have this effect, even after twenty-five or more years on unopposed estrogen. The scientists deduced that HRT has to contain progesterone (they really meant *progestin*) to promote breast cancer growth. This study is one of many that have come to this conclusion, but no other study has tracked people on unopposed estrogen for such a long period of time.

Did you know that women who are on estrogen replacement therapy when they are diagnosed with breast cancer tend to fare *better* than those who aren't? They also tend to live longer, disease-free lives following their diagnosis. Studies of women who survive breast cancer and choose to go on low-dose ERT suggest that these women live longer, with fewer disease recurrences, than survivors who don't use estrogens.

More reassuring data comes from the Nurses' Health Study. Harvard researchers observed just under 29,000 of the subjects in this cohort for about twenty years.

> **Cohort Study**
>
> A cohort study involves a group of people followed over a period of time to deduce any connections between behavior, diet, lifestyle, the use of medications, and the incidence of disease and mortality.

All had had hysterectomies and some were using estrogen-only HRT. They found that:

1. A total of 934 invasive breast cancers occurred in the cohort;
2. Breast cancer risk increased with how long unopposed estrogen was used, with a higher risk for estrogen receptor-positive tumors;
3. Women who used ERT for up to fifteen years had no increase in risk, and those who took ERT for fifteen years

or more only had an increased risk of ER+/PR+ cancers, and that increase was small—about a 1.5-fold risk compared to the other subjects.

This figure amounts to a very small overall number of breast cancers. Other animal, cell-culture, and human studies strongly suggest that natural progesterone would counteract any increase in risk with unopposed ERT. And at least three small observational studies have found that women who are on estrogen and also use progesterone have a lower-than-expected incidence of breast cancer. Other studies also indicate the protective effects of progesterone.

1. A study by researchers at Johns Hopkins reported that, of 1000 women followed for at least twenty years, those who had a measurable progesterone deficiency had a 5.4-fold increase in the incidence of breast cancer.
2. Women who had breast tumors surgically removed were enrolled in a study where they were instructed to rub a progesterone gel on the affected breast for ten to thirteen days prior to surgery. The cell growth within the normal and cancerous breast tissues was slower than expected with this therapy.
3. Women who have breast cancer surgery during the luteal phase of the menstrual cycle, when progesterone levels are at their highest, have significantly less abnormal cell growth and a lower incidence of metastatic disease. Higher concentrations of progesterone in the body helps to reduce the chances that any cancerous cells missed by the surgery will take hold and grow into new tumors.

The clincher, in terms of progesterone's benefits to the breast, comes from a 2004 study published in the American Cancer Society's journal, *Cancer*. In this study, from the highly regarded M. D. Anderson Hospital in Houston, Texas, scientists tracked 383 women who had all been diagnosed with breast cancer prior to age thirty-five. They all had surgery and chemotherapy for their cancer. Forty-seven of the 383 women subsequently gave birth to babies.

The incidence of breast cancer recurrence in the women who had babies after breast cancer treatment was 50 percent less than the women who did not get pregnant. Women who got pregnant and did have recurrence had significantly less metastatic disease and lower-grade tumors than the women with recurrent cancer who did not have a pregnancy between the initial surgery and chemotherapy and the recurrence of the disease. This study lends strong credence to the theory that the heavy-duty progesterone bath a pregnant woman receives protects the breasts.

Perhaps the most convincing evidence comes from the very large study involving 54,548 French women published in 2005 in the *International Journal of Cancer*. These women (average age: 54.8) had not used HRT for one year before enrolling in the study, and the average duration of HRT use in the study was 2.8 years. As might be expected, women who used estrogen plus progestin HRT had a 40-percent increase in breast cancer incidence, which is consistent with the rise in risk seen in women on estrogen plus progestin in the WHI study and the Nurses' Health Study. Estrogen alone did not significantly increase the risk, and the estrogen plus progesterone arm of the study revealed a 10-percent *decrease* in the incidence of breast cancer over the same period.

In Europe, bio-identical HRT is more widely accepted, and these investigators were smart enough to do an analysis comparing the use of bio-identical micronized progesterone with that of progestins. Here's what they found—*estrogen plus natural, bio-identical progesterone significantly reduced the women's risk of breast cancer.*

The next step would be to do a study on women who have had breast cancer to see if bio-identical progesterone therapy would lower their risk of recurrence. Although I don't know where the funding would come from for such a study, it's the logical next step in the learning curve that I hope will someday cement the idea in the minds of the medical world that *progestins are not progesterone,* and that progestins are carcinogenic but *progesterone is not.*

A number of my female patients who have had breast cancer are now on HRT. It took a leap of faith for them to pursue this route because they have all been told since diagnosis that they should avoid HRT at all costs. However, if you look at the cold hard facts about HRT and breast cancer, and if you use *only* bio-identical hormones, it becomes a much more reasonable option for women who have conquered breast cancer and decidedly do *not* want to fight another bout with the disease.

Here's another way of looking at the HRT/breast cancer issue. In a 2005 review article, one Belgian researcher pointed out that the increase in the risk of developing breast cancer because of *conventional* progestin-Premarin HRT is, according to a good-sized body of research, equivalent to the increased risk found in women who started their periods before the age of eleven. And, according to the WHI results, having a first pregnancy after the age of thirty-five increases your risk of breast cancer about as much as postmenopausal HRT does. Statistically, obesity or moderate consumption of alcohol will have the same effect on your breast cancer risk as PremPro. It is not really a very big absolute increase in risk. Now, consider that the risk with appropriate doses of estrogen alone is basically nonexistent. *Bioidentical* hormones, given in doses approximating those of a normally cycling woman, are not going to harm your breast health.

Does Testosterone Raise Breast Cancer Risk?

In the summer of 2006, a study was published in the *Annals of Internal Medicine* that seemed to be a potential death blow to testosterone therapy in women. The study looked at the 121,700 participants in the Nurses' Health Study, examining associations between hormone replacement and breast cancer. It was performed by researchers at Brigham and Women's Hospital and Harvard Medical School, and they concluded that women who had gone through natural menopause and used methyl-testosterone plus estrogen had 2.5 times as much breast cancer as women who took no hormones. Women who used estrogen plus methyltestosterone (Estratest) and progestin had a 77-percent higher risk of breast cancer than women who had never used hormones. Women who took estrogen only had a 15-percent increase in breast cancer, and women who took estrogen and progestin only (no testosterone) had a 58-percent increase.

In their discussion of the study, the researchers write that women's bodies may be transforming the extra testosterone into estradiol in the breasts, which they suspect might enhance the risk of breast cancer. Here are two relevant points on this study:

1. They used Estratest, a pill containing esterified, *non-bio-identical* estrogen and methyl-testosterone, which is *not* bio-identical testosterone;
2. The women who had the most significantly increased risk in this study were the ones who took *progestin-containing* formulations.

In an as-yet-unpublished study by a colleague of mine in California, almost 1000 postmenopausal women received subcutaneous bio-identical hormone pellets for up to twenty-five years. All of them received both estradiol and testosterone pellets, and 70 percent of them were also taking natural progesterone in some fashion. At the conclusion of the ten-year period for which these women were tracked, they had been on pellets for six months to twenty-five years.

During that ten-year period, only one of the women was diagnosed with breast cancer. She had gotten the bio-identical pellets once, and six months later was diagnosed with breast cancer, which indicates that the cancer preceded the pellets. The *expected* incidence of breast cancer in these women would have been at least one in thirty; according to this expected incidence in the general population of menopausal women, at least forty of them *should* have gotten breast cancer.

And, finally, a study published in the *Journal of the North American Menopause Society* in 2007 examined ninety-nine postmenopausal women who were given estrogen and progestin plus either a testosterone or placebo patch. Biopsies were performed to remove breast tissue at the study's outset and again after six months of hormone therapy; these samples were examined for any changes that suggested increased cell growth (proliferation), a precursor to cancer. The results were remarkable: in women who got the placebo patch with their estrogen and progestin, proliferation increased *more than five-fold.* Women who got the testosterone patch, on the other hand, had *no significant increase in proliferation.*

In spite of the fact that, microscopically, male and female breast tissue is the same, men rarely get breast cancer. Why the discrepancy? Some say it's because men don't have as much estrogen and progesterone, and they see this as evidence that these hormones increase breast cancer risk. Men have high testosterone and low estradiol, women have high estrogen and low testosterone. But keep in mind that women's greatest increase in the incidence of breast cancer occurs *in the five years prior to menopause.* This just so happens to correspond with the time when progesterone and testosterone levels are *decreasing* in women. This is probably not a coincidence. During those perimenopausal years, estrogen can remain dominant, and it's not a good idea to add more estrogens to the mix until menopause comes along for real, as evidenced by measurably low levels of this group of hormones, or such menopausal symptoms as hot flashes, low libido, night sweats, and vaginal dryness.

The evidence is convincing that the right form of HRT—balanced, bio-identical estrogen, testosterone, and progesterone—not only does *not* increase the risk of breast cancer, but may decrease it instead.

A woman who is at a high risk for breast cancer, or who is concerned about its recurrence, should be sure to have her hormone levels carefully tested, and should be sure to use replacement only if it's bio-identical and in a dosage carefully designed to do no more than replace what is missing.

It is my hope that, in the near future, more attention and money will be spent on the prevention of breast cancer. Presently, only about 5 percent of the budget of the National Cancer Institute is spent on prevention. That's not enough for a disease that has a mortality rate of 89.2 per 100,000 women in the United States—the nation with the highest breast cancer mortality in the world. Hopefully, the strategies presented here will help lower your chances of developing this most dreaded disease.

Other Avenues to Breast Cancer Prevention

What else can you do to lower your risk of breast cancer right now, today? In women who are nearing, or in, menopause, I believe the two most important environmental influences on breast cancer risk are diet and *xenoestrogens.*

Diet and Breast Cancer Prevention

Eating well is the most vital step you can take to living a

long, healthy life. You have more control over your diet than you have over any other aspect of disease prevention. Most cancers tend to strike more often in people with poor nutritional habits, and breast cancer is no exception. Here are some dietary pointers specifically for the woman who wants to avoid a diagnosis of breast cancer.

Lose weight by cutting calories and exercising. Losing excess weight and exercising daily or almost daily can reverse early insulin resistance, where cells stop listening to insulin's message to allow sugars out of the bloodstream and into the cells. Women who are obese and insulin resistant have more risk of breast cancer. Even if you are not insulin resistant, but are more than twenty or thirty pounds beyond the weight your doctor says you ought to be, lose the weight anyhow because overweight is likely to boost your risk. Simply eating fewer calories each day will help decrease your risk of most cancers, and heart disease as well.

Reduce or eliminate sugar and flour, and other refined carbohydrates. Refined carbohydrates are the big culprits in raising calorie intake well beyond what is healthful. I'm not suggesting you give up these foods entirely; instead, find ways to cut back on them so you can still have the enjoyment without the consequences of weight gain. Eat one piece of bread instead of four, have a small piece of gourmet chocolate instead of a giant pastry, or pull the bready middle out of a roll before putting a burger inside. Know that refined carbohydrates create cravings for more of the same, and that the less of these foods you eat, the less you'll crave them.

Drink alcohol in moderation. Take it easy with the alcohol. Drinking more than one alcoholic drink a day will raise your risk of breast cancer.

Eat cruciferous vegetables as often as possible. It's looking as though women who eat a lot of *cruciferous* vegetables (broccoli, Brussels sprouts, cabbage, cauliflower, garlic, and onions, also known as *Brassica* vegetables) can reduce their risk of breast cancer. Cruciferous vegetables contain abundant *indole-3 carbinol*, which promotes the body's ability to process and get rid of any excess estrogen that might otherwise hang around in the body after being metabolized, and possibly create an imbalanced situation that could stimulate cell growth and cancer formation.

This might seem to counter my assertion that estrogens are not as dangerous to the breasts as most medical authorities seem to believe, so let me explain further. In the body, estrogens enter at receptor sites and then circulate in the blood to the liver, where they are broken down into *metabolites*, such as 16-alpha-hydroxyestrone, 4-hydroxyestrone, and 2-hydroxyestrone. The first two metabolites are carcinogenic, while the last is protective against breast cancer (and other cancers, as well).

When you eat foods rich in indole-3-carbinol (I-3-C), they affect liver enzymes in a way that pushes more of these *spent* estrogens into the production of 2-hydroxyestrone, the *good* estrogen metabolite. I-3-C also inhibits the production of 4-hydroxyestrone. As if that weren't enough to recommend it, I-3-C further affects liver enzymes in ways that increase the body's production of important antioxidants, such as glutathione, and has been found to modulate the breakdown of carcinogens, such as aflatoxin (found in a mold that naturally grows on peanuts) and benzo(a)pyrene (found in burnt, charred food) in ways that help prevent cancer. It has been found to up-regulate apoptosis, the good kind of cell death that works against cancer, in several cancer-cell lines. And I-3-C even appears to help stave off heart disease by decreasing inflammation in the blood-vessel walls and reducing the affects of a free-radical attack on bad LDL cholesterol. LDL oxidation is believed to be a major initiating factor in the development of heart disease.

So, bust out that broccoli! Whip up some cole slaw! Drag out your German great-grandmother's red-cabbage recipe! And it might be time to try Brussels sprouts again if you've turned up your nose at them since childhood. If you toss them in extra-virgin olive oil and sprinkle on some sea salt and pepper, then roast them at 400 degrees until the edges of the outer leaves start to turn brown, you'll be stunned by how good they taste.

Eat more vegetables, fruit, and fiber-rich whole grains and beans. A diet that meets those government recommendations for seven servings of vegetables and fruit per day will aid in breast cancer prevention. Fiber-rich whole grains and beans are great sources of the B vitamins, too. These foods are packed with antioxidants and fiber, both of which are known to protect against just about every kind of age-related disease. Besides, if you are full of fresh, crisp, leafy greens with an olive-oil vinaigrette and a side of seasoned brown rice and beans, you're not going to be so quick to reach for the pint of Haagen-Dazs when the meal is over.

Try some flaxseed. Flaxseeds and other seeds, as well as fruits and vegetables, contain weakly estrogenic compounds called *lignans,* which many studies indicate have protective effects against breast cancer. In the gastrointestinal (GI) tract, lignans are broken down by microorganisms, producing a phytoestrogen called *enterolactone.* Studies find that higher dietary intake of lignans and higher blood levels of enterolactone translate to a substantial reduction in breast cancer risk.

Cell-culture studies find that flaxseed reduces the tendency for breast cancer cells to grow and spread. It is available as pre-ground flaxseed meal or as whole seeds. It needs to be ground to make it digestible—you can grind your own in a coffee grinder. Stir flaxseeds into yogurt, add them to hot cereals, or sprinkle them over salad.

Flax oil is not as good a choice as the whole seeds, although it is rich in omega-3 fatty acids—a beneficial type of fat that most Westerners need a lot more of than they are getting (*see* Chapter 11 for details). The fiber in flax is an important part of its benefit.

Fat in your food is fine—as long as it's the right kind of fat. What about fat? A lot of studies have linked dietary fat to breast cancer, suggesting that a diet low in fat is the best route to prevention. But most of these studies have not looked at the *type* of fat women eat.

Overall, a diet that contains plentiful monounsaturated fats from olive oil is protective against breast cancer. Saturated fats from butter, full-fat dairy, and meat are not such a good idea in excess—use them only in small amounts to add flavor. Avoid hydrogenated oils (found in most processed foods), which contain carcinogenic, artery-clogging trans fatty acids; and avoid liquid polyunsaturated oils, such as those from corn, cottonseed, soybeans, and sunflower.

What about soy foods? Soy foods are a low-fat, high-fiber addition to a breast-protective diet. Unfortunately, they've been over-hyped because of evidence that the phytoestrogens—plant estrogens—they contain might help reduce every female problem, from hot flashes to breast cancer. Soy is no miracle food, and there is actually some debate about whether too many of the estrogenic chemicals found in soy could enhance breast cancer risk in a very small, high-risk subset of women. However, adding a serving of a fermented soy food, such as miso (soybean paste, which you can use to make dressings or soups), tofu, or tempeh to your diet two or three times a week will definitely do you more good than harm.

Recommended Diet and Lifestyle Changes for Breast Cancer Prevention

- Lose weight by cutting calories and exercising more or less daily
- Reduce or eliminate refined sugar and flour
- Drink alcohol only in moderation (one drink or less per day)
- Eat lots of cruciferous vegetables (cabbage, broccoli, Brussels sprouts, cauliflower)
- Eat more vegetables and fruit; add more fiber-rich whole grains and beans to your diet
- Eat ground flaxseeds to increase lignan intake
- Choose monounsaturated fats like olive oil over polyunsaturated nut/seed oils
- Avoid hydrogenated oils
- Eat soy foods two to three times weekly
- Choose organic food whenever possible to avoid xenoestrogens

Eat organic foods, avoid xenoestrogenic chemicals. Eating organic food is a difficult step towards breast cancer protection—primarily because organic food costs so much more and may be more difficult to find. This step is crucial, however, because of the *xenoestrogenic* chemicals that have invaded our non-organic food supply.

Among the world's women, those in America have the dubious honor of being most likely to develop breast cancer, and a large part of that risk is probably found in the environment. Women who immigrate from countries where breast cancer risk is low have been found to have a risk equal to their American-born counterparts within two generations. And exposure to xenoestrogens, along with an overabundant diet that encourages obesity and insulin resistance and is deficient in anti-cancer antioxidant nutrients, is probably a major culprit.

Xenoestrogens are man-made substances that have estrogenic activity in living cells. Everyone in this culture is exposed to these chemicals. They are found in herbicides, household chemicals, pesticides, solvents, and industrial wastes, and they've managed to wiggle their way into virtually everything that slithers, flies, swims, crawls, or walks the planet. Their actions in the body tend to mimic those of estrogen, but some resemble mutant versions of this class of hormones that can interfere with the action of the body's own hormones. Some of these toxic xenoestrogens are strongly linked to birth defects, cancer, immune dysfunction, infertility, nervous system damage, or other serious problems.

They get into your body and stimulate estrogen receptors just as the estrogens do—only xenoestrogens are harder to eliminate from your body. Many chemicals used in the growing and processing of *non*-organic foods contain xenoestrogens that have been definitively shown to have carcinogenic effects.

It would be impossible to avoid these chemicals and still live in the United States, but eating organic food as often as possible will help protect you against a major source of exposure. In particular, try to eat organic foods rich in fat—dairy, eggs, fish, meats, poultry, and oils—that have been raised and processed without chemicals.

Trapped Toxins and Underarm Odor

There is some evidence suggesting that antiperspirants and underwire bras conspire to prevent the release of toxins from breast tissue into sweat and the lymphatic system. It seems sensible for women to avoid antiperspirants and wear underwire bras infrequently. While I'm not exactly an expert, female patients and colleagues have told me that camisoles with shelf bras sewn in are comfortable, supportive alternatives.

Eating a clean, pure, nutritious diet will reduce underarm odor, and there are many natural, organic deodorants available. Instead of perfumes and deodorants, try dotting essential oils, such as jasmine, lavender, rose, or vanilla, under your arms. And, if necessary, use a non-talc powder to reduce underarm wetness.

9

Menopause Isn't Just for Women Anymore

Andropause and Testosterone for Men

I include this chapter knowing full well that a woman in the man's life may well end up being the one to read it on his behalf. As most doctors will tell you, it's almost always women who read these kinds of books. Most of the men who end up in my office for hormone evaluation and replacement are dragged in by their wives or other women who see that spark going, going, gone, and who care enough to persuade them to at least try and get themselves feeling good again.

Men are often too proud to admit, even to themselves, that they might be sliding into andropause, the male version of menopause. They don't want to admit that they're bothered by their lack of libido or any difficulty getting and maintaining erections. Or they might believe themselves to be too busy doing other, more manly, things to read up on testosterone-replacement therapy—things like sitting in a chair, remote in one hand, beer in the other, a bowl of chips perched atop their growing midsections, trying to avoid going to bed and facing their libidinous wives.

In my experience, many men reflect this attitude of not recognizing or wanting to admit they have a testosterone-deficiency problem. The symptoms characteristic of testosterone deficiency come on gradually, and therefore, most men don't recognize them as anything more than getting old.

Even if it occurs to them there could be a deficiency, they can't always get their doctor to make a proper diagnosis. Most men who tell their doctors about symptoms that, to me, *scream* andropause, get a response something like, "These symptoms are just a normal part of aging, there's nothing that can be done." Even those physicians willing to perform blood tests of testosterone almost always report that the results are in the normal range. But a measurement in that range is often non-physiological in the extreme—their testosterone is at a level in the body that may fall within so-called normal ranges, but is far from optimal.

Gentlemen, in case you *are* reading this chapter yourselves, I'm going to talk man to man and give you a whirlwind, man-friendly crash course on andropause and testosterone. You'll learn how to clue in on a deficiency, how to find out whether it's safe for you to replace it, and how your health, longevity, and sex life will most probably benefit dramatically if you do.

Harold—Eighty-Eight Years Young and Not Ready to Lose His Spark

Men young and old can be low on testosterone. Some lucky bucks maintain decent levels all the way into very old age. Others could benefit from replacement at a much younger age, even in their mid- to late thirties. Can a man in his sixties, seventies, or even eighties, benefit from bio-identical testosterone replacement? You bet.

Take Harold, for example, one of the most fascinating people I've ever met. Harold was born in 1919, which made him eighty-eight on the day he limped into my office with the aid of a cane. A friend of his, who had been a long-term patient of mine, had persuaded Harold to come in and see me. Although he was hunched forward and moving quite slowly and deliberately, Harold's voice was impressively strong and clear.

Finding a person over the age of eighty-five with no symptoms of dementia is pretty rare, but Harold was articulate and sharp, really on the ball. As we chatted, I could see he had a clear grasp of events both recent and distant.

Harold had been a vaudeville performer for more than sixty years, and had performed all over the world with his wife. She had died about a year before he walked into my office. He informed me that their sex life had continued to be good until about two years before her death, at which point he had lost his libido and, in his words, "hit the wall." After eighty-six years of vim and vigor, he had begun to feel weak, tired, achy, and impotent; and he wasn't ready to feel that way.

After his wife died, Harold could feel his physical status deteriorating even more than expected in response to the loss of his lifelong partner. For a year, his many close friends told him that his experience was perfectly normal for an eighty-plus-year-old man who had lost his wife. Eventually, he bought into their beliefs and assumed that his active life was behind him.

Fortunately, he had one friend who believed there was more to his decline than passing the eighty-year mark. She had started with me on BHRT several years before, and had felt great since, so she hoped her good friend might have the same *Youth Effect* experience she had.

I would love to know what Harold's testosterone level was at eighty-six when he was still feeling good and enjoying sexual intimacy with his wife; but he stated that, as far as he knew, no one had ever measured his testosterone level. The assays we took showed very low levels of testosterone. His PSA and estradiol levels were also low, which made him a great candidate for testosterone-replacement therapy. (More later on why PSA and estradiol are concerns in male HRT.) After we discussed his options, he chose to use a compounded testosterone cream twice daily.

When I followed up with him, he reported that he had no trouble using the cream as directed. "It's easy to use," he said, "and I feel noticeably better. More energy, fewer aches and pains." On re-assessment six months later, his testosterone levels were in a more optimal range, and his PSA and estradiol levels were unchanged.

Harold tells me he feels like his old self, and I certainly hear a spark in his voice and see more spirit in his walk. The ladies in his nursing home best beware.

Male HRT—A Brief History

Testosterone therapy for men isn't new. In fact, its history extends further back than estrogens and progesterone in women. In 1889, a renegade French physiologist named Charles Edouard Brown-Séquard announced to a group of physicians that he had been injecting himself with a concoction made from the testicles of dogs and guinea pigs, and he claimed that, as a result, his physical strength, his intellectual energy, and the arc of his urine had all increased dramatically. The idea of using testicular extracts to improve men's health and vigor caught on quickly, and interest was strong.

Leo L. Stanley, M.D., had a less-than-free market for a procedure he developed in 1918: For forty years, he transplanted the testicles of executed prisoners into healthy ones at San Quentin Prison. He claimed that the transplants restored health and potency. When the surgery became popular and human testicles ended up in short supply, he began using testicles from rams, goats, and deer. Hundreds of men underwent his procedure, and his papers on the subject were published in the renowned journal *Endocrinology*.

Testosterone was isolated in 1935. Physicians began to inject it into athletes (to make their muscles bigger); women with breast cancer (to decrease tumor size); homosexuals (to "cure" them); and trauma patients (to increase their red-blood-cell production in an attempt to minimize blood loss). In 1939, The *Journal of the American Medical Association (JAMA)* published an article entitled, "The Male Climacteric," which led to greater use of this hormone in aging men.

In 1944, Drs. Keller and Myers published a study in *JAMA* about treating a group of men who had low testosterone levels and symptoms of andropause with testosterone injections. After six weeks, almost all these men had a resolution of most of their symptoms, and some had complete relief.

Unfortunately, widespread use of this therapy was delayed for several decades by the advent of anabolic-androgenic steroids (AAS) in competitive athletics and bodybuilding.

Altered, Anabolic-Androgenic Steroids vs. Bio-identical Testosterone

By the 1950s, Russian athletes had discovered synthetic testosterone as an anabolic aid. They started winning competitions left and right, and Americans wanted a piece of that action. Anabolic-androgenic steroids (AAS)—the true name of the synthetic, and powerful, forms of chemically-altered testosterone and related hormones used to get *huge and strong* fast—were widely available to athletes by 1960. The *non*-bio-identical AAS stimulate growth in both muscle and bone.

The scientists responsible for introducing AAS to American athletes realized too late that these drugs had terrible side effects. But, in spite of a very long list of serious side effects, including alterations in heart valves, baldness, cancer, gynecomastia (growth of female-like breasts due to the transformation of excess testosterone to estrogens), high blood pressure, jaundice, liver toxicity, severe acne, testicular atrophy, and unfavorable shifts in blood cholesterol, the demand for anabolic steroids grew throughout the rest of the twentieth century. A few deaths were publicly linked to the use of these drugs, including Lyle Alzado's from a brain tumor. Reputed 'roid rages' and other psychological effects were common cautions against the use of these steroids.

Some of the testosterone now used by athletes is actually bio-identical testosterone. However, the stacking regimens they often use can raise testosterone levels to several times the natural, physiological levels.

All forms of testosterone, bio-identical or not, are currently classified as Schedule III controlled substances and are closely regulated. This means that all testosterone prescriptions are tracked by the Drug Enforcement Agency (DEA). Non-bio-identical testosterone still has a few medical uses, including stimulating the appetite and building muscle mass in men with such wasting conditions as AIDS and cancer. But more of these steroids are used by athletes and bodybuilders than are prescribed by physicians because a huge black market exists for them, despite the fact that possessing them without a prescription is a federal crime.

The furor over these steroids has given testosterone a bad

name. This is unfortunate because the benefits of *physiological, bio-identical* testosterone replacement for men who are measurably low in this hormone—particularly at a young age—are indisputable. This is the First Tenet of male testosterone replacement, first mentioned way back in the Introduction. This therapy has significant health benefits for aging men. There have been positive outcomes using bio-identical testosterone since the 1980s.

FSH, LH, and the Manliness of Men

In men, follicle stimulating hormone and luteinizing hormone (FSH/LH), both hailing from the pituitary (a gland situated just below the brain), stimulate cells of the testes to secrete testosterone. This hormonal duo also promotes the production of sperm. At *andronarche*— male puberty—this mechanism cranks up, causing testosterone to rise to its highest lifetime levels.

Ideally, FSH and LH keep the testosterone volume cranked up to high-normal levels all the way into a man's 70s or 80s. A man is better off healthwise, and performs better sexually, when his testosterone levels stay within optimal ranges throughout his life. His risk of dementia, heart attacks, impotence, and osteoporosis is reduced, muscles stay harder, and less weight is gained as fat.

There are two cell types in the testes: *Leydig* and *Sertoli* cells. LH stimulates the Leydig cells to produce testosterone. FSH stimulates the Sertoli cells to produce binding proteins, which bind to and transport testosterone to other parts of the testes where sperm are produced and developed.

Andropause—What It Is, Who's Affected

Andropause. Male menopause. Menpause. Viropause. Low-testosterone syndrome. Male climacteric. Partial androgen deficiency of the aging male (PADAM). These are all terms for the same entity—a very real and disabling shift that affects a large percentage of men middle-aged and older.

Since andropause is the most commonly used term now, and it's a little catchier, it's the one I'll use. Low testosterone syndrome is, however, probably the most descriptive term, as the condition boils down to low testosterone levels in the majority of cases.

The changes with male menopause are gradual, but distinct. By the age of fifty-five, *50–75 percent of men are low in bioavailable testosterone*. They experience a broad range of symptoms—erectile dysfunction (ED), loss of energy and vigor, loss of muscle, low libido, weight gain—and an increased risk of age-related diseases, such as cancer, diabetes, and heart disease. All these issues are often chalked up to just plain getting old.

A substantial age-related reduction in men's testosterone levels is often accompanied by an increase in the production of estrogen. In some men, testosterone falls as FSH and LH rise; in others, testosterone appears to drop because of a drop in LH. In other words, some andropausal shifts start in the brain, and others start in the testes.

Although it was once believed that higher testosterone in aging men was largely to blame for heart disease and prostate cancer, it now appears more likely that lower testosterone and higher estrogen (perhaps even lower progesterone)—the common shift that occurs with andropause—is more harmful.

Why Isn't Testosterone Replacement More Commonly Prescribed for Men?

In spite of numerous scientific articles confirming the many benefits of testosterone-replacement therapy for men, the public and medical community have been very slow to take advantage of this life-enhancing treatment. From what I've seen, there are three basic misconceptions that prevent men from trying testosterone therapy.

First, and probably foremost, is a failure to recognize that testosterone deficiency exists. Denial and pride are huge issues for men. If I had a dollar for every woman who has tried unsuccessfully to get her husband to come and see me for evaluation, I could retire a rich man. And if they're finally dragged in here, most men are shocked by the finding of low testosterone, in spite of having virtually *every symptom* of testosterone deficiency. "Me? Low testosterone? No way."

For most men, the onset of andropausal symptoms is gradual

rather than abrupt. You might just get used to feeling lousy, tired, absentminded, and asexual, and you might forget how it felt to be young and sharp and raring to go. But a little bio-identical testosterone, appropriately delivered, can do a lot to bring you back to being your old, more vital self.

Even doctors astute enough to order tests of testosterone levels in men with andropausal symptoms tend to under-diagnose low testosterone. They look at the lab's *normal* range for total testosterone, which happens to be a very wide range. According to that range, just about every man is normal.

Normal is average. It's determined by sampling the hormone levels of a large number of men, figuring out the range their measurements span, and then taking off the top and bottom five percent. Average is, very often, far from optimal. Optimal feels better, looks better, and is likely to extend your healthy lifespan.

Is Testosterone Replacement Safe?

Yes, definitely.

The safety of testosterone in men who are deficient has long been accepted as proven. My Second Tenet of testosterone replacement for men is built on this premise: Using testosterone in a bio-identical form and in a physiologic manner will not increase a man's risk of heart disease, prostate cancer, or any other adverse consequence.

In this chapter you will learn why adequate testosterone is *good* for men's hearts. The only real question is whether it's safe for men with prostate cancer, whether the hormone could accelerate the growth of a prostate tumor. In the next chapter, I'll discuss this important issue; for now, let me assure you that high testosterone is not a cause of prostate cancer.

Hopefully, with more and more positive information being published, physicians will become more proactive in diagnosing and treating andropause.

Are You Andropausal?

Andropause isn't a midlife crisis. Andropause doesn't make you want to cheat on your wife with a woman half your age, get a hairpiece, or buy a sports car. It makes you want to give up on all that. It's often characterized by a pronounced loss of libido and energy. Erectile dysfunction, fatigue, loss of muscle mass, depression, and an overall feeling of *why bother?* can all point to andropause.

Most men believe if they don't have erectile dysfunction or a decreased libido, then their testosterone level must be fine, and andropause isn't a concern for them. While ED and low libido may well be a direct result of low testosterone, they are only two of a great many symptoms provoked by low testosterone. Because the hormonal actions of testosterone affect virtually every organ system, a lack of testosterone can cause a wide variety of physical and mental complaints.

St. Louis University Questionnaire on Symptoms of Testosterone Deficiency

In 1990, a group of researchers at St. Louis University developed a questionnaire that is commonly used to screen men for low testosterone syndrome. Try it yourself and see how you do.

1. Do you have a decrease in sex drive?
2. Do you lack energy?
3. Have you experienced a decrease in strength and/ or endurance?
4. Have you lost height?
5. Have you noticed a decreased enjoyment of life?
6. Are you sad or grumpy?
7. Are your erections less strong?
8. Has there been a deterioration in your ability to play sports?
9. Are you falling asleep right after dinner?
10. Has there been a deterioration in your work performance?

If you answered *yes* to questions one or seven, or if you answered *yes* to at least three of the other questions, your testosterone levels could use a checkup. And keep in mind that even if your test results come back in the average range, your symptoms could still merit a trial of bio-identical testosterone replacement to put you into a more optimal range.

How do you know if you've got low testosterone syndrome? Sounds simple enough—just get a blood testosterone level and see what it shows. Unfortunately, it's not that simple. There are three problems with this approach.

1. ***The problem of SHBG***. Testosterone travels in the bloodstream mostly bound to proteins called *albumin* and *sex-hormone-binding globulin* (SHBG). These proteins effectively take testosterone out of play, and only the portion that is not bound to a protein is available to cells to have an effect on receptors. We call this active testosterone in the bloodstream *unbound* testosterone. This is a very important concept to understand in the treatment of testosterone-deficiency states, as the level of testosterone binding to proteins can make a big difference in testosterone's availability at the cellular level. We have to measure both total and unbound testosterone to get a picture of a man's andropausal status.
2. ***The estrogen issue***. Although a certain amount of estrogen is necessary for hormone balance in men, an excessive amount can overwhelm normal testosterone levels. As men get older, they tend to convert more and more testosterone into estradiol through *aromatization*, an enzyme-mediated process. Aromatization of testosterone into estradiol lowers the ratio of testosterone to estrogen, which can—*even when testosterone levels seem adequate*—induce andropausal symptoms. So, it's imperative to know what is happening with estradiol levels in a man's body, both prior to, and during, treatment with testosterone. A man who is overweight or obese is more likely to aromatize excessively because aromatization happens in fat cells. If adding testosterone to the man's body ends up increasing estradiol levels, that's a problem—but one that can be solved (more on this in a bit).
3. ***Normal is not optimal, and never shall the twain meet***. Ninety percent of people will fit into the normal testosterone range for their age group. But is normal what you want? No way—an *optimal* level, the one that existed when you were at your physical best, is what you want.

The best-case scenario would be to get a hormone test when

you're at that physical best, so you have a baseline value to refer to later on. If your testosterone level during your most healthful, most energetic time of life was 800 and you've dropped to 400, you are not going to function optimally. Conversely, if your optimal level is 400 and it is unchanged twenty years later, you're most likely still functioning at a high level. But, since no one does that, it is not really known what that optimal level is for any individual. Until getting this baseline test when you're at your physical best becomes standard practice, symptom relief is the most important guide to that optimal level. Symptoms are the first barometer, and then the hormone levels are checked to make sure testosterone is a viable solution for relieving those symptoms.

Mike's Story—Young Doctor, Heal Thyself

The week after I started seeing men as patients for the first time in my professional life, Mike, another local physician, made an appointment to see me. His wife had been a patient of mine for several years, and we had been successfully treating her for hormone-imbalance issues. At the time, Mike was thirty-eight. He'd been a general surgeon in a very busy small group practice for about six years, and had been working very hard, putting in long hours. It also happened that he had a strong family history of heart disease, and was already on two cholesterol-lowering medications by the time he turned thirty-six.

Mike's symptoms included decreased libido, erectile dysfunction (ED), fatigue, sleep problems, unexplained weight gain, and difficulty exercising. He had initially thought most of these symptoms were side effects of his medications, but when the ED hit, his wife did a little research and suspected a different cause—low testosterone.

The hormone assays I performed on Mike revealed, not surprisingly, that his testosterone levels were very low. I also found that his insulin levels were higher than desirable for a man his age—a sign of blood-sugar imbalances that could have led to type 2 diabetes over time. We decided, after a thorough discussion of his treatment options, that he would try testosterone replacement in the form of subcutaneous pellets.

Almost overnight, the testosterone replacement gave him more energy and zest than he'd had in years. He shed about fifteen pounds in two months, and was able to exercise for longer and at a level of intensity he hadn't achieved since his early twenties. It took about three months for his libido to surge back completely, and the erectile dysfunction he was dealing with was no longer an issue.

Around the time he started with the testosterone pellets, Mike had to discontinue the statin drug he was taking (statins are cholesterol drugs, such as Zocor and Lipitor) because of muscle pain, a well-known side effect of these medicines. The pain disappeared when the drug was stopped, but his cholesterol remained stable, even without the statin. His insulin level decreased to an acceptable level within a month of getting his first testosterone pellets, and it has stayed in an ideal range since then.

Mike is a different person now. He has been on the regimen for about two years, and feels he is healthier than he has been in years. I recently saw him and his family at a local restaurant—they're a great-looking group, and he and his wife both had *big* smiles on their faces. Life is good when your hormones are cooking.

How Common Is Low Testosterone—and What Are the Risks?

In his excellent book, *The Testosterone Syndrome*, Dr. Eugene Shippen has created an expanded questionnaire for men that divides andropausal symptoms into four basic categories. I utilize his questionnaire in my office because I have found it is well-suited to my practice, and is extremely accurate at predicting which men are andropausal. I can also administer the test again after a few months of testosterone treatment to get an idea of how well it's working to eradicate symptoms.

In June 2006, Dr. Thomas Mulligan of the Malcolm Randall Veterans' Administration Medical Center in Gainesville, Florida released the results of testosterone assays in 2,162 men who had visited primary care physicians. He found that 38.7 percent—about four in every ten of these middle-aged men who were age forty-five and up at the time of their tests—had testosterone levels below 300 nanograms per deciliter (ng/dL).

Overall, the research suggests that 25–75 percent of men over fifty-five have low, or at least, sub-optimal, testosterone levels. Because a large percentage of the male patients in my practice come to the office as a result of symptoms suggestive of andropause, greater than 95 percent of these men turn out to have sub-optimal testosterone levels. Again, this is going to vary from man to man, and individual evaluation by a skilled physician is important. Virtually all of them have resolution of at least some of their symptoms when I get their testosterone levels into the optimal range.

Testosterone levels below 300 ng/dL have been linked with depression, diabetes, high blood pressure, high cholesterol, osteoporosis, and obesity. Obese men had, in fact, the greatest risk of *hypogonadism* (low levels of testosterone)—they were over twice as likely to test low on testosterone as men who maintained a more healthful weight.

In a five-year study of veterans published in the *Archives of Internal Medicine* in 2006, investigators measured testosterone levels in male veterans age forty and older. They found that low testosterone levels were strongly associated with the risk of death during the course of the study.

A man who has had prostate cancer is likely to be told he shouldn't even *dream* about putting this hormone into his body. This is not necessarily true for every man. Even if you've been warned not to use this hormone, keep reading—you might be in for a pleasant surprise.

In Praise of Testosterone

Testosterone is what makes little boys little boys. It's what makes young men the energetic, virile, horny, macho guys that they are.

A man with a more masculine, muscle-bound appearance who tends towards aggression has higher testosterone levels than a softer, rounder, more sensitive fellow. The same goes for women—a soft, round, stereotypically feminine woman has lower testosterone levels than a hard-bodied, aggressive, forceful woman.

A man's body produces roughly ten times more testosterone

than the body of a premenopausal woman. Well before that pubertal surge of testosterone that deepened your voice, caused acne to spring up on your face, and made your world seem filled with appropriate targets for sexual desire, you were a fetus that was bathed in testosterone produced by the bud of cells that would eventually turn into your testicles. Once those testes developed and the fetal you became the infant you, LH from the hypothalamic/pituitary system stimulated your Leydig cells to produce testosterone. In boys and men, small amounts of testosterone are also produced in the adrenal glands from DHEA.

No testicles, no testosterone. And although that might give you great potential as an operatic soprano (male castrati and their natural soprano voices were once celebrated in the European opera world; at that time and place, if you had dreams of singing stardom for your boy, you could have his testicles removed at the barber shop), the lack of this hormone would also reduce bone mass, facial and body hair, muscle mass, penis size, and physical and mental energy.

Under the influence of FSH, sperm production and maturation take place in the Sertoli cells of the testes. This begins around puberty and continues indefinitely, as long as there is adequate FSH. This is why you can probably father a child at eighteen, forty-eight, or seventy-eight, as long as your hormones are balanced properly and you're engaged with a fertile companion.

Once the puberty-related acceleration in testosterone production arrives, a man's highest levels are reached and maintained in the mid- to late teens. After that point, levels usually remain high for ten to twenty years.

Great variability exists with regard to how long testosterone keeps cranking at optimal levels in men. Unlike menopause in women, which is relatively predictable, andropause—where testosterone levels drop below physiological range—can occur at any time. Personally, I've seen it as early as age thirty and as late as eighty-seven.

What Testosterone Can Do for Your Heart

In 2004, according to pharmaceutical sales tracker, IMS Health, some 2.4 million prescriptions for testosterone replacement were filled in pharmacies in the United States. IMS Health did not distinguish between male and female testosterone prescriptions, but their numbers did show a doubling of the number of prescriptions between 2000 and 2004. Despite the chorus of voices warning about all that's still not known about testosterone therapy, people are willing to give it a shot—probably because the benefits are so pronounced.

For most of my medical career, most physicians have assumed that testosterone is an enemy of the cardiovascular system. This is usually traced back to the known fact that a man is at greater risk of heart attack earlier in life than a woman, whose heart-attack risk only approaches that of a man's once she has gone through menopause. Although men make more testosterone than women, I am not aware of any study that has shown a negative relationship between testosterone and the heart. The evidence is strong that coronary heart disease should not contraindicate testosterone therapy.

A decent-sized body of research actually suggests that higher testosterone in men has a protective effect when it comes to heart disease. For example, men with lower testosterone are more likely to have high cholesterol, high triglycerides, and hypertension, and are more likely to be obese—all well-known risk factors for heart disease. Several recent studies have shown that testosterone has many beneficial effects on the heart.

Risk Factor

A risk factor is something that can increase the risk of developing a disease. With some risk factors, science is not entirely sure whether the factor is the cause or the effect of disease. For example, high cholesterol is widely considered a cause of heart disease, but some evidence suggests it may instead be an *effect.*

Men who have angiographically proven coronary artery disease—clogged or narrowed arteries shown in a high-tech test called an angiogram—have *lower* testosterone as a group than men with normal coronary arteries. When men who have angina are treated with testosterone, their blood vessels dilate, enhancing blood flow to the heart and other tissues throughout the body.

As I was in the final stages of completing this book, scientists at the University of California at San Diego (UCSD) came out with the results of a study that suggests a major role for adequate testosterone in male longevity. They shared these results with the public at the 2007 Endocrine Society meeting in Toronto.

They tracked testosterone levels and lifespan in a group of men, and found that those with the lowest testosterone had an 18 percent lower chance of living past the age of 50 than men with the highest testosterone. Men with low testosterone were about three-fold more likely to have high blood pressure, high "bad" cholesterol, and belly fat – all signs of *metabolic syndrome,* which is a predictor of heart disease and type 2 diabetes. Those with low testosterone also had lower quality of life.

Another study looked at the effect of testosterone therapy after insertion of a *stent* – a tiny, rigid mesh tube that props open clogged coronary arteries. The men in the study all had coronary artery disease; some got testosterone injections once a week for three weeks before surgery, and some got standard therapy. Men who got testosterone had much lower levels of two inflammatory markers, C-reactive protein (CRP) and interleukin-6 (IL-6) – markers that are predictive of the re-closing of arteries following heart surgery. These results were so compelling that pre-treatment and post-treatment with testosterone may become standard practice in stent surgeries.

In a study by Hugh Jones, MD, and co-workers in Great Britain, men with chronic, stable angina underwent three months of testosterone therapy and had several treadmill tests. After the three months, the men were able to walk for almost a minute more on average before their hearts lacked oxygen to the extent of having angina. The men who started out with lower testosterone had more dramatic improvement, and in a follow-up study, men with very low testosterone levels were enrolled. Their walking times improved by seventy-three seconds over the three-month period.

Dr. Jones found that testosterone works in the cardiovascular system much the same as the calcium-channel-blocker medications commonly used to relieve angina and reduce high blood pressure. He reports anecdotally that men who have remained on testosterone long-term (for two to three years) have continued to have cardiovascular benefits.

Weight Loss and Testosterone

Testosterone has a marked anabolic effect in men, increasing bone and muscle mass and decreasing body fat. Deepening of the voice, thickening of the skin, and a whopping libido are other effects of high-flying testosterone.

Everyone knows that losing weight is good for heart health. What many don't know is that testosterone can help protect your heart by helping you lose weight, and that losing excess pounds can help free up more testosterone.

A study of healthy older men with testosterone levels on the low end of normal, or just below normal range, found that testosterone replacement increased lean body mass and decreased body fat significantly. Another study of previously obese men who had lost a great deal of weight, either through stomach-stapling surgery or dieting, found a significant drop in plasma sex-hormone-binding globulin (SHBG), a protein that takes testosterone out of its active state—meaning their free testosterone levels rose. Their fasting insulin levels fell, which means a decrease in heart risk, and their levels of good HDL cholesterol went up.

The Cortisol Connection—One Way Stress Hurts Your Heart

The type-A personality has long been linked with high blood pressure and heart disease, and testosterone appears to play a role in this equation.

Research has found that men who have a higher ratio of cortisol—the stress hormone made by the adrenal glands in response to chronic stress—to testosterone tend to have a greater risk of a heart attack and death from a heart attack. The study, published in the July 19, 2005 issue of *Circulation,* found that in men who are under chronic stress, cortisol levels tend to stay higher than normal, and this has the effect of suppressing testosterone production.

High cortisol also pushes your body towards gaining weight in the midsection and developing insulin resistance—two of the main signs that you're on your way to developing type 2 diabetes. If that happens, your risk of dying of a heart attack or having to contend with kidney failure, blinding eye disease, and nerve damage goes up exponentially.

The investigators who performed this study at the University of Bristol in the United Kingdom conclude that by working to control the cortisol-to-testosterone ratio, a great deal could be done to reduce a man's risk of cardiac disease. In plain terms, that means learning to cope better with whatever stresses life hands you—maybe with the help of meditation, yoga, or relaxation techniques, some of which I'll tell you about in Chapter 11—and, if necessary, bringing testosterone levels into more youthful ranges. If testosterone is low, even mild elevations in cortisol will send your ratio in the wrong direction.

What's Good for Your Heart Is Good for Your Sex Life

Erectile dysfunction can be related to a lack of testosterone, and the common denominator is blood-vessel health. When a man's heart vessels are occluded by plaques, as they so often are—heart disease being the number-one threat to the lives of aging men—the blood vessels that bring blood into the penis during an erection are probably not in great shape either. When you enhance erections with drugs, you're doing so by allowing those vessels to fully dilate and let more blood flow through. Testosterone's *vasodilating* effects probably help in this regard. A man low in testosterone has fewer erections while sleeping and tends to have a weaker, or nonexistent, morning erection; restoring optimal testosterone levels helps restore this youthful pattern.

This hormone has been blamed for creating more aggressive, angry, showily masculine, confrontational behaviors in all kinds of creatures. Does adding testosterone to the body of a man who finally seems to be mellowing and finding his feminine side—

perhaps to the great pleasure of the partners in his life—return him to his old, macho ways? No, it does not appear that *replacing testosterone in men who are deficient* has this effect. Giving a man many times more testosterone than he probably would have made naturally in his youth may make him cranky and more prone to road rage, but giving him just enough will not change his moods or psychological profile for the worse. In my clinical experience, these change for the better.

Depression, Dementia, and Deficient Testosterone

Dan - Testosterone as Brain Booster

Dan, an investment banker, is a typical patient in my practice who turned out to have low testosterone. He's not so typical in that, for all of his fifty-four years, he has taken extremely good care of himself—eating well, exercising five days a week despite working long hours, and maintaining his body-fat levels at less than 15 percent. Unlike most fifty-four-year-old American men, Dan was taking no prescription medicines. He came to see me because of decreased energy, libido, stamina, and strength.

Dan's lab work revealed that he did, indeed, have very low testosterone, and he was started on testosterone replacement therapy in the form of subcutaneous pellets. Two months after initiating the testosterone therapy, I got his follow-up labs, which indicated a vast improvement in his testosterone level.

My office generally calls my patients after their follow-up lab work results are interpreted, to get the patient's story on how she or he is doing, discuss the results of the tests, and make any changes that seem appropriate. When my nurse called Dan to inform him of the findings, he told her he was feeling "great." She said he probably didn't need to come in for his scheduled appointment the following week, but he replied, "No – I really want to come in and tell Dr. Brown about how I'm doing." I assumed he was having some sort of problem that he wanted to discuss with me only.

Three days later, when I walked into the room to talk with Dan, he got the prize for biggest smile of the week. He was *beaming*. (One thing I love about my job is seeing the smiles and hearing the stories about how much better people are feeling and functioning when they have good hormone effect.) Dan proceeded to tell me that he was, indeed, incredibly better—his energy, erectile function, libido, stamina, and zest for life were all back in high gear. "I can work out like I did when I was thirty years old," he told me, "but that's not why I wanted to come see you." Again, I thought, uh-oh, something must be wrong.

"You told me I might experience an increase in cognitive function," Dan said. "I pretty much dismissed that, since I felt that my brain was already working great—no problems with memory, concentration, or anything else. But…wow! Within two weeks of getting the pellets, I had a phenomenal increase in awareness and concentration. The only problem was, it made me aware that my brain hadn't been working as well as I'd thought."

The brain has a lot of hormone receptors, and they're there for a reason. Without proper hormone effect, the brain just doesn't perform as well, and there probably is an increased risk of degenerative changes in the brain. Prevention of brain diseases, dementia in particular, may ultimately prove to be the greatest benefit of testosterone-replacement therapy.

Researchers from many nations have correlated testosterone deficiency in aging men with anxiety, depression, difficulty concentrating, insomnia, irritability, and memory impairment. There is, in fact, a substantial overlap between the signs and symptoms of insufficient testosterone and major depression.

This is not a coincidence. Studies show a strong relationship between the testosterone level and male depression, and further show that giving a hypogonadal, depressed man a replacement dose of testosterone lifts his depression.

In aging men with sub-optimal testosterone levels who start to have a lot of senior moments, where they become absent-minded and lose cognitive skills, adding testosterone back in brings improvements in those cognitive skills, and in attention span, memory, mental status, and spatial abilities.

A good deal of research has linked dementia in older men to an excess of estrogen, which, as I mentioned earlier, can create an imbalance that resembles a lack of testosterone. A study of 2,974 Japanese-American men, the Honolulu-Asia Aging Study, showed that the higher a man's estradiol levels, the greater his risk of Alzheimer's disease and vascular dementia (memory loss caused by occluded blood vessels in the brain that cause mini-strokes, which reduce oxygenation to the brain).

More recent studies have found that testosterone is *neurotrophic* (brain-cell and nerve-cell-building) and neuroprotective, and that it may play a role in preventing the growth of the beta-amyloid plaques that eat away at the brains of Alzheimer's victims. Other studies have found a lower incidence of Alzheimer's in men on testosterone replacement and a higher incidence of this disease in men with low testosterone levels.

One intriguing study, performed at USC, and described in a letter to the editor published in the *Journal of the American Medical Association (JAMA)* in September 2004, involved examining the brains of forty-five deceased men. Some of the brains were from men who had normal cognitive function and no sign of any brain disease (control subjects); some had a mild neuropathology that was suggestive of early dementia; and some had Alzheimer's disease. The investigators found that the brains of the men with the mild neuropathology had significantly lower testosterone levels than the controls, and that the brains of men with Alzheimer's had levels that were lower still. The investigators write that, "our finding strongly suggests that normal age-related testosterone-depletion is one of the important changes that promotes Alzheimer's disease in men." Low testosterone "creates a hostile neural environment that promotes accumulation of toxic beta-amyloid protein, leaving neurons less able to survive the insult."

Testosterone and Male Osteoporosis

By age ninety, about 17 percent of men will experience a hip fracture caused by thinning bones (women up to age ninety have almost double the chance of hip fracture). Research shows that men with the lowest levels of bioavailable (free) testosterone are 2.5 times more likely to have bone fractures related to osteoporosis. Even young men who are hypogonadal—low in testosterone and other gonadal steroids—have lower bone-mineral density and are more likely to end up with osteoporosis as they age. Testosterone replacement increases bone-mineral density in men with low blood-testosterone levels.

Estrogen and the Male Body—A Delicate Balance

Estrogen is a necessary hormone in the male of the species, but there is a real paucity of research on exactly what all of its roles are. One thing that is known is its essential role in sperm production—so much so that the interference of such xenoestrogenic chemicals as DDT on the action of a man's own estrogens may cause sperm counts to plummet. Semen contains a lot of estrogen, and men require estrogens for bone health, too.

Women who have concluded that the man in their life is so brainwashed by testosterone that he may as well be a separate species might be surprised to know that estrogen has a large role in the workings of the male brain. In fact, parts of the brain are known to have high concentrations of *aromatase,* the enzyme that converts testosterone into estrogen.

Finger Length, Testosterone, and the Geeky Scientist Stereotype

Men, take a look at your hands for a moment. Is your index finger shorter than your ring finger, or are both fingers the same length? Believe it or not, research has shown that the relative length of your index and ring fingers gives information about the balance of testosterone and estrogens you developed while still a fetus—a balance that sets the precedent for the balance of these hormones in your body the rest of your life. If your index finger is longer than your ring finger, or the same length, you are likely to have higher estrogen levels than a man whose ring finger is longer than his index finger.

A study at the University of Bath in England built on this research, and found that male scientists whose finger length reflected higher estrogen levels during development were more likely to work in the *hard sciences*, such as mathematics and physics.

The investigators suggest these higher estrogen

levels may enhance development of the right brain—the half that deals in spatial, analytic skills. The same research group, interestingly, found heightened testosterone levels in female social scientists, and discovered that men with more typical finger-length reflection of testosterone and estrogen levels were more likely to work in the social sciences. In the male scientists, they also found that lowered levels of testosterone, relative to estrogens, could be to blame for the *geeky-scientist* stereotype, reducing the male science-nerd's ability to use language, grow big muscles, stand up against the oaf who kicks sand on him at the beach, and relate socially with others. On the other hand, these men may be blessed with a sensitivity that makes them great life partners.

In men, areas of the brain that control sexual function are believed to have the highest levels of estradiol. For young, libidinous males, this flow of estradiol probably acts as an off switch for sexual desire to help moderate the overwhelming role of very high levels of testosterone. As a man ages, testosterone naturally decreases; this shift, in conjunction with increasing estradiol, causes most of the problems associated with male menopause. A man in andropause can have estrogen levels that exceed those of a menopausal woman.

To summarize—although the roles of estrogens in men are not well-understood, they appear to be intimately involved in men's reproductive and cognitive function.

Table 9.1

Roles of Testosterone in Men

What Doctors Say	Plain English Translation
Enables development of male genitalia and secondary sex characteristics	Transforms a genetically male fetus into a boy and a boy into a teenager

Production and maturation of sperm	Makes it possible for a man to pass on his superior genes to the next generation
Libido enhancement	—and have fun doing it
Erectile function	Sexual performance; ability to get and keep an erection
Increases lean body mass	More muscle
Decreases body fat	Less flab; able to look down and see your shoes in a standing position
Lowers LDL	Helps promote healthier cholesterol levels, aiding in prevention of heart disease
Increases energy	Maybe not able to leap tall buildings in a single bound...but definitely able to work, workout, have a satisfying family life, and otherwise enjoy an active, busy life
Vasodilation of coronary arteries	Improves flow of blood to heart by relaxing the arteries that bring oxygen-rich blood to the walls of the heart muscle
Decreases insulin resistance	Protects against the onset of type 2 diabetes—a disease that causes massive damage to the cardiovascular and nervous systems and dramatically shortens life expectancy
Improves cognitive function, lowers risk of Alzheimer's disease	Not only can you please your significant other in the bedroom, you can also have a great conversation, or beat her at chess
Reduces inflammation	Helps balance immune function in a way that is believed to aid in prevention of Alzheimer's disease, cancer, heart disease, and many other diseases linked with advancing age

More about Testosterone Testing and Therapy for Men

A thorough evaluation to determine whether a man is andropausal includes blood measurements of free and total testosterone, SHBG, estradiol, follicle stimulating hormone (FSH) and luteinizing hormone (LH). We also do a complete blood count and prostate-specific-antigen (PSA) measurement at the outset and for continual monitoring throughout the course of testosterone therapy. Some practitioners use saliva testing for testosterone levels.

As you've seen, optimal testosterone levels vary widely from one person to another. They will usually run between 200 and 800 ng/ml, but there's more to testosterone availability than just testosterone levels. Estradiol levels for all men should be less than 50 nanograms per milliliter (ng/ml) and ideally between 20–30 ng/ml. Also, sex-hormone-binding globlin (SHBG) is key—the higher it is, the less testosterone is able to leave the bloodstream and get into cells to be effective. In my practice, I look at SHBG and total T to calculate a free androgen index (FAI). Any value below 1.0 is considered less than optimal.

Once I get the results of the lab tests, I evaluate them and decide on the cause of the man's andropausal symptoms. I find myself almost always dealing with one of three separate diagnostic issues.

1. ***Primary hypogonadism.*** The failure of the testes to produce testosterone, with decreased testosterone and normal FSH and LH.
2. ***Secondary hypogonadism.*** The failure of the pituitary to stimulate the testes to make testosterone, with low testosterone and low FSH and LH.
3. ***Increased estrogen levels.*** Normal or low testosterone and increased estradiol and SHBG.

If total testosterone is very low, there's no doubt about the proper course of treatment—it is to restore healthful testosterone levels. A lot of men with low-normal testosterone levels have symptoms and also warrant treatment.

Testosterone Replacement Options for Men

When faced with a simple case of insufficient testosterone, I give men a few different options for replacement. Five forms are currently available—intramuscular injections, patches, subcutaneous pellets, sublingual drops or lozenges, and transdermal gels and creams. But take note—if you are considering fathering a child, you should know that testosterone replacement can reduce sperm production.

Intramuscular (IM) Injections

IM injections are initially quite effective, but the standard dosing is every two to three weeks...and they hurt, plus they eventually cause scarring in the buttocks muscles. The injections yield a sharp rise in testosterone, which often leads to increased conversion to estradiol. It's like pouring too much water into a cup at once—the overflow is transformed to estradiol.

Patches

Transdermal testosterone patches are worn on the arm and must be changed daily. Some complain of skin irritation and inconvenience. Patches produce fairly steady levels of testosterone, but high physiological levels of testosterone are sometimes difficult to attain with this approach. I personally believe that testosterone patches are on their way out unless the technology of the patch changes.

Subcutaneous Pellets

Pellets of bio-identical testosterone are inserted under the skin of the hip or buttocks area after numbing the area with a local anesthetic. The pellets are very effective at raising testosterone levels, and, as with the pellets in women, they more closely simulate the action of the failed gland. The activity of the hormone is more physiological, resulting in sustained, steady testosterone levels.

Pellets are more convenient. They last at least four to six

months, sometimes even longer, and they provoke fewer problems with aromatization to estradiol than other methods.

My experience with pellets has been the most positive of any mode of testosterone therapy. My male patients on pellets generally feel better than on any other treatment, despite the fact that their levels match those of men on other forms of testosterone. Presumably, this is due to the steadier levels of testosterone produced by the pellets. The body may be utilizing the repository of testosterone as it needs it, creating a more physiologic hormonal state.

Sublingual Lozenges or Liquid Drops

These can be quite effective, but they need to be taken two to three times per day, which can be inconvenient. Lozenges or drops also generally produce a roller-coaster effect with a lot of peaks and valleys in the blood levels.

Transdermal Gels and Creams

Androgel is a commercially available prescription product that can be found at any pharmacy. It is probably the most frequently prescribed form of testosterone replacement for men because it is commercially available and is known by more physicians than any other method. However, it is not generally as good an option for testosterone replacement therapy as compounded cream or pellets. For adequate absorption, a large amount of gel has to be applied to a large area of skin surface, and this can be a messy situation that often ends up on sheets, clothes, and loved ones. It comes as one concentration only, and most of the time it doesn't raise testosterone levels very much.

Creams formulated by compounding pharmacists can be obtained in any strength desired. Generally, a small amount applied to the skin once or twice a day is quite effective at raising testosterone levels.

Unfortunately, creams and gels may provoke an increase in estradiol levels, as some men's skin may contain a large amount of aromatase, the enzyme that converts testosterone into estrogen. Not good.

Testosterone Replacement Options For Men	
Delivery Method	**Frequency Used**
Pellets	Replaced every 4-6 months
Cream	Once or twice daily
Patches	Once daily
Gel	Once or twice daily
Sublingual lozenges/ drops	Two to three times daily
Intramuscular injections	Once every two to three weeks

Treatment Options for Secondary Hypogonadism

Men who turn out to have secondary hypogonadism—a failure of the pituitary gland to produce enough gonadotrophins (FSH and LH) to stimulate the Leydig cells of the testes to produce adequate testosterone—may be able to return to optimal testosterone levels if the Leydig cells of the testes can be stimulated. This can be achieved by raising FSH and LH levels in the body.

FSH and LH can be given as injections, but these hormones are expensive. Fortunately, there is a relatively inexpensive bioidentical hormonal substitute: *human chorionic gonadotrophin* (HCG), which is very similar in chemical structure to LH and may effectively stimulate the Leydig cells to produce testosterone.

HCG has to be given as an injection. It can be given either as weekly intramuscular injections or as intramuscular injections in the thigh two to three times per week. Most people are able to self-administer these shots with some training. In the past six months, I have been using a new regimen of subcutaneous HCG injections of small amounts, 3-5 days per week and have had good results when the testicles are able to respond.

While HCG injections treat the underlying cause of the problem, some men with secondary hypogonadism still choose to use testosterone replacement therapy instead. Some men prefer to use a cream, patch, or pellets instead of giving themselves frequent injections, but the end result is the same—higher testosterone levels.

In this situation, some physicians advocate using testosterone and HCG on a rotating schedule. When these two hormones are rotated, one of the possible consequences of continuous testosterone therapy is avoided—atrophy of the Leydig cells and testes, which can adversely affect sperm production.

If you are diagnosed with secondary hypogonadism, but are still interested in optimizing sperm production in order to have children with the woman in your life, then the choice is clearly HCG. If adequate sperm production is not an issue, testosterone replacement therapy may be a reasonable choice for secondary hypogonadism.

Excessive Estradiol in Men—Why It Happens

If a man's estradiol levels come back high, I suspect that excessive conversion of testosterone to estrogen is a major contributor to his state of andropause. To effectively treat andropause, a physician must understand this concept and know how to deal with this kind of hormonal imbalance. Check in with your doctor about this, and if he or she doesn't know what you're talking about, you'd best find another doctor for your problem.

Estrogen is, as I said, an essential part of the hormone balance in both men and women. On the other hand, too much estrogen not only causes symptoms of andropause, but there is also strong evidence that excess estrogens have a major role in benign and malignant prostate disease. Keeping estradiol levels down does a lot more for you than enhance your sex drive.

Elevated estradiol levels can be caused by several different factors. Some are avoidable, all are treatable.

Increase in Aromatase Activity

Aromatase is the enzyme that converts testosterone into estradiol. The most common reasons for increased aromatase activity are aging, certain drugs (such as the diuretics commonly used to treat high blood pressure), obesity, and zinc deficiency.

In aging men, there is a natural tendency towards increased

aromatase activity. The mineral zinc is a natural inhibitor of aromatase, but because dietary sources of zinc are limited, I always recommend zinc supplementation for men with andropause who start testosterone therapy—at least 50 mg per day. If the man's estradiol levels increase with the therapy, I then raise that dose of zinc to 50 mg twice a day.

> Any andropausal man who uses testosterone replacement should take 50 mg of zinc once or twice daily to help prevent aromatization.

The reasons why estrogen levels rise in men who take diuretics are not well understood, but it's presumed that a zinc deficiency is one cause.

Obesity

Obese men have more and larger fat cells than non-obese men. Aromatase is concentrated in fat cells. The fatter you are, the more aromatase your body has to convert testosterone into estrogen. Without question, obese men have a greater likelihood of high estrogen levels and lower testosterone levels. The solution here is, of course, weight loss.

Xenoestrogens

Abnormal liver function can be one cause of higher-than-optimal estrogen levels in men and the andropausal symptoms that usually result. When the liver isn't up to par, it can't rid itself of certain toxins and chemicals, including estrogens with an attitude, otherwise known as xenoestrogens, that are found in food and commonly used chemicals. As discussed (*see* Chapter 8 on breast cancer), xenoestrogens are found in abundance in our American environment—in herbicides, household chemicals, pesticides, plastics, and solvents, to name a few sources. Since these chemicals are just about impossible to avoid, you need to have good liver function to facilitate their detoxification and elimination.

To improve the function of your liver, stop drinking more than one alcoholic drink a day. Too much booze can damage this vital organ. Don't use over-the-counter drugs (particularly acetaminophen—Tylenol—which is overused and wreaks havoc on the liver, especially when used with other drugs or alcohol), or prescription medications if you don't really need them, because they have to be processed by your liver, and this creates wear-and-tear that can eventually reduce the organ's function.

The herb milk thistle (*Silybum marianum*) has been used to promote better liver function for hundreds of years, and research demonstrates that it improves antioxidant protection in the liver, helps move toxins out of the body, and promotes the growth of healthy new liver cells.

> Supplements containing milk thistle, artichoke, dandelion root, and turmeric may be used to promote better liver function; this can aid in reducing the body's toxic burden.

Supplements that support liver function may also contain the herbs artichoke, dandelion root, and turmeric. All of these promote bile production by the liver, which in turn helps bind fat-soluble toxins, such as xenoestrogens, and move them out of the body. A liver-support formula may also contain the nutrient cysteine, or garlic/onion extracts. Both are helpful for increasing the liver's production of antioxidants, which in turn protect the organ against the damage that can be done by free radicals produced during the detoxification process.

As mentioned in Chapter 8 on breast cancer, indole -3 carbinol also aids in the proper metabolizing of estrogens, especially those that are difficult for the body to get rid of, such as xenoestrogens.

Treatment Options for Men With Excess Estradiol

High-estrogen andropause sometimes requires a few different treatments. Eliminating zinc deficiency with a supplement, eating a healthful diet and exercising to eliminate extra body fat, avoiding excessive alcohol, discontinuing the use of unnecessary prescription drugs, and being aware of, and eliminating, as many xenoestrogens as possible are all helpful in reducing estrogen levels.

Most of my men patients who end up with high estrogen levels have been using testosterone replacement because of a suboptimal testosterone level, and are aromatizing too much of it to estrogen. As I pointed out earlier, some forms of testosterone replacement are more likely than others to increase aromatase activity, and pellets seem to be least likely of any form of testosterone replacement to have this effect. The slow, steady trickle of the hormone into the bloodstream makes it far less likely to overflow into the production of excess estradiol. If I have a patient on some other form of testosterone replacement and I see their estradiol levels rising, I suggest they switch to subcutaneous pellets.

If the man switches to pellets and his estradiol levels still remain high, I will then add an aromatase inhibitor—a pharmaceutical drug that inhibits the activity of aromatase enzymes. There are several alternatives, but the one I most commonly use is anastrozole. The brand-name drug, **Arimidex,** is sometimes quite expensive, so I often have a compounding pharmacy formulate capsules which can be taken three to five times a week, for a total weekly dose of one to two milligrams.

> A prescription drug, anastrozole – an aromatase inhibitor – may be needed to maintain optimally low estrogen levels in men who tend to turn testosterone into estrogens.

Often, lowering estradiol levels is not a quick deal—it can take months to get those levels down to an acceptable level where symptoms of andropause finally abate. Persistence is key here.

10

Testosterone and Your Prostate

Every day in my office, I hear some variation on this theme: "I thought testosterone *caused* prostate cancer."

The question of a relationship between cancer of the prostate—the second most common cause of cancer death in American men—and testosterone is not as simple as you may have been led to believe. You need to understand the relationship between testosterone and the prostate so you can make an informed decision about the benefits and risks of testosterone replacement.

Each year, about 220,000 American men are diagnosed with prostate cancer and some 37,000 men die from the disease. There is a hopeful side to these numbers, however. With today's screening methods, prostate cancer is diagnosed in its earliest and most curable stages, and early detection makes the disease almost 100-percent survivable. Many men turn out to have prostate tumors that are small and slow-growing, and never grow large enough to become a threat.

Although at one time surgical treatments for prostate cancer were almost certain to cause erectile problems, impotence, or incontinence, in the past decade or so, the science of prostate cancer surgery has surged forward. Treatment options for men with this disease are much more varied and targeted today than ever before. And if impotence does result from treatment for prostate cancer, there are now better remedies for that problem than ever before.

The American Cancer Society recommends that all men age fifty and older have a digital rectal exam (DRE) and a prostate-specific antigen (PSA) blood test every year to screen for prostate cancer. African-American men, and men who have a family history of the disease should begin screenings at age forty-five.

The conventional wisdom in the medical community is that testosterone not only has a role in prostate cancer, but that testosterone-replacement therapy can increase a man's risk of prostate cancer, just as estrogen supposedly increases a woman's risk of breast cancer. I believe, however, that there is overwhelming evidence to the contrary, and that men need not dismiss the possibility of using testosterone, which is likely to protect them against Alzheimer's disease, heart disease, osteoporosis, and erectile dysfunction, because of this putative relationship between testosterone and prostate cancer.

Testosterone and Prostate Cancer—Evidence Against a Causative Link

In very recent years, several high-caliber studies have shown no increase in the risk of prostate cancer or benign prostatic hypertrophy (BPH) in men who have been on testosterone-replacement therapy. In fact, the tide of medical opinion is turning, with the consensus starting to inch towards a *protective* role for testosterone-replacement therapy against prostate cancer and BPH.

Benign Prostatic Hypertrophy (BPH)

Benign prostatic hypertrophe (BPH) is a non-cancerous swelling and growth of the prostate that can restrict the flow of urine from the bladder. It is extremely common in aging men, and can become severe enough to require surgical intervention. In the research, no relationship has been found to exist between BPH and testosterone replacement in andropause.

This comes as no great surprise, considering that the risk of prostate cancer *increases* with age, just as a man's testosterone level is *decreasing*. And the scientific data from the past decade indicate that low, not high, levels of testosterone correlate with a higher incidence of prostate cancer. In these studies, high levels of testosterone do not correlate with a higher incidence of prostate cancer.

In the January 2000 issue of the journal *Mayo Clinic Proceedings*, Dr. J. E. Morley reported, "there is no clinical evidence that the risk of either prostate cancer or benign prostatic hypertrophy increases with testosterone replacement therapy." In a meta-analysis of studies published in the past ten years that was reported in the January 2004 *New England Journal of Medicine*, Drs. Rhoden and Morgentaler, two prominent Harvard researchers, concluded that there is, "no compelling evidence at present...[to] suggest that men with higher testosterone levels are at greater risk of prostate cancer or that treating men who had hypogonadism with exogenous [replacement] androgens increases this risk. In fact, it should be recognized that prostate cancer becomes more prevalent exactly at the time of a man's life when testosterone levels decline."

Meta-Analysis Study

A meta-analysis is a type of study that combines data from several studies on a topic, such as testosterone levels and prostate cancer. This allows the pooling of a lot more data in one study, enabling researchers to draw more accurate conclusions than smaller studies can.

Growing ranks of andropausal men are now being treated with testosterone-replacement therapy. For the most part, their physicians are not interested in doing clinical research; they are more interested in helping people live healthier, happier lives. These doctors network with one another and exchange anecdotal information. Many of them have patients who have been on testosterone for a number of years. The consensus among these physicians reflects the current wisdom from scientific research—that testosterone replacement therapy does not increase the risk of prostate disease, and that it appears instead to significantly decrease the incidence of prostate cancer and BPH, long-term.

Low Testosterone—The Real Culprit in Prostate Cancer?

A few early studies showed possible links between higher testosterone levels and the risk of prostate cancer, but this finding is not supported by the majority of studies. Some recent studies suggest that, to the contrary, high testosterone levels are *protective* against especially aggressive forms of prostate cancer.

In one study, Australian researchers measured total testosterone, DHEA (another androgen), estradiol, and sex-hormone-binding globulin (SHBG) in 17,049 men. Of that large group, 524 were diagnosed with prostate cancer during the mean 8.7 years of follow-up. Here's what they found:

1. A small (roughly 30 percent) decrease in risk of prostate cancer in men whose estradiol levels were twice that of men with the lowest estradiol levels (an association the researchers called weak);
2. No relationship between any of the other hormones and a risk of unaggressive (slow-growing) prostate cancer;
3. Almost half the risk of aggressive prostate cancer in men with higher levels of testosterone (double that of the lowest levels);
4. A 37-percent reduction in the risk for men with double the DHEA levels of men with the lowest levels of that hormone.

They conclude that, "High levels of testosterone and adrenal androgens [DHEA] are thus associated with decreased risk of aggressive prostate cancer but not with nonaggressive disease."

Another intriguing study, published in the *Journal of the American Medical Association (JAMA),* looked at the effect of testosterone replacement (as testosterone enathanate, injected intramuscularly every two weeks) on prostate tissue and PSA measurements. The subjects were forty-four men aged forty-four to seventy-eight, and all started out with testosterone levels below 300 and had related andropausal symptoms. About half got testosterone and the other half got a placebo injection. Men who got the injections had their testosterone levels rise to mid-normal. Over the six months of treatment, no significant changes (compared to placebo patients) were found in prostate volume, or serum PSA, and prostate biopsies showed no changes in the gland.

Circulating androgens have *not,* by and large, been positively associated with prostate-cancer risk. Anyone who says otherwise hasn't been paying attention to the research.

A Plan for Lifetime Prostate Health

A great deal of money is presently being spent on research to cure prostate cancer. Unfortunately, as with breast cancer, most of this money is spent on the treatment of prostate cancer with chemotherapy or radiation. If we spent as much money on prevention, I think we would be much closer to a cure—but that's not the way the great American medical/industrial complex works. In the meantime, I'd like to apprise you of what you can do to lower your risk of prostate disease.

DRE and PSA tests should be done at least every year after age fifty. A man on testosterone therapy who gets frequent PSA tests and DREs is going to catch signs of prostate cancer sooner than a man *not* on testosterone therapy who isn't getting that kind of care.

The Key Role of Nutrition for Prostate Health

Maintain a healthy weight and eat a moderate diet that isn't too rich in fats from meat or dairy products. A diet chock full of antioxidant-rich, colorful vegetables and fresh fruits will protect you against most illness. To protect your prostate specifically, focus on tomatoes, red peppers, cruciferous vegetables, such as broccoli, Brussels sprouts, cabbage, and cauliflower, and soy foods, such as miso tempeh, and tofu. You will benefit from drinking green tea. Take supplements that contain lycopene and green tea if you prefer them to the foods themselves.

Prostate-Protective Supplements

Saw palmetto. This is a natural extract from a type of dwarf palm tree. Saw palmetto has been widely studied and has been shown to be beneficial for the prostate, especially for preventing or treating BPH. It may also have a role in lowering the risk of prostate cancer. Saw palmetto is a 5-alpha reductase inhibitor, a substance that blocks conversion of testosterone into dihydrotestosterone (DHT), a more powerful testosterone. Saw palmetto also inhibits estradiol activity and reduces inflammation in the prostate, both of which are believed to be important elements in the genesis of prostate cancer. Take 160 mg twice a day.

> To reduce symptoms of enlarged prostate, take 160 mg of saw palmetto extract twice daily.

Omega-3 fatty acids. These are essential fatty acids found in high concentrations in fish and flaxseeds. These fats tend to be severely lacking in contemporary diets, and adding them back into your diet with a supplement may be one of the most crucial steps you can take for your general health and well-being. Omega-3s are metabolized and used by the body to make specific hormone-like biochemicals that act like anti-inflammatory drugs, without the side effects. These fats have been shown to inhibit the growth of prostate-cancer cells and to control inflammation in the joints, the blood vessels, and throughout the body. More detail about omega-3s in Chapter 11, but for now, know that the best source of supplemental omega-3 fatty acids comes from pharmaceutical grade fish oil. I recommend 2.5 grams of EPA and DHA every day.

> Take 2.5 grams (2,500 milligrams) of EPA + DHA daily to protect your prostate.

Herbal chemoprevention. Aaron Katz, M.D., is a urologist and founder of the Holistic Urology Center at Columbia-Presbyterian Hospital in New York City. He also happens to be one of the world's most respected urological surgeons. Dr. Katz and his colleagues have been doing some interesting research into the use of specific herbs to slow the progression of prostate cancer. In particular, they've been studying an herbal combination that contains highly concentrated turmeric, ginger, holy basil, green tea, oregano, rosemary, and a couple of lesser-known Chinese herbs.

A combination of turmeric, ginger, holy basil, green tea, oregano, and rosemary can reduce inflammation and may help reverse pre-cancerous growth in the prostate.

All these herbs have documented anti-inflammatory effects, and Dr. Katz, along with other experts in his field, strongly suspects that inflammation plays an important role in the genesis and progression of prostate cancer. Dr. Katz says this herbal combination may reverse a precancerous condition in the prostate gland (prostatic interepithelial neoplasia, or PIN); and even when the herbal remedy doesn't reverse PIN, it can slow the progression into prostate cancer—test-tube studies show that the herbal combination stops or slows the growth of prostate-cancer cells. You can buy this herbal supplement in any health food store or online. If you have prostate disease, or would like to do all you can to prevent it, *Dr. Katz's Guide to Prostate Health*, is a thorough resource on both prevention and treatment.

Be proactive. You *can* lower your risk of prostate disease. If you take good care of that little gland at the base of your bladder, it will make life a whole lot more livable and enjoyable.

11

There's More to It Than Hormones

Ten Simple Pointers for Healthy Living—for Real

In the twentieth century, when medicine began to make incredible leaps and bounds, life expectancy increased dramatically over a period of decades. In light of this astounding progress, it has seemed to some that a cure for death must be just around the corner.

Ray Kurzweil, a modern-day inventor who lives in Wellesley, Massachusetts, believes this cure is forthcoming, and he has written a book on this subject with Terry Grossman, M.D., called *Fantastic Voyage: Live Long Enough to Live Forever.* In it, he advises readers on diet, how to use supplements, and other interventions to live long enough to see the advances in *nanotechnology* (the science of creating and using super-microscopic particles) that he believes will eradicate the infirmities of old age, as well as death itself. He envisions microscopic *nanobots* that would travel around in our bodies repairing damage, and downloads from the Internet that would improve our genetic cod ing.

Kurzweil has been lauded for his work in the growing field of nanotechnology. He has won a $500,000 grant that has been called the Nobel Prize for inventors, as well as the 1999 National Medal of Technology Award. It is widely agreed this man is a genius on a par with Thomas Edison. Kurzweil is about sixty, and with his regimen of 250 daily supplement pills, lots of green tea, and constant tracking of his body's workings, he has every intention of living long enough to live forever. (I hope bio-identical hormones are part of his regimen.)

The physical changes that come with aging are the subject of a great deal of research effort on the part of many brilliant scientists, including Cambridge University professor Aubrey de Gray, Ph.D., and University of Chicago professor Jay Olshansky, M.D. Professor deGray cuts a striking figure, with long reddish-brown hair, a beard, and a penchant for floral-patterned shirts. He is also a brilliant, well-respected, visionary academic scientist who claims that the extension of human life span to Methuselah-like dimensions of 1000 years or beyond is a realistic prospect. He insists it is possible, although it won't happen quickly—he anticipates that several generations of costly work are needed to extend lifespan this much. He has said that the first person to live 1000 years may already be sixty-years-old. (Maybe it will be Ray Kurzweil.)

Olshansky, a professor at the University of Chicago's School of Public Health, looks more like your standard university medical school professor (close-cropped, thinning, greying hair and beard). He thinks deGray's predictions are more a fascinating theoretical exercise than an actual possibility. In an article for the BBC News, he remarked that all the people in ancient history who maintained that immortality was possible have one thing in common—they're all dead.

My view is that eternal life is probably not in the cards for humanity, but that lifespan—and, especially, *healthy* lifespan—will continue to be stretched past limits once thought impossible. Hormones will play a role, but exactly how is not yet known. Regardless what technology is used, a part of the formula for healthy longevity will be to keep hormones in an optimal range—because cells simply don't function as well without them.

The Present and Future of Healthcare

Today, doctors prescribe thousands of drugs every day to treat allergies, anxiety, attention deficit, depression, high cholesterol, hypertension, menopausal symptoms, PMS, and many other conditions. Many news stories about the adverse effects of prescription drugs—cancer, heart failure, impotence, liver damage, muscle wasting, restless legs, suicide, you name it—are filtering into the mind of the general public and bringing the troubling realization that all drugs have inherent risks. Drugs are not always safe. Even when properly prescribed and used, they have very real potential to cause significant problems, even death.

On the other hand, I have yet to see a study on any bio-identical hormone (estrogen, insulin, progesterone, testosterone, thyroid) that is given as a replacement for a hormone deficiency, with maintenance of hormone levels in a physiological range, that indicates this mode of treatment is anything but safe.

Presently, we are in a phase of medicine where drug therapy is the *standard* of care. Even BHRT is modeled on drug therapy. As I've repeatedly pointed out, the drug companies have a powerful foothold right now, and probably will for years to come, but eventually things will change. If you accept the commonly cited figure that our knowledge of science doubles every 3.5 years, it's not a stretch to assume that whatever we're doing today in medicine will be ancient history—and rightly so—in twenty years. What will we be doing then?

I don't think we'll be using the same pellets, creams, and patches forever. The ways in which we treat disease, aging, and hormone deficiencies will certainly change, thank goodness. We may end up using stem cells to rejuvenate the body's own production of steroid hormones. We might also find ways to lengthen telomeres (those tags at the end of DNA strands that seem to create an aging clock for each cell) and otherwise utilize futuristic technologies in genetic bioengineering, nanotechnology, and adjustment of the body's electrical fields (biofields) rather than giving people drugs. If this seems far-fetched, think about this—only 250 years ago, we didn't have a clue as to what causes most diseases. Now look at how much more we know today, and consider the exponential pace at which we continue to learn.

I have no doubt that continuing study in the areas of genetic bioengineering, nanotechnology, and stem cells may soon allow us to medically treat such diseases as Alzheimer's, autoimmune conditions, cancer, and Parkinson's more successfully without those primitive chemical agents known as pharmaceutical drugs.

Until that time, here's what there is to work with to create *The Youth Effect*: bio-identical hormones, diet, exercise, supplements, and reduced exposure to toxins. Sometimes, drugs can be a part of the longevity picture, too, but pharmaceuticals are greatly overused at this juncture, particularly cholesterol-lowering statin drugs, and drugs to combat anxiety and depression. Most people would benefit from using medicines less often and turning instead to non-pharmaceutical alternatives that don't just mask symptoms, but actually work *with* the body to create a more appropriate, healthful balance.

Here, I'd like to give you a cursory glance at strategies (aside from BHRT) I advise my patients to utilize to help them feel young, energetic and vibrant, and look their best. To maximize *The Youth Effect* in your life, it is imperative to have a good balance of all these other modalities.

I could write a book about each of these factors. Others have done just that, however, so the pointers I am giving you are simple and easy to incorporate in your life—you don't have to read book after book to implement them.

Play Good Defense

College basketball is a big deal in my home state of North Carolina, where I still practice medicine. Dean Smith, Mike Kryzcewski, and Roy Williams are legendary coaches who have made their living winning NCAA championships. How'd they do it? By emphasizing defense.

Keys to good defense of your health:
Kick tobacco
Avoid sun overexposure
Protect your hearing
Avoid environmental toxins, especially xenoestrogens
Drink filtered water
Avoid biofield disruptions
Eat organic dairy, eggs, and meat

You, too, must start thinking in terms of playing good defense to survive the onslaught of toxins and other environmental insults that Americans are exposed to every day. I think it's important to understand that this advanced industrialized country, while very creature-comfortable, comes at a price—and a high one at that. Some of the byproducts of industry and advanced technology may well be zapping your vitality, youth, and longevity. Some of the current comforts most people indulge in—cigarettes, eating junk or fast food, killing household pests or weeds with chemicals, going to a manicurist's salon, sunbathing—come at a price, too.

Here's a quick hit list of all the ways in which you ought to get on the defensive and stay there for the rest of your born days.

Kick the tobacco. If you're using tobacco in any form, you've got no business doing anything else for your health until you quit.

Avoid overexposure to sun. Fifteen minutes of direct sun on your skin two or three times a week will give your body adequate vitamin D, which it needs to maintain bone mass, but more than that is going to prematurely age your skin and contribute to skin cancer. Self-tanning sprays, creams, and lotions are O.K as far as anyone knows now, but they haven't really been around long enough to know for sure. Protect your skin against the sun with shade, sunscreen, and appropriate clothing, and don't go to tanning booths. You also need to defend your eyes against UV rays. The leading cause of blindness in older people is macular degeneration, and it is a direct result of sun exposure to the delicate retinas of the eyes. Wear UV-blocking sunglasses at all times while outside, and don a hat, while you're at it.

Protect your hearing. Avoid chronic exposure to loud noise. Loud noises of all kinds—otherwise known as noise pollution—can rob you of your hearing. Deafness is on the rise, and people are becoming deaf at ever-earlier ages because of noise pollution from earphones, loud music, and machinery. Be especially careful with personal music players, which have been found to damage the eardrums, when played at even moderately high volume. Reduce your exposure by avoidance altogether, but when you can't avoid high-volume noise, muffle it with earplugs.

Do what you can to avoid environmental toxins. Environmental toxins are a very big subject, too big to thoroughly address here. You probably know about asbestos, dioxins, furanes, PCBs, and radon, all of which are well-documented sources of adverse health consequences, including cancer, cardiovascular disease, respiratory diseases, and damage to the nervous and immune systems. Most of these chemicals are fairly ubiquitous. Every person on the planet has them in their tissues to some extent. Keeping yourself as healthy as you can with appropriate diet, hormone balance, lots of clean drinking water, and supplements can help your body rid itself of some of its chemical burden.

Mercury is seriously damaging to the nervous system and has been implicated as a contributing cause of Alzheimer's dementia. Eating too much fish of the large, predatory variety (king mackerel, shark, swordfish, tilefish, tuna) can raise your mercury levels too high. Anchovies, sardines, shellfish, and and wild-caught salmon are much lower in mercury. Another obvious source of mercury contamination is the amalgam fillings you may already have in your teeth. Don't let your dentist use them, and consider having any that are already in your teeth removed.

Drink filtered water. Some toxic chemicals, such as chlorine and fluoride, are purposely put into the water supply to purify it and reduce dental cavities, but significant evidence suggests these chemicals may be causing more harm than good. Drinking chlorinated tap water has been linked to an increased risk of cancer because the chlorine reacts with organic compounds in the water to create carcinogenic chemicals. Fluoride in excess can weaken bones and has been linked to cancer, neurological damage, and reproductive problems. Fluoridation is not needed for dental health, it only has decay-preventive effects when actually *applied to the teeth,* not when swallowed. Fluoridated water has actually been implicated in an epidemic of dental fluorosis (discolored teeth) in children.

Drink only filtered water, and don't trust that any old bottled water is adequately filtered—some are just tap water poured into fancy bottles. Your best bet is a reverse osmosis/carbon-block filter, a home water-filtration system that gets rid of chlorine, fluoride, and other toxins. Buy some fancy bottles of your own and fill them with your own pure, clean water if you like. If you don't have a whole-house system, a filter for chlorine on your shower is a good idea too, as you breathe it in every time you stand in that steamy spray.

Beware the xenoestrogens. Xenoestrogens are mostly petroleum-based. They increase abnormal estrogen activity in your body, and exposure to these chemicals is a well-established risk factor for breast and prostate cancers. Major sources include antiperspirants, deodorants, fabric softeners, insecticides, nail polish remover, pesticides, plastics (all of them), and some building materials.

Buy green products, which are usually non-toxic and made in ways that are kind to the environment. Use natural, non-toxic cleaning supplies, cosmetics, and personal care products. When you paint, put down new flooring or otherwise fix up your home, investigate non-toxic building products—they're more expensive, but worth it, just as organic foods are. Don't spray chemicals to kill bugs or weeds—the cure is *far* worse than the disease. Use natural, organic methods. You might deal with some more bugs and weeds, but you will also improve your chances of biting into that 100th birthday cake someday.

Avoid disrupting your biofield. Sounds like something out of Star Trek, which may explain why this concept has taken so long to gain broad acceptance in the scientific community. But it is now established fact that each person's body is surrounded by a weak electromagnetic field (EMF). When intact, this biofield—the name given it by none other than the National Institutes of Health (NIH)—has a significant role in maintaining normal body function. In Eastern medicine, the biofield has long been recognized as a key component of well-being. The energy field of the body is what acupuncture treats; in Ayurveda, the doshas are energetic forces with a strong impact on health and disease; and in the popular natural-healing methods of homeopathy and therapeutic touch, energy fields play an important role. Over the centuries, these fields have been variously recognized as auras, chakras, chi, and prana. Western medicine has been slow to accept this concept, but recent revelations have led to increased interest on the part of well-respected institutions in this part of the world, which are now engaging in noteworthy research in these areas.

Disruption of biofields by outside sources of electromagnetic energy—types of EMF that interfere with weaker biofields—has been linked to increased rates of cancer, including brain tumors, breast cancer, and leukemia; to childhood cancers; and to increased rates of miscarriage in women who had exposure to EMFs in their homes. Weak evidence also supports a role of exposure to these fields in mood disorders and insomnia.

What disrupts a biofield? Basically, anything that uses electromagnetic energy—cellphones, high-tension electrical wires, microwaves, TV. Any wire or plug that carries a current has an electromagnetic field. Since these entities are impossible to avoid, what you need is something to deflect or mute their effects, such as devices for a cellphone and computer that reduce the EMF emissions from these now indispensable gadgets. At websites selling such devices, you can also purchase a Gauss meter to find hot spots in your home where faulty wiring is creating an amplified EMF current. If you do find such a spot, getting it fixed by an electrician will enhance the health of everyone who spends time in that place.

Eat organic dairy products, eggs, and meats to avoid non-bio-identical hormones. Most animal sources of food in the United States are contaminated with synthetic growth-enhancing hormones administered to fatten the animals or increase milk production. Cattle, chickens, dairy cows, and pigs are all pumped full of these non-bio-identical hormones. Hormone balance is a complex enough business without the addition of this extra hormone burden, and scientific evidence leans to the conclusion that eating these hormones is a bad idea—or, at the very least, a participation in an uncontrolled scientific experiment. You now know how potent hormones can be. Don't chance it. Organically raised and free-range animals are not exposed to such chemicals. Sure, they're pricey, but you can, and probably should, eat smaller portions.

Nutrition and *The Youth Effect*

Hippocrates, considered the father of medicine, wrote 2500 years ago, "Let medicine be your food, and let food be your medicine." That was sound advice then, and it still ranks among the best bits of medical advice I've ever heard. So many of the ills that aging people just expect to encounter as a matter of course are actually precipitated by a poor diet—and they can be prevented by a good diet.

What can I possibly say about nutrition that hasn't already been said in one of several hundred books on the subject written in the last twenty years? If you're one of the many who has read stacks of them, and you're still wondering how to best feed yourself and the people who eat your cooking, you might agree that it's hard to know what to believe about nutrition anymore, with all the contradictory advice that's been swirling around in books, magazines, newspapers, and on the Internet.

Eating Moderately Enhances *The Youth Effect*

The science on caloric restriction, where longevity can be improved and age-related disease forestalled by eating roughly 30–40 percent fewer calories than you have an appetite for, is conclusive. The lifespan of an animal can be dramatically extended by underfeeding it. Eating fewer calories means less wear and tear, less free-radical formation, and less inflammation in your body.

Most people just plain eat too much, and most underestimate the number of calories they consume on any given day. Just an extra 100 calories a day—that's a glass of juice, or a cookie, or a few extra French fries—adds up to ten pounds of body fat in a year. If everyone could just get rid of the *all-you-can-eat* mentality, and could approach food as sustenance and nourishment, rather than getting all wrapped up in those fun packages and intense sweet, salty, or fatty flavors, that could do a lot to curb the obesity epidemic everyone's so hysterical about right now.

Of course, this is much easier discussed than done.

And being half-starved—which those calorically restricted experimental animals were—puts an enormous crimp in your mood. It's just not something the average person can maintain through sheer willpower. (Another tack that has been taken throughout history is to fast periodically—it appears that eating almost nothing for several days or longer can make up for eating plentifully on other days.)

If you can shave just 100–200 calories off of your daily food intake, or reduce your weekly food intake by a few hundred calories, and if you can increase the bulk of the food you eat *without* increasing calories—by eating more whole foods, such as vegetables, fruits, and whole grains—you can slow the aging process, and probably live longer, too.

No doubt, there are a lot of differing opinions on what constitutes a good diet—some more extreme than others. My personal favorite among health-promoting, youth-effect-actualizing diets happens to be what I call a "Zone-type" diet.

Barry Sears, Ph.D., wrote his very first Zone book, *The Zone,* in 1995. It became a *New York Times* #1 bestseller. And not because it was easy to read or well-written—a lot of people who tried to read his books complained that his program was too complicated—but because it advocated a nutritionally sound eating plan that had fifteen years of science behind it. I've had personal success with the Zone plan, and a great number of my patients have done equally well with it.

If you want to know more about Dr. Sears' approach, you'll find he's written several more books. Instead of the original book, I strongly recommend *A Week in the Zone*_(the paperback costs about seven dollars). The first thirty-five pages are a comprehensive wrap-up of all the essential points of excellent nutrition.

Entering Dr. Sears' *Zone* involves eating a balance of *macronutrients* (carbohydrates, fat, and protein) to maintain a proper balance of your internal hormonal response (eicosanoids, glucagon, and insulin). He advocates an emphasis on low-glycemic-index carbohydrates—carbohydrate foods that are broken down slowly in the body and don't cause a sudden spike in blood sugars and insulin levels. *The Zone* also recommends that you eat adequate amounts of lean proteins, and monounsaturated fat (mostly from nuts and certain oils, especially olive oil). Obviously, it's a little more complex, but you can learn more from the book. I don't need to reinvent the wheel here, Dr. Sears has done an excellent job creating a diet that works to encourage weight loss, wellness, and longevity.

Having declared myself a *Zone* fan, I'll say that I am primarily in favor of a lifestyle diet plan that works well for *you*. Most of the top-selling diet books out there have helped a lot of people who felt the plans advocated in their pages were a good fit for their lifestyle and food preferences. The approaches might be radically diverse, but most have been designed based on sound science and will work just fine. The main point to keep in mind is that your diet has to be something you can maintain comfortably and long-term. (*See* Recommended Reading section in back to read further on how to clean up your diet.)

If you've been trying to adhere to a diet plan and you keep backsliding into fast food and junk food, your plan needs to change. A good lifetime diet should be uncomplicated, un-extreme, and easy to maintain. You and I both know you won't stick with a diet that requires drastic reductions in foods you love, or one that requires you to eat a lot of foods you dislike or are too time-consuming to prepare. Any diet, however, should go heavy on vegetables and fruit and light on meat and dairy.

The key is to get on one of these diets, and let it become the way you eat—not just for a period of time to lose weight, but forever. You're going to be eating for the rest of your life, so you need to do it well for the rest of your life. My other favorite resources are Ann Kulze's *Dr. Ann's 10-Step Diet*, and Mo Bethea's *The New Sugar Busters*.

Now put down that diet book. It's time to get some exercise.

Workout Q and A

Everyone knows that exercising regularly is a good thing.

Those who exercise know this because they feel better and generally enjoy better health. Those who do not exercise can easily see how those who do seem so much healthier than they are. If you still haven't gotten on the workout bandwagon, don't hate them because they're beautiful...get off your rear and join them.

Once you've made the commitment to working out regularly, the following questions might arise:

Q. How often is enough?

A. The federal government's guidelines state that ninety minutes of exercise or physical activity a day is best. This is the closest we can come to matching the amount of daily physical activity the human body evolved to perform. As a species, people have only been sitting on their duffs for fifty years or so. Before that, the days were filled with intense and moderate physical activity. But to go from no exercise to ninety minutes every day is a bit of a stretch, so it's best to ease into it.

Most experts advise three to five sessions per week, thirty to sixty minutes in duration. They recommend exercising at an intensity level that raises your heart rate into a target range that's usually based on age.

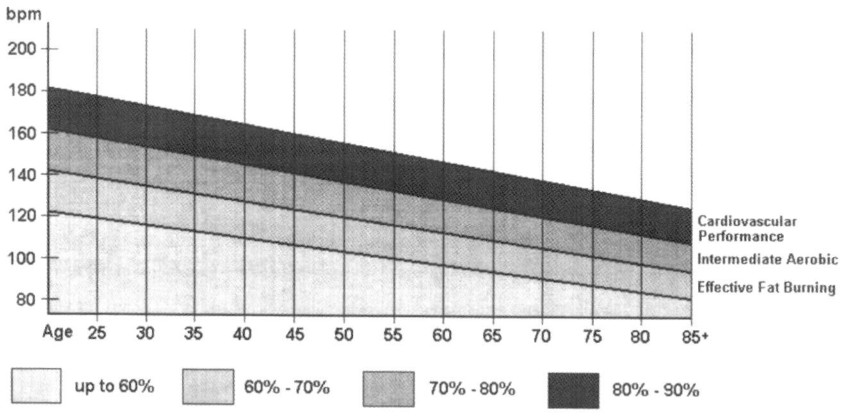

BPM = beats per minute—the number of times your heart beats each minute. Resting heart rate is usually between 60–90 BPM, with a lower BPM likely when you're in better cardiovascular shape. Maximum heart rate depends on your age; the graph shows how it declines over the years.

Low-intensity exercise to burn fat can be done at 55–65 percent of maximum heart rate; moderately intense exercise happens at 65–85 percent; and high-intensity exercise will boost heart rate to 85–100 percent of maximum.

To use this chart, find your age along the bottom; trace up to the level of exercise you think you would prefer. (Keep in mind that a lower intensity of exercise will require longer duration to effectively train your body and aid in weight loss; also keep in mind that high-intensity exercise isn't a good idea if you are out of shape—it's something you'll need to build up to.) Then, trace your finger to the left to see where your heart rate should be to get you in that range. Divide the numbers at the top and bottom of the range (each range has its own shade) by six to get a 10-second count. When you do cardiovascular exercise, check your pulse and count it for 10 seconds; if you're in the range, you're working at the proper intensity. If you're below it, work harder.

Q: What kind of exercise should I do?

A. You can divide your pursuit of fitness into three categories: aerobic (cardio-respiratory) , strength, and flexibility. A good exercise program emphasizes all three; they are all important for your overall ability to function. It's possible to engage in all three categories at the same time—dance, martial arts, Pilates, and some forms of a more athletic power yoga come closest to incorporating all three types of fitness into a single activity.

Try new things. Shake it up. Try walking and lifting weights one day, yoga the next, an aerobic dance class with strength training the next, and lap swimming after that. You can rent countless DVDs or videos of different workouts to try at home. Aside from keeping exercise interesting and staving off boredom, a varied program will train a variety of muscle groups and help ensure that you touch on all three types of fitness training at least twice a week. It'll also help keep the neural connections between brain and body crackling as you learn to move your body in new and challenging ways—connections that you either use or lose.

My general advice is, when you start an exercise program, get proper instruction, and walk before you run. This means starting out slowly and gently, setting goals, and working towards those goals—whether they are to lose inches off your waistline, get tighter arms, perform in your community theater's production of the *Nutcracker,* enter a 5K race, or do the Ironman triathlon. Exercise is its own reward—it can become almost addictive and can be part of your life for as long as you live it.

Pace yourself. The people who jump in too fast are the same people who quit workout programs. They get sore or injured, or expect quick results that are just not realistic, and they end up backing out before they really get going. A qualified trainer to start you off on the right foot is a worthwhile investment—you can enlist her or his help periodically as you expand your workout horizons.

Just *do something that gets you moving*—every day if you possibly can.

Vitamins and Supplements

With all the supposedly indispensable lifesaving supplements advertised today, you could spend all your time (and money) taking pills. The truth of it is that a person who eats a truly optimal diet doesn't need to take absolutely every new, trendy supplement that comes down the pike.

As of now, scientific research strongly backs only a few nutritional supplements for everyday use in the prevention of disease. Many supplements contain very concentrated doses of nutrients, and we really don't know the long-term consequences of taking nutrient doses that are many times greater than that required for basic physiological functioning. For now, it seems that a conservative approach to nutritional supplements, along with a highly nutritious diet, is the safest bet.

Here's what I recommend:

1 A multivitamin/mineral supplement;

2 Pharmaceutical grade fish oil.

That's right—just two supplements for everyday use. Pretty

simple, right? You can use any multivitamin/mineral that contains at least the RDA of essential nutrients. (*See* Resources in back for for further information.)

Juice Plus+

Another supplement about which I've heard good things from people I trust: Juice Plus+. The Juice Plus+ line consists of capsules, chewables, or "gummi" supplements that contain highly concentrated dehydrated vegetables and fruits – the foods lacking in most diets. They have an Orchard Blend that contains seven kinds of fruit (apple, orange, pineapple, cranberry, peach, acerola cherry, and papaya) and a Garden Blend with concentrated vegetables and fibers (carrots, parsley, beets, kale, broccoli, cabbage, spinach, tomatoes, barley/rice fiber). You get all the antioxidants, vitamins, and minerals of several servings of these foods without the calories, and they go into the body in the same synergistic combinations found in healthy whole foods.

Several university research centers have done research into the health benefits of Juice Plus+; in fact, it's the most widely researched nutraceutical in the world. The results of this research are very positive.

These supplements raise levels of antioxidants and the B vitamin folate in the bloodstream; they've been found to help maintain heart health by reducing homocysteine (a toxic amino acid that's neutralized by B vitamins like folate) and improving blood flow. Other studies have found that these concentrated food capsules enhance immune system function and help protect DNA against cancerous changes. Other ongoing research is investigating its use in lengthening survival in cancer patients, reversing periodontal (gum) disease, and reducing markers of systemic inflammation.

If this sounds interesting to you, you will need to contact a Juice Plus+ distributor; the products are sold through multi-level marketing. Go to https://www.juiceplus.com/+rb04207 to purchase these supplements. Or, you can click on the "Contact Us" link on that page and fill out the information, and a distributor will contact you.

If you only want to take one supplement, I recommend fish oil. Good-quality pharmaceutical-grade fish oil is the best single source of the omega-3 fatty acids, which are highly beneficial to the health of your heart and brain. Omega-3s reduce silent inflammation, which we now know to be the basis for most chronic disease.

In recent years, an explosion of studies has supported fish oil's power to lower your risk of Alzheimer's and heart disease—and do so at least as well as the major drugs available from drug companies. Fish oil has these protective effects without causing any abnormal changes to body chemistry or physiology, and without any of the adverse consequences that can result from drug therapy. This is because the omega-3s found in fish oil are used to make anti-inflammatory biochemicals in the body that naturally reduce inflammation at the cellular level.

Testing for Intracellular Nutrient Deficiency

Spectracell Laboratories in Houston has developed a unique method for measuring intracellular levels of vitamins, amino acids (protein building blocks), and antioxidants. This method gives you exact information about nutrient levels where they really count—inside your cells. It involves an analysis of white blood cells, which enables you to determine whether you have a deficiency in a particular entity and treat it accordingly. The cost of the test is offset by the savings you reap when you stop taking supplements you don't actually need.

Check out their website at <http://www.spectracell.com/>. It contains full information about the company, and lists clinicians who do this testing.

Again, Dr. Barry Sears deserves credit, this time for his work on omega-3 fatty acids. Two of his books, *The Omega Zone* and *The Anti-Inflammation Zone,* give in-depth information on the science behind omega-3 fatty acids. If you find the science behind the value of fish oil intriguing, both are informative reads, but if you're willing to trust me that omega-3 is the most important nutritional supplement you can take, you don't need to read them.

Health Benefits of Fish-Oil Supplements

Fish oils rich in the omega-3 fats docosahexaenoic acid (DHA) and eicosapentaenoic acid (EPA) have the following benefits. They:

1. Are beneficial for the treatment of arthritis, asthma, eczema, hypertension, migraines, psoriasis, and ulcerative colitis;
2. Decrease the growth rate of plaques that develop along artery walls;
3. Decrease the risk of heart arrhythmias, which can lead to sudden cardiac death;
4. Decrease triglyceride levels;
5. Help treat depression, bipolar disorder, and ADHD;
6. Positively modify inflammatory markers in autoimmune diseases, such as lupus and rheumatoid arthritis;
7. Slightly lower blood pressure.

If you take fish oil, be sure it is pharmaceutical grade. A pharmaceutical-grade fish oil undergoes extensive processing to ensure that it is free of contaminants and unlikely to cause gastrointestinal distress with high doses. It also has a higher potency (more omega-3s per gram of oil) and contains *exactly* the amount of DHA and EPA the labeling claims it does. (*See* Resources in back for more information.) Because omega-3 fats spoil easily—they are delicate fats that are easily oxidized, creating free radicals—take vitamin E (100–400 IU) daily in a multivitamin or as a separate supplement. (Some fish oil supplements contain extra antioxidants to deal with this problem.) Don't take cod liver oil, which contains enough of vitamins A and D to create toxicity with long-term use.

How much fish oil should you take each day? A healthy person can get by with a dose of 2.5 grams of EPA plus DHA a day. That can be a handful of capsules in *non*-pharmaceutical grade fish oil, but pharmaceutical-grade oil can pack this much omega-3 into three or four capsules, or a teaspoon of liquid. If you have heart disease or any other chronic disease, you may want to try taking more—up to 5.0 grams per day is a safe dose that doesn't necessitate any special testing.

Take enough fish oil to deliver 2.5 grams (2,500 milligrams) of DHA plus EPA daily. Take it with 100-400 IU of vitamin E if it does not contain an antioxidant to protect against free radical formation.

A Matter of Taste?

Some patients have told me, "I tried fish oil and I won't take it anymore. I had a fishy taste in my mouth after I took it." Others complain colorfully of "fish burps."

Here's what I tell them: "First of all, use a pharmaceutical-grade oil—you'll be less likely to have a fishy aftertaste. Second of all, if you still have the aftertaste, *get over it.* Fish oil is so good for you—are you going to let a little thing like fish burps keep you from taking it?"

One patient of mine told me she had figured out a trick to reduce the fish-oil-burp problem. She purchases concentrated liquid chlorophyll—the same stuff that makes plants green—to which mint has been added. Chlorophyll is a natural breath freshener and a detoxifying agent used in natural medicine. This person says she puts a tablespoon of this green liquid in an eight-ounce glass of water and uses that to swallow her fish-oil capsules. (As is true of many dogs, hers had bad breath, so she started putting her chlorophyll in his water and reports that it worked to freshen his breath...and the rest of his digestive tract.)

> To prevent "fish oil burps," add a tablespoon of chlorophyll with mint to the water used to swallow the capsules.

One sharp, very healthy, energetic older lady I know used to swallow a clove of garlic with her fish oil each day. She'd take a big, fat, freshly peeled clove of garlic, partly crush it, and split it the long way with a knife. Then she poured a teaspoon of cod liver oil into a glass, dropped the garlic clove into it, and swallowed the whole thing down. And you think just a little pharmaceutical-grade fish-oil tablet gives you bad breath?

The Big Picture of Healthcare—Disease-Mongering vs. Preventive Medicine

Some years back, the term *disease-mongering* was coined by a journalist to describe the transformation of normal life changes, such as aging and menopause, into diseases. Disease-mongering expands the boundaries of disease, so someone who might once have been considered a little down in the dumps is now diagnosed as clinically depressed. Someone with blood pressure or cholesterol levels once considered to be at the upper edge of healthy is now said to be pre-hypertensive or borderline high risk. A child who can't sit still was once seen as just that—a child who can't sit still. Today, he/she is diagnosed with ADHD. A woman who once just had a headache, usually, mysteriously, right around the time her partner was feeling amorous, is now said to have female sexual dysfunction.

The result of this shift in today's medical focus is a dramatic increase in people's reliance on prescription drugs—those patented chemicals that abnormally alter your biochemistry to try and squelch individual symptoms or risk factors. People once considered healthy are now taking handfuls of pills every day because their blood pressure or their cholesterol fell just beyond the current bounds of normal, or their bad mood was given a medical diagnosis and targeted with a prescription.

How about intervention in the aging process? Is it disease-mongering? No—it's intelligent preventive medicine. If *prevention*—which consists of the judicious and scientific identification of risk factors and early signs of disease, and the safe, effective steps taken to slow or stall the progression of disease in those early stages—starts to be seen as disease-mongering, we'll be throwing the baby out with the bathwater.

I admit that, in the case of pharmaceutical companies colluding with doctors and government to expand the markets for drugs, the line between disease-mongering and preventive medicine can get downright fuzzy. Risks are inherent with such pharmaceuticals as Celebrex, Lipitor, or Prozac, because they are synthetic molecules with potent and targeted effects in the body. There is a growing push to try and *prevent* disease with pharmaceuticals, such as Celebrex (studied as a preventive against colon cancer) and Lipitor (used to prevent heart disease). Risks are inherent with such pharmaceuticals, because they are synthetic molecules with potent and targeted effects in the body. As they were with Vioxx, another drug strongly considered to be a candidate for disease prevention (Alzheimer's disease, colon cancer), these risks are often underplayed or even hidden by those who stand to profit from increased sales of those drugs. The public has an incomplete understanding of the risk-to-benefit relationship of using prescription drugs to *prevent* disease. In general, and more specifically, in connection with the theme of this book, it is far safer to approach prevention with bio-identical hormones and dietary shifts than with prescription drugs.

Consider that ancient medical practices, such as traditional Chinese medicine (TCM) and Ayurveda, the Indian form of medicine, focus strongly on prevention. They have detailed tools, such as acupuncture, nutrition, and herbs, for diagnosing imbalances in the body and mind that can be corrected with gentle, natural remedies. These imbalances are the very earliest indications of disease, and by remedying them, it may be possible to avoid falling ill altogether.

It is said that doctors in ancient China would not receive

payment for their services if their patients actually got sick. They were paid to *prevent* disease, not fix a person's body after it had become broken. This is an intelligent application of knowledge to maintain health. And today, we know vastly more about how to prevent disease and slow its progression.

If it is to survive, the healthcare system in America will have to embrace a preventive approach. The current model doesn't work at all well, as you probably know—and far too many people are uninsured and can't afford even the most basic healthcare. This has to change if we are not going to burden our children and grandchildren with a mostly sick, disabled, and rapidly ballooning population of unhappy senior citizens who need constant medical care.

In the upcoming final chapter, I'd like to pitch my two cents' worth about the broken healthcare system and how, unlike Humpty Dumpty, it *can* be put together again.

12

Follow the Money

The Economic Forces of Medicine

I helped recruit Martin to our hospital because we were in need of someone with his skills—he had spent much of his first thirty-five years training intensely to be a gynecologic oncologist, a specialty that requires incredible competence and compassion. I quickly became impressed with his expertise and his dedication to his patients, staff, and duties. It didn't matter what time it was, or what day of the week—if you needed his help, he'd be there. We operated together on numerous occasions, and his surgical skills were second to none. He loved to perform surgery, but never did so unnecessarily or aggressively.

One day, he phoned to give me some follow-up on an endometrial cancer patient we had operated on together. After giving me her information, he asked if I'd heard his news. "I'm leaving," he said. I thought he meant the hospital, or perhaps Charlotte, and sadly asked where he was going. "I'm leaving medicine," he told me.

After picking myself up off the floor, I think I said, "You can't *do* that!"

"I just can't take it anymore," he replied. "The endless battles with insurance companies and Medicare, the progressive decrease in reimbursements...among other things...it has just overwhelmed my desire to take care of people."

Once before, he'd mentioned to me his increasing disenchantment with the system. He had complained about spending far too much valuable time fighting the forces that be—mostly the insurance companies and Medicare. I understood all too well, just as I understood his issues with the nightmarish coding game all physicians have to deal with—a game he had obsessively tried to make work for himself and his patients. I hadn't thought all this would be enough to make this remarkable, dedicated, skilled physician leave the profession altogether, but he made good on his word and left soon after.

What a sad day that was. Since then, I've seen many others like him take the early-retirement route out of a medical system in which caring, competent, intelligent medical practice seems increasingly impossible to deliver. The loss of Martin was most poignant to me, and the biggest loss to medicine I have personally experienced.

Thankfully, there will always be good, dedicated, bright people who want to go into medicine, even though the bureaucratic tangles have turned a lot of young people away. As with Martin, this system has led to disenchantment among the ranks of those who have practiced under better circumstances.

The American healthcare system is sick. In fact, it may have an ultimately fatal disease unless a cure is found in the near future. This crisis involves rapidly escalating costs, especially when compared to gross domestic product, and a population that is living longer, at least for now. As reported in an article about lifestyle in the Science section of *The New York Times*, April 17, 2007, "a 2005 study in *The New England Journal of Medicine* predicted that average life expectancy in the United States would decline in the next twenty years as a result of unhealthy lifestyles, reversing a trend dating to the 1850s."

The American healthcare system, once just a bothersome and inefficient bureaucracy, has evolved into a nasty behemoth. You know this as a consumer, and I'm painfully reminded of the mess it creates every day I practice medicine. Undoing the system's monstrous complexities and inefficiencies is a daunting task that has, so far, flummoxed the many experts who have been summoned to come up with a solution.

I could write an entire book on this topic alone, and if I ever come up with a solid solution, I'll do just that. In the meantime,

I want you to know who the players in this game are, what economic forces motivate them, and how they affect what is going on with your healthcare today. And, of course, I'd love to see you avoid getting mired in the tar pit that is our healthcare system by taking spectacular care of yourself, using the advice found in this book—staying fit and healthy really is the best revenge against a monstrous system that would as soon swallow you up as look at you.

Government Red Tape Threatens to Bury Good Medical Practice

In my thirty years of practicing medicine, I've watched the gradual infiltration of government into the day-to-day operations of doctors and hospitals. It's been disconcerting, to say the least, as one acronym after another has been thrown at us—HMO (*Health Maintenance Organization*), PPO (*Preferred Provider Organization*), EMTALA (*Emergency Medical Treatment and Active Labor Act*), OSHA (*Occupational Safety and Health Act*), HIPAA (*Health Insurance Portability and Accountability Act*), JCAH (*Joint Commission on Accreditation of Hospitals*), and CLIA (*Clinical Laboratory Improvement Amendments*).

In each doctor's practice, every one of these acronyms translates into stacks of ever-changing paperwork, which increases every year, piling higher and higher and higher. The effect of all this bureaucratic red tape has been a major stifling of doctors' ability to practice the art of medicine—plus a dramatic increase in the cost of doing business. It has been estimated that HIPAA alone cost doctors $150 million in the first two years of its existence, and I can't for the life of me see how it's worth it.

Medicare and Medicaid

Medicare and Medicaid have both been around for nearly forty years now. These programs have enabled Americans who are older, or indigent, to enjoy state-of-the-art medical care, which they could not otherwise afford. Unfortunately, as will happen with any such government bureaucracy, both programs have also generated massive costs, paperwork, and regulations.

Perceptions of inequity in provider compensation have been an issue since the inception of these programs. Every few years, there are alterations made in the compensation scale, but the overall trend for the past thirty years has been downward. The end result is that providers work harder and harder to make fewer and fewer dollars. As a physician, I can tell you this has not created a very happy scenario, especially as our economy has enjoyed its greatest growth in history during this same time period—the same economic growth that has allowed Medicare and Medicaid to remain solvent.

Speaking of solvency, it's hard to know what this word really means with a government program, because money moves from one entity to another so freely. It's almost impossible to follow the money in these situations. My prediction is that Medicare's solvency is going to be short-lived with the passage of the new Medicare prescription drug bills. I'm afraid we may have opened Pandora's box with this one.

Socialized Medicine is Not the Answer

As the current system has moved further and further towards intractability, doctors have been almost universally terrified that the government would take over medicine. Socialized medicine is a concept I've heard about since I was in college, and I'm fairly sure the fear of it lurking in the shadows as a political agenda has kept a lot of good people from going into medicine. I can assure you, the establishment of socialized medicine in America would lead to a huge shift in the type of person who goes into the medical field.

Given the track record of Medicare and Medicaid, I think most people understand that a federally run healthcare system for all Americans would be a disaster in every way. It could well bankrupt the government (especially without tort reform), and it would create a level of care that is inferior to the present one. Federalized healthcare in countries like Canada is moving in the direction of privatization. There, it is not unusual to wait months or years for a surgery, and increasing numbers of Canadians are flying to India to have prompt, affordable surgeries.

I believe that the less government involvement there is in

the healthcare system, the better. In fact, if Medicare/Medicaid could be privatized, a few billion dollars a year could be saved. Unfortunately, once the government gets their fingers into something, it tends to hang on permanently.

Insurance Companies—a Necessary Evil

This is not to say the insurance companies are doing a bang-up job. Their mistakes are clearly evident, as millions more Americans become unable to afford insurance with every passing year.

Don't be fooled by all the slick, warm, fuzzy advertisements about how such-and-such insurance company took care of so-and-so when she was sick. No one at an insurance company has ever done anything to provide care to you or any other person. It's against the law for them to provide care of any kind, but they would rather be seen in a caring and giving role than in their true light, as moneychangers.

Still, I think of insurance companies as a necessary evil. They're probably the only thing preventing government take-over of the healthcare system. Although insurance companies do not provide care to you, they do have a definite impact on what type of care *is* provided to you.

Insurance companies have varying degrees of power to select who your provider is (doctor and hospital), what kind of evaluation is done (lab, x-rays, and other tests), and what treatment is performed (including surgery, hospitalization, medication, and physical or occupational therapy). These influences have not only dictated how doctors treat problems, but more subtly—and perhaps more importantly—insurance company guidelines dictate a doctor's full approach to a person's health as a whole.

A doctor's reimbursement is based on a complex coding system, which is devised by good old Uncle Sam. Non-adherence to any of the many federal rules and regulations about healthcare billing can result in late payment or non-payment to the physician for services rendered. Sometimes, paperwork snafus lead to a situation where a patient ends up having to pay for something that should have been covered. To avoid these problems, doctors have been relegated to concentrating on what the insurance companies want, which often is not what's best for the patient.

Doctors have no avenue through which to effectively fight this. If they want to get paid by insurance companies, they must play the insurance companies' game, on their home court, by their rules. And this benefits no one but the insurance companies.

Insurance companies are really in the catbird seat. No matter how high the cost of healthcare goes, they still make money, as long as they collect more in premiums than they pay out in benefits. Since they control both ends of that equation, from their standpoint, the risk is really minimal. Insurance company CEOs rake in multi-million-dollar compensations each year, even as thousands of subscribers see their claims denied and their families' financial health sent the way of the dinosaurs.

Preventive Medicine Could Solve the Problem

If insurers were interested in lowering the cost of healthcare and providing the best benefit to your health and well-being, they would embrace preventive medicine.

For the most part, insurance companies have not done this because they perceive that wellness programs are costly, providing little or no benefit in terms of profit margins. And since people are more likely to change insurance companies throughout their lifetimes than they once were, a long-term return on investment in a wellness program may not be realized by the insurance company.

I think this is not only shortsighted, but dead wrong. At least two studies done in the last several years have shown a positive return on a health insurer's investment within the first year after a wellness program was instituted.

Since insurance companies have such a great influence on the type of care people receive, the greater good would best be served if they did all they could to emphasize preventive medicine. I only hope they will grasp this concept before it is too late.

Follow the Money...Into Drug Company Coffers

Government and insurance companies impose their own

guidelines for practicing the art of medicine on doctors. Then, drug companies swoop in and try to convince doctors that their products are the best way to treat their patients' problems. I tell you, for physicians these days, it can feel like being between rocks and hard places everywhere you turn.

A 1996 AMA survey of physician members revealed that 80 percent of doctors admitted to getting all new information on pharmaceuticals from drug reps who visit their offices regularly. The other 20 percent reported getting most of their information from medical journals and scientific meetings. But the kicker here is that authors of the articles, and conductors of the studies, are on drug company payrolls, and journals are financially supported by drug companies' ads in their pages. The meetings that all physicians go to are most often subsidized by drug companies, and virtually all the speakers are being paid by one or more drug companies.

Don't get me wrong, I'm not saying everyone is on the take, or that these people are bad and dishonest. I am merely pointing out that the drug companies' influence on what a doctor believes, and how she or he treats a problem is totally pervasive. For many doctors, not believing drug companies' information is almost impossible today, but I would like to see more doctors critically question where the drug companies are taking us—aside from the figurative poorhouse. Skyrocketing drug costs are the greatest contributor to rising medical costs.

Believe it or not, *there are almost always alternatives to drug therapy*. In the end, a drug could turn out to be the most beneficial alternative, but generally speaking, with good nutrition, adequate exercise, the right nutritional supplements, and yes, bio-identical hormone replacement, drug therapy can be avoided. Your mindset needs to shift in this direction, because the current thinking that a pill is what's best for an ill—"Here, take this drug and everything will be okay"—is not good for you at all. Drugs are more costly than preventive measures and their harmful side effects can often lead to other, more serious, problems that, in an insane downward spiral, often necessitate other medications. According to a survey released in 2005 by the U.S. Department of Health and Human Services, one in six Americans takes *three or more* prescription medications.

Does giving a drug to treat drug side effects, then another drug to treat the side effects of the second drug, sound more like fiction than reality? Trust me, it happens every single day in every single town in the United States. And a lot of people incur a lot of damage—even death—every day from *properly prescribed and administered* prescription drugs. Every year, tens of thousands of people are killed by errors in prescribing and administering FDA-approved medications.

Prescription drugs have their place in medicine and have saved many lives. I am very thankful for our diverse pharmacopoeia; however, too often, drugs are pegged as the only solution to any health problem, and that's a stab in the heart of the physician's true calling. Over-hyping of drugs to doctors and the general public has led to their overuse and abuse, and from the standpoint of cost or overall health, this doesn't serve anyone.

For the well-being of our healthcare system, it behooves everyone—provider and consumer alike—to become less reliant on drugs and more dependent on natural, less costly means of controlling disease processes. *Drugs should be the last resort, not the first response.*

Trial Lawyers and Tort Reform

Our entire way of life is hamstrung by the threat of being sued, and this is especially true for doctors and hospitals. No single factor will do more in a shorter period of time to reduce healthcare costs than meaningful tort reform—changes in the laws that currently allow outrageous sums to be awarded in malpractice lawsuits.

The economy in general would be strengthened if frivolous lawsuits could be reduced. No other economy in the world has to deal with this menace. In a global economy, other countries are able to deliver goods and services with far more cost-efficiency than Americans can, unless tort reform becomes a reality here. If a politician tells you that tort reform will *not* reduce the cost of medical care, look to see who his or her major contributors are. I would bet a stack of bills that trial lawyers are in there somewhere.

Doctors who are struggling with rapidly escalating malpractice insurance rates would gain a measure of relief. With tort reform, the benefits to medical care costs would be vast. Doctors would be freed up to practice medicine based on our education, our experience, our minds, and our clinical instincts, rather than in a way designed to protect ourselves against malpractice lawsuits. We could deal with the patients in front of us and do what's right for each individual, rather than practicing defensive medicine.

In my twenty-five years of delivering babies, I saw ever-increasing costs associated with, among other things, more and more testing, and a greater tendency to deliver by cesarean section. Two wonderful obstetricians who were friends of mine quit obstetrics shortly after a bad outcome resulted in a major lawsuit. On both occasions, the doctor was present at the mother's side, but the available technology did not absolutely confirm there was a problem with the baby. Both babies ended up with neurological problems. Both doctors were determined in court to be at fault. One of these judgments was for 23 million dollars.

The threat of a huge lawsuit doesn't prevent medical mistakes. Of course, people who were hurt because of a doctor's carelessness are entitled to receive damages, but the current system is akin to killing a flea with a hydrogen bomb. I'm all for people who have been injured having compensation and support, but today's environment of defensive medical practice is too expensive and hurts more than it helps.

Relief from these threats will have an incredible impact, allowing doctors to do the *right* thing—not just the thing that covers their rear ends and results in much higher medical costs without making things any safer for their patients. One way in which doctors cover themselves is by employing every possible technological diagnostic and treatment tool available to them. This need has fueled an unbelievable boom in technological medical advances over the past fifteen years. Some of these advances have netted cost savings, while others have significantly increased the cost of doing business, without necessarily offering a corresponding benefit to healthcare.

Sometimes a simpler, older technology works better than a newfangled, pricey gizmo. Often, simple changes in diet or exercise habits are better interventions than drugs. Contrary to opinion, high-tech is not always better than low-tech, and some would say it is seldom better. Doctors need to do a better job of deciding which technologies result in better medicine at lesser cost. This may not always be a simple task, but it is just not possible to afford every newfangled device that comes down the pike.

Corporate America to the Rescue?

Here's my conclusion: The corporations of the United States have to be the saviors of the healthcare system.

With the exception of government-funded healthcare, the bulk of the healthcare costs in the United States is shouldered by corporate America, the employer of American workers. It's on their shoulders that this problem ought to get solved.

Prior to World War II, essentially every individual American paid for his own healthcare expenses. During WWII, when wage and price controls were instituted on private corporations by the government, it became economically advantageous for companies to offer certain employees the benefit of healthcare insurance. The corporate expense for this insurance was essentially tax-deductible, enabling corporations to use this benefit to retain and hire key employees.

The rest is history. Over the past sixty years, corporations have absorbed more and more of the cost of healthcare coverage for their employees and employees' dependents. While this may sound like a good thing for the large number of employees who need coverage, a number of bad consequences have come about.

Ever-Increasing Costs for Employee's Healthcare Insurance

Since corporations have set a precedent, it is expected that a certain percentage (if not all) of an employee's healthcare insurance is paid for by the corporation. Once a certain percentage is covered, it is difficult to cut this back. To remain competitive with other companies' benefit packages, corporations have felt the need to maintain this practice, which has led to ever-increasing costs. Today, after payroll, the largest expense item for most companies is healthcare. In most parts of the United States, companies are now paying twice as much for healthcare coverage as they were five years ago.

All of a sudden, companies are panicked by this rising cost, which they perceive as something they have very little control over. While cutting costs and becoming more efficient in every other department has been a hallmark of most successful American companies, healthcare costs are like a cancer for which there is no known cure.

Disproportionate, Unfair Costs to Small Companies and the Self-Employed

Small companies and self-employed individuals, regardless of their health status, pay a disproportionately higher cost for healthcare insurance. This is because they have fewer employees and are thus lumped into a higher risk pool. The end result is significantly higher insurance rates and deductibles, and often less effective coverage, even though the covered individuals may be younger and healthier than their counterparts at a large corporation. This is flat-out unfair and must end; it makes small companies unable to compete with the big boys, and ends up leading to all kinds of adverse consequences for American business—and, ultimately, for consumers.

The Growing Ranks of the Uninsured

Uninsured Americans—including the unemployed, the working poor, or those who just cannot afford healthcare insurance—are really getting the shaft. That's some 42.6 million Americans, including 10 million children. These Americans don't have anyone negotiating on their behalf with providers, so when they need care they end up paying full, non-discounted rates for everything. They tend not to seek medical care, until they're too sick not to, because they can't afford to pay for it, so when they finally stagger into the clinic or the emergency room, they require very costly catastrophic care. *The very people who need and generally deserve a discounted rate do not get one.*

No Economic Incentive for Preventive Medicine or Good Self-Care

Our present system has virtually destroyed any economic incentive for individuals to take good care of themselves. I believe, until every individual takes responsibility for her or his own healthcare, the current system is doomed to failure. This is where corporations *must* change the way they do business. If they don't, they're going to continue to pay the consequences of rising healthcare costs.

Presently, many ideas to help companies deal with skyrocketing healthcare costs are being proposed. However, if those ideas do not make the individual employee and their covered dependents accountable for their own health and wellness, they *will not* result in a long-term solution.

In my state, one large corporation has instituted a plan to charge the higher-paid employees more for their healthcare insurance than the lower-paid employees, irrespective of their health status or age. While this approach might sound like a nice gesture on the part of management, and has earned them points for political correctness, it does not solve the underlying problem. In fact, it is doomed to failure because it creates no incentive for the lower-paid employees to take better care of themselves.

Companies need to institute plans that *allow employees to participate in how they receive healthcare,* and that *give them the financial incentive to make positive, healthful decisions.* This accountability will result in healthier employees and lower long-term healthcare costs. Companies, such as Microsoft, who have made these changes have seen a positive effect on their bottom line. It's all about wellness and preventive medicine—always a better, less expensive alternative.

Appendix

The Ultimate Physical

If you've read this book to this point, odds are you are in an age group that grew up watching the TV program Star Trek. Being a premed student during the early days of Star Trek, I was always intrigued by the futuristic methods of diagnosis and treatment that were utilized by Bones, the doctor on the starship Enterprise.

As you probably remember, Bones would use a hand-held device for diagnosing virtually every medical problem. He would run the device over the entire length of the patient, and he would get a readout of what the problem was. This is of particular interest today because this basic capability is actually available now. There may not yet be a hand-held device that can do all that Bones did, but it's close. Imaging techniques, such as CT scans, MRIs, and ultrasound, have all emerged since Gene Roddenberry aired the first episode of Star Trek in 1966. Today, these techniques are thought of as old hat, but in fact they are all relatively new when you consider the history of medicine and the history of x-rays—basically the only imaging technique for seventy-plus years. Do you really think it's a stretch to think that sometime in the not-too-distant future there will be a hand-held device to perform diagnostic imaging and even treatment of many disease states?

In light of the relatively brief history and the rapid evolution of imaging techniques, it is interesting to note that the foundation of the American healthcare system, the annual physical everyone is told they need, hasn't changed a whole lot in the past hundred years. Sure, stethoscopes are fancier and a little bit more sophisticated, ophthalmoscopes have better light sources, and tongue depressors are now disposable, but the basic physical exam hasn't really been upgraded to meet the times.

Why is it that people go to the doctor to get a physical in the first place? For some, it's because their school or work or insurance company makes them, but for most, it's because they're hoping that, if they do have some occult disease process, it will be picked up early enough to be treated and effectively cured.

In my opinion, another reason to see a physician on a routine basis is for them to give you current information about what you can do to *prevent* a disease process from taking hold, but most people don't expect that, and it's not what they usually get at an annual physical. So if you're expecting to find any occult disease process—something you can't tell is there without the help of a doctor—do you think your basic routine physical is the best way? Or do you think the best way is to use an up-to-date technique, which is far more likely to find disease months, or even years, before it becomes manifest? I think the answer is obvious.

Mind you, I'm not saying the annual physical is a waste of time and money. I have always believed that face-to-face communication, the laying on of hands, the bedside manner, and the doctor-patient relationship, are not only meaningful, but have immense value in ministering to sick people—and in encouraging people who are well to do what's necessary to stay that way.

But I also think everyone should expect value from the time, effort, and money they spend, and I think every doctor should use the annual physical as an opportunity to make a real difference in the health and well-being of those in their care. The *outdated* traditional physical is not, however, the best way to accomplish this end.

There are certainly different levels of diagnostic capability, and what I'm going to outline in these next few pages is what I call the *ultimate physical*. It is, admittedly, not for everyone, but I believe that finances are the only valid reason not to have this entire series of tests performed every one or two years, once you've entered your fifties. If everyone had an unlimited budget, then I would advise every person over the age of fifty to have this physical on a regular schedule.

In fact, because it would find diseases so much earlier, thereby leading to cures, or elimination, of the diseases before they became life-threatening, such a physical could become cost-effective after a few years if it could be standardized and used for just about everyone fifty and up (though I don't think we'll realize that level anytime soon). For those who prefer a bare-bones basic annual physical, you'll find out below how to update the traditional version with your doctor's help. I've marked these basics with an asterisk(*).

Anatomical vs. Functional

A diagnostic evaluation can basically be divided into two categories—anatomical and functional. Both types are of value. An anatomical test looks directly at your anatomy, at the physical characteristics of the machinery and upholstery that make up your working physical body. Anatomical tests include imaging (such as CT scans), a physical exam, mammograms, and a colonoscopy. A functional test measures your body's function—its levels and utilization of hormones and nutrients, as well as its biological (as opposed to chronological) age.

ANATOMICAL TESTS

Physical Exam*	A physical exam by a licensed practitioner, with emphasis on a total body/skin exam. The skin exam may be the most important part of the actual physical exam, because it really can't be duplicated in any other way. Also included in the physical exam would be the vital signs (blood pressure, heart rate) and calculating a body mass index (BMI).
CT Scan Imaging	CT scans of head, neck, chest, abdomen and pelvis. This technique is fairly expensive, costing between $2,500 and $4,000, but it will find occult disease years before it is manifest or is picked up by the usual physical exam. There is some radiation exposure, and there is also a chance of finding changes that

	may lead to further medical evaluation, but prove to be nothing harmful in the end. These *false-positive* results are known and accepted liabilities of using this highly sensitive tool.
Cardiac Scoring with Electron Beam Tomography (EBT) and Helical CT Scan*	This test alone is worth a whole book. I think it is the greatest single innovation in the fight against heart disease—ever. It utilizes two basic technologies: EBT (electron beam tomography) and helical CT scan. Both do the same thing—they measure calcium in the coronary arteries. The amount of calcium in the inner lining of the arteries is a direct reflection of the formation of a substance called plaque. This can lead to the obstruction of the artery, which is what causes a heart attack. This test is non-invasive and relatively inexpensive ($100–$350), with minimal or no radiation exposure, and it can be a lifesaver. All the other non-invasive tests that have been done in the past—the EKG stress test, echocardiograms, nuclear stress test—pale in comparison to the predictive value of this simple procedure. If you have a high risk of heart disease or are a man of fifty or woman over fifty-five, *make sure you get this test done.*
Doppler Flow Study of Carotid Arteries*	This imaging test allows physicians to see how well blood is flowing through the carotid arteries, the vessels that move oxygenated blood to the brain. Carotid-artery

	occlusion (clogging with plaques) or weakness can both lead to catastrophic medical events. Catching these problems early is possible with this test.
Ultrasound of Testicles (men)	This allows doctors to see testicular tumors when they are still small and are unlikely to have spread.
DEXA Scan of Spine and Hips	Women should have this test done by age fifty; men, by age sixty. It shows whether osteoporosis is a concern.
Mammograms*	For women, every year or two after age forty. You may need fewer if you have minimal risk factors. Talk with your medical team about this.
Virtual Colonoscopy	This is less expensive and less risky than a regular colonoscopy, but the preparation for the procedure is the same. If something is found, then you have another prep and a regular colonoscopy is done.
Pap Smear	If a woman has had a hysterectomy, with removal of the cervix and no history of cervical disease, she doesn't need a Pap smear. Women with documented HPV should have a Pap every six months. Your OB/GYN can talk with you more about the frequency of this test. Depending on your sexual history and other factors, you may need it either less or more often.
Routine Blood Work*	The standard blood work you

	should have yearly includes a CBC (a measurement of blood cell count), lipids (cholesterol and triglycerides), metabolic profile.
Other Blood Work	CRP, homocysteine, LPa, hemoglobin AIC, Insulin, essential fatty acid analysis.
PSATest*	Men require a PSA yearly after the age of fifty to check for prostate problems.
Ovuchek	A new screening test for ovarian cancer, available in some areas for women who are at high risk for ovarian cancer or who are over age fifty. If Ovuchek isn't available, you can ask for another screening test, a CA-125, a pelvic CT scan, or ultrasound.
Routine Urinalysis*	Screening for kidney disease.
24-Hour Urine Analysis	The twenty-four-hour urine test checks for metals and creatinine. Excess metals, such as mercury and lead, are a threat to overall health, increasing the risk for Alzheimer's disease and heart disease. Creatinine is a measurement of kidney function.
Pregen+*	This is a substitute for a colonoscopy, or it can be done in the years between colonoscopies. It checks a stool sample to pick up DNA specific to colon cancer or polyps.
Colonoscopy*	Follow the current recommendations for one colonoscopy every five years after the age of fifty.

FUNCTIONAL TESTS

Audiometry	Hearing tests.
Hormone Assays*	To determine hormone balance, your doctor looks for deficiency states. This can be done through measurements of hormone levels in blood, saliva, or urine. My preference is blood testing.
Intracellular Analysis of Vitamins, Amino Acids, and Antioxidants	This testing is done on white blood cells, which are grown in tissue culture by a company called Spectracell. I believe it is the most accurate way of obtaining information regarding the bioavailable levels of vitamins, amino acids, and antioxidants.
Tonometry* and Visual Acuity Testing	Tonometry is a test for glaucoma. And no matter how much you want to avoid wearing glasses, you need to ensure that you can see well enough to drive. So go get that eye exam. The ophthalmologist can also evaluate you for age-related macular degeneration (ARMD) and cataracts.
Pulmonary (Lung) Function Testing	A very telling sign of physiological age. Below-average lung function can cause fatigue. It's best to identify the problem early on and treat it to avoid damage to the lungs and airway that can accelerate over time.
EKG*	You can have a resting EKG to ensure that your heart is beating regularly and normally; or you can take it a step further and have an EKG with exercise stress test. The

	latter is a more sensitive diagnostic tool for heart problems.
Measurement of arterial elasticity and heart rate variability	Both of these measurements are early predictors of cardiovascular disease.
Fitness Evaluation	This can be done as a fairly simple test in the office. No sophisticated equipment is necessary to determine your level of fitness in three areas: cardio-respiratory, strength, and flexibility.
Nutrition Evaluation*	Some sort of evaluation and counseling on nutrition should be a part of every annual physical, even if it's just a thirty-second pep talk about the importance of eating well. I have patients keep a food diary so they can be evaluated by a nutritionist who can give them guidance on what dietary changes to make to preserve or better their health.

Resources

Physicians

American Academy of Anti-Aging Medicine (A4M)
1510 W. Montana Street
Chicago, IL 60614
Ph: 1-773-528-1000
Fax: 1-773-528-5390
e-mail: info@worldhealth.net
Website: http://www.worldhealth.net/p/51.html

If you have difficulty finding a physician in your area who is willing to prescribe BHRT, contact the Academy of Anti-Aging Medicine. This is not a blanket endorsement of all physicians in the A4M. Generally speaking, I think most women are best served by finding a gynecologist who uses bioidentical hormones. For the most part, gynecologists understand more about hormones and are better equipped to handle potential problems which can arise with BHRT. Urologists are usually the best choice for men who are in need of HRT.

Carolina Healthspan Institute
Ronald Brown, M.D.
423C South Sharon Amity Road
Charlotte, NC 28211
Ph: 1-703-333-4817
Fax: 1-704-333-4879
e-mail: info@carolinahealthspan.com
Website: www.carolinahealthspan.com

This is the author's medical office. If you would like information, or want an appointment or a consultation, please call or write him or his staff.

Website

Johnleemd.com/Hormones Etc., Inc.
e-mail: info@johnleemd.com
website: http://www.johnleemd.com

Although Dr. Lee died in October 2003, his work lives on in his best-selling books, his audio and video tapes, and on this website, where you'll find a wealth of information about natural hormones, from Frequently Asked Questions for beginners, to biochemistry for experts.

Compounding Pharmacies

For information regarding compounding and compounding pharmacies, I would recommend that you contact one of the two organizations listed below. Generally speaking, it is likely that, with their help, you can find a pharmacy in your area who can provide you with compounding services.

International Academy of Compounding Pharmacists (IACP)
PO Box 1365
Sugar Land, TX 77487
Ph: 1-281-933-8400
Fax: 1-281-495-0602
Website: www.iacprx.org

Professional Compounding Centers of America (PCCA)
9901 S. Wilcrest Drive
Houston, TX 77099
Ph: 1-281-933-6948 or toll-free 1-800-331-2498
Fax: 1-281-933-6627 or toll-free 1-800-874-5760
Website: www.pccarx.com/

Nutritional Supplements

Vital Nutrients
45 Kenneth Dooley Drive
Middletown, CT 06457
Ph: 1-860-638-3675 or toll-free 1-888-328-9993
Fax: 1-888-328-9993
e-mail: sales@vitalnutrients.net
Website: www.vitalnutrients.net

I have dealt with this company for several years, and in my opinion, it is the best. Their products are of the highest quality, their quality control is peerless, and their website contains a lot of great information.

Vital Nutrients sells only to physicians, but they've given me permission to give out a code—5032—that you can use to order their supplements. You can also order these directly from me, as I buy them in bulk to supply the more than 1200 patients in my practice. In doing so, I am able to offer them at a significant discount.

Products and Services

Culligan International
One Culligan Parkway
Northbrook, IL 60062-6209
Ph: 1-800-CULLIGAN or 1-847-295-6000
e-mail: feedback@culligan.com
Website: http://www.culligan.com

Contact your local Culligan dealer to figure out how best to keep your house's water clean; or shop around for whole-house or single-faucet water filtration systems you can install yourself.

Spectracell Laboratories
10401 Town Park Drive
Houston, Texas 77072
Ph: 1-800-227-5227 or 1-713-621-3101
Fax: 1-713-621-3234
Website: http://www.spectracell.com
e-mail: spec1@spectracell.com

This company measures intracellular levels of vitamins, amino acids, and antioxidants. Its website lists clinicians who do the testing.

TYE Products
Charlotte, NC 28270
704-365-0700
Website: www.typeproducts.com
Youthifying products for the skin and heart and for cancer prevention.

Recommended Reading

Female HRT and Women's Health

Lee, J, Hopkins, V. *What Your Doctor May NOT Tell You About Menopause.* New York, NY: Warner Books, 2004.

Lee, J, Zava, D, Hopkins, V. *What Your Doctor May NOT Tell You About Breast Cancer: How Hormone Balance Can Save Your Life.* New York, NY: Warner Books, 2002.

Rako, S. *The Hormone of Desire: The Truth about Testosterone, Sexuality, and Menopause.* New York, NY: Random House, 1999.

Smith, K. *Kathy Smith's Moving Through Menopause: The Complete Program for Exercise, Nutrition, and Total Wellness.* New York, NY: Warner Books, 2002.

Green, Y. *Weight-Bearing Workouts for Women: Exercises for Sculpting, Strengthening, and Toning.* Berkeley, CA: Ulysses Press, 2003.

Male HRT and Men's Health

Katz, A. *Dr. Katz's Guide to Prostate Health.* Topanga, CA: Freedom Press, 2005.

Schuler, L, Mejia, M. *Men's Health Home Workout Bible.* Emmaus, PA: Rodale Books, Inc., 2002.

Shippen, E, Fryer, W. *The Testosterone Syndrome: The Critical Factor for Energy, Health, & Sexuality— Reversing the Male Menopause.* New York, NY: M. Evans and Co., 2001.

Personal Growth, Marriage, and Relationships

Men and women who are moving into and through the menopausal/andropausal transition may find that their relationships and inner lives are ripe for examination and renewal. These books can help you get started.

Bly, R. *Iron John: A Book About Men.* Cambridge, MA/New York,

NY: Da Capo Press, 2004.
Goldenson, M. *It's Time: No One's Coming to Save You*. Los Angeles, CA: Deverani Publications, 2003.
Hendricks, K, Hendricks, G. *Lasting Love: The 5 Secrets of Growing a Vital, Conscious Relationship.* Emmaus, PA: Rodale Books, Inc., 2004.
Keen, S. *Fire in the Belly: On Being a Man.* New York, NY: Bantam, 1992.
Northrup, C. *The Wisdom of Menopause: Creating Physical and Emotional Health and Healing During the Change.* New York, NY: Bantam, 2006.

Diet

I believe there's more than one way to eat to foster The Youth Effect. It's easier to stay slim and satisfied on a diet that's lower in carbohydrates, but an appropriately designed high-complex-carbohydrate diet can also keep you healthy and at your ideal weight.

Agatston, A. *The South Beach Diet.* Emmaus, PA: Rodale Books, Inc., 2003.
Kulze, A. *Dr. Ann's 10-Step Diet: A Simple Plan for Permanent Weight Loss and Lifelong Vitality.* Charleston, SC: Top Ten Wellness and Fitness, 2004.
Pratt, W, Matthews, K. *Superfoods Rx: Fourteen Foods That Will Change Your Life.* New York, NY: HarperCollins, 2006.
Sears, B. *A Week in the Zone.* New York, NY: Regan Books, 2000.
Sears, B. *Enter The Zone.* New York, NY: Regan Books, 1995.
Sears, B. *The Anti-Inflammation Zone.* Los Angeles, CA: Regan Books, 2006.
Sears, B. *The Omega Rx Zone.* New York, NY: Regan Books, 2002.
Steward, HL, Bethea, M, Andrews, S, Balart, L. *The New Sugar Busters!* New York, NY: Ballantine Books, 2003.

Living with Fewer Toxins

Berthold-Bond, A. *Home Enlightenment: Practical, Earth-Friendly Advice for Creating a Nurturing, Healthy, and Toxin-*

Free Home and Lifestyle. Emmaus, PA: Rodale Books, Inc., 2005.

Colborn, T, Dumanosky, D, Meyers, JP. *Our Stolen Future: How We Are Threatening Our Fertility, Intelligence, and Survival—A Scientific Detective Story.* New York, NY: Plume Books, 1997.

References

Note: Each reference is cited only once. Those in Chapters 3–13 were also used as foundations for Chapters 1 and 2. References are in alphabetical order.

Chapter 3

Antunes, CM, et al. "Endometrial cancer and estrogen use. Report of a large case-control study." *New England Journal of Medicine.* 300(1):9–13, Jan 4, 1979.

Barrett-Connor, E, Slone, S, Greendale, G, et al. "The Postmenopausal Estrogen/Progestin Intervention Study: Primary Outcomes in Adherent Women." *Maturitas.* 27(3):261–274, Jul 1997.

Collaborative Group on Hormonal Factors in Breast Cancer. "Breast cancer and hormone replacement therapy: collaborative reanalysis of data from 51 epidemiological studies of 52,705 women with breast cancer and 108,411 women without breast cancer." *The Lancet.* 350(9084):1047–1059, 1997.

Curb, JD, Prentice, RL, Bray, PF, et al. "Venous thrombosis and conjugated equine estrogen in women without a uterus." *Archives of Internal Medicine.* 166:772–780, April 10, 2006.

"Effect of hormone therapy on bone mineral density: results from the postmenopausal estrogen/progestin interventions (PEPI) trial. The writing group for the PEPI." *Journal of the American Medical Association (JAMA).* 6:276(17):1389–1396, Nov 1996.

"Effects of estrogen and estrogen/progestin regimens on heart disease risk factors in postmenopausal women: the Postmenopausal Estrogen/Progestin Interventions (PEPI) Trial," *Journal of the American Medical Association (JAMA).* 273(3):199–208, Jan 18, 1995.

Elliot, Carl. "A World of Our Own Making: Medical Enhancement and the Pursuit of Happiness." *Dissent.* http://

www.dissentmagazine.org/article/?article=355 Summer 2004.

Goddard, MK. "Hormone replacement therapy and breast cancer, endometrial cancer, and cardiovascular disease: risks and benefits." *British Journal of General Practice.* 120–125, Mar 1992.

Grodstein, F, Manson, JE, Stampfer, MJ."Postmenopausal hormone use and secondary prevention of coronary events in the Nurses' Health Study." *Annals of Internal Medicine.* 135:1–8, 2001.

Hammond, CB, et al. "Effects of long-term estrogen replacement therapy. II. Neoplasia." *American Journal of Obstetrics and Gynecology.* 133(5):537–547, Mar 1, 1979.

Hulley, S, Grady, D, Bush, T, et al. "Randomized trial of estrogen plus progestin for secondary prevention of coronary heart disease in postmenopausal women. Heart and Estrogen/progestin Replacement Study (HERS) Research Group." *Journal of the American Medical Association (JAMA).* 280(7):605–613, 1998.

LaVecchia, C, Gallin, S, Fernandez, F. "Hormone replacement therapy and colorectal cancer: an update." *Journal of the British Menopause Society.* 11(4):166–172, Dec 2005.

Vongpatanasin, W, Tuncel, M, Wang, Z, et al. "Differential effects of oral versus transdermal estrogen replacement therapy on C-reactive protein in postmenopausal women." *Journal of the American College of Cardiology.* 41(8):1358–1363, 2003.

Chapter 4

Adams, MR, Williams, JK. "Medroxyprogesterone acetate antagonizes inhibitory effects of conjugated equine estrogens on coronary artery atherosclerosis." *Arteriosclerosis, Thrombosis, and Vascular Medicine.* 17:217, Jan 1997.

Anderson, GL, Limacher, M, Assaf, AR, et al. "Women's Health Initiative Steering Committee. Effects of conjugated equine estrogen in postmenopausal women with hysterectomy: the Women's Health Initiative randomized controlled trial." *Journal of the American Medical Association (JAMA).* 291(14):1701–1712, 2004.

Gambrell, RD. "The Women's Health Initiative Report: Critical

Review of the Findings." Epigraph. *The Female Patient.* 29:23–30, Nov 2004.

Grant, Ellen. "Cancer in a cream?" *What Doctors Don't Tell You.* 6–9, May 2006.

Fournier, A, Berrino, F, Clavel-Chapelon, F. "Unequal risks for breast cancer associated with different hormone replacement therapies: results from the E3N cohort study." *Breast Cancer Research and Treatment.* Feb 27, 2007.

Hopkins, Virginia. "Dr. Ellen Grant and Lynne McTaggart Launch Progesterone Attack." *The Virginia Hopkins Health Watch* (formerly *The Hopkins Health Watch*). e-mail to the author, August 7, 2006.

Magliano, DJ, Rogers, SL, Abramson, MJ, et al. "Hormone therapy and cardiovascular disease: a systematic review and meta-analysis." *British Journal of Gynecology.* 113(1):5–14, Jan 2006.

Miyagawa, K, Hermsmeyer, K. "Medroxyprogesterone interferes with ovarian steroid protection against coronary vasospasm." *Nature Medicine.* 3:324, March 1997.

Raloff, J. "Hormone therapy: issues of the heart." *Science News Online.* www.sciencenews.org/pages/sn_arc97/3_8_97/fob1.htm

Rossouw, JE, Anderson, GL, Prentice, RL, et al. "Risks and benefits of estrogen plus progestin in healthy postmenopausal women: principal results from the Women's Health Initiative randomized controlled trial." *Journal of the American Medical Association (JAMA).* 288(3):321–333, 2002.

Speroff, L. "The future of postmenopausal hormone therapy: it's time to move forward." *Maturitas.* Mar 17, 2007.

Strickler, RC. "Women's Health Initiative results: a glass more empty than full." *Fertility and Sterility.* 80(3):488–490, 2003.

Veiga, S, Melcangi, RL, Doncarlos, LL, et al. "Sex hormones and brain aging." *Experimental Gerontology.* 39(11–12):1623–1631, Nov–Dec 2004.

Vongpatanasin, W, Tuncel, M, Wang, Z, et al. "Differential effects of oral versus transdermal estrogen replacement therapy on C-reactive protein in postmenopausal women." *Journal of the American College of Cardiology.* 41(8):1358–1363, 2003.

Williams, JK, Adams, MR. "Estrogens, progestins and coronary artery reactivity." *Nature Medicine.* 3:273, Mar 1997.

Wilson, R. *Feminine Forever.* New York, NY: Evans and Lippincott, 1966.

Chapter 5

Archer, DF. "Percutaneous 17-ß estradiol gel for the treatment of vasomotor symptoms in postmenopausal women." *Menopause.* 10(6):516–521, 2003.

Bushnell, CD. "Estrogen and stroke in women: assessment of risk." *Lancet Neurology.* 4(11):743–751, Nov 2005.

Canonico, M, Oger, E, Plu-Bureau, G, at al. "Hormone therapy and venous thromboembolism among postmenopausal women: impact of the route of estrogen administration and progestogens: the ESTHER study." *Circulation.* 115(7):840–845, Feb 20, 2007.

Chan, J, Meyerhardt, J, Chan, A, et al. "Hormone replacement therapy and survival after colorectal cancer diagnosis." *Journal of Clinical Oncology.* 24:5680–5686, 2007.

Chetkowski, RJ, Meldrum, DR, Steingold, KA, et al, "Biologic effects of transdermal estradiol." *New England Journal of Medicine.* 314:1615–1620, 1986.

Cirillo, DJ, Wallace, RB, Wu, L, et al. "Effect of hormone therapy on risk of hip and knee joint replacement in the Women's Health Initiative." *Arthritis and Rheumatism.* 54(10):3194–3204, Oct 2006.

Connell, EB. "Transdermal estrogen therapy." *Postgraduate Medicine.* 101:11–116, 122, 128–130, 1997.

Cryer, B, Bauer, DC. "Oral bisphosphonates and upper gastrointestinal tract problems: What is the evidence?" *Mayo Clinic Proceedings* ;77(10):1031–1043, Oct 2002.

Curb, JD, Prentice, RL, Bray, PF. "Venous thrombosis and conjugated equine estrogen in women without a uterus." *Archives of Internal Medicine.* 166:772–780, Apr 10, 2006.

deGroen, PC, Lubbe, DF, Hirsch, LJ, et al. "Esophagitis associated with the use of alendronate." *New England Journal of Medicine.* 335:1016–1021, 1996.

Dupont, A, Dupont, P, Cusan, L, et al. "Comparative endocrinological and clinical effects of percutaneous estradiol and oral conjugated estrogens as replacement therapy in menopausal women." *Maturitas.* 13:297–311, 1991.

Fackelmann, K, "Forever smart: does estrogen enhance memory?" *Science News.* 147(5):74–78, Feb 1995.

"Fosamax (alendronate sodium tablets)" [package insert]; West Point, PA: Merck Co., Inc., 1996.

Grodstein, F, Stampfer, MJ, Colditz, GA, et al. "Postmenopausal hormone therapy and mortality." *New England Journal of Medicine.* 336(25):1769–1775, 1997.

"Hormone replacement therapy hurts hearing, study finds." *EurekAlert.* http://www.eurekalert.org/pub_releases/2006-09/uorm-hth090506.php

Jewelewicz, R. "New developments in topical estrogen therapy." *Fertility and Sterility.* 67:1–12, 1997.

Laufer, LR, DeFazio, JL, Lu, JK, et al. "Estrogen replacement therapy by transdermal estradiol administration." *American Journal of Obstetrics and Gynecology.* 146:533–540, 1983.

Liu, SL, Lebrun, SM. "Effect of oral contraceptives and hormone replacement therapy on bone mineral density in postmenopausal women: a systematic review." *British Journal of Sports Medicine.* 40(1):11–24, Jan 2006.

Hodis, HN, Mack, WJ, Azen, SP, et al. "Hormone therapy and the progression of coronary artery atherosclerosis in postmenopausal women." *New England Journal of Medicine.* 349:535–545, Aug 7, 2003.

Lobo, RA. "Benefits and risks of estrogen replacement therapy." *American Journal of Obstetrics and Gynecology.* 173(3 Pt 2):982–989, Sep 1995.

Murphy, DG, et al. "The Women's Health Initiative Memory Study: Findings and implications for treatment." *Lancet Neurology.* 4(3):190–194, Mar 2005.

"Neonatology Research Leads To Better Understanding Of How Estrogen Protects Against Heart Disease." http://www.scienceblog.com/community/older/1999/E/199904236.html

Nilsen, J, Morales, A, Brinton, RD. "Medroxyprogesterone acetate exacerbates glutamate excitotoxicity." *Gynecologic Endocrinology.* 22(7):355–361, Jul 2006.

Shumaker, SA, Legault, C, Rapp, SR, et al. "Estrogen plus progestin and the incidence of dementia and mild cognitive impairment in postmenopausal women: the Women's Health Initiative Memory Study: a randomized controlled trial." *Journal of the American Medical Association (JAMA)*. 289(20):2651–2662, 2003.

Simon, JA, Wehren, LE, Ascott-Evans, BH, et al. "Skeletal consequences of hormone therapy discontinuance: a systematic review." *Obstetrical and Gynecological Survey*. 61(2):115–124, Feb 2006.

Sowers, MF, et al. "Estradiol and its metabolites and their association with knee osteoarthritis." *Arthritis and Rheumatism*. 54:2481–2487, 2006.

Spector, TD, Nandra, D, Hart, DJ, Voyle, DV. "Is hormone replacement therapy protective for hand and knee osteoarthritis in women? The Chingford Study." *Annals of the Rheumatic Diseases*. 56:432–434, 1997.

Tang, MX, et al. "Effect of estrogen during menopause on risk and age at onset of Alzheimer's disease." *The Lancet*. 348:429–432, 1996.

"Thousands of Patients to FDA: Don't Let Wyeth Rob Us of Our Hormone Treatments; Responses to Wyeth Citizen Petition Likely to Top 30,000." posted 4/12/06. http://www.iacprx.org/site/PageServer?pagename=Press_Releases#040406, accessed 8/7/06."

Ultra-low dose estrogen patch improves bone, appears safe for the uterus." http://www.health.harvard.edu/newsweek/Ultra-low_dose_estrogen_patch_improves_bone.htm

Verdier-Sevrain, S, Bonte, F, Gilchrist, B. "Biology of estrogens in skin: implications for skin aging." *Experimental Dermatology*. 15(2):83–94, Feb 2006.

Wu, O. "Postmenopausal hormone replacement therapy and venous thromboembolism." *Gender Medicine*. 2 Suppl A:S18–27, 2005.

Yaffe, K, Barnes, D, Lindquist, K, et al. "Endogenous sex hormone levels and risk of cognitive decline in an older biracial cohort." *Neurobiologic Aging* 28(2):171–178, Feb 2007.

Yates, J, Barrett-Connor, E, Barlas, S, et al. "Rapid loss of hip fracture protection after estrogen cessation: evidence from the National Osteoporosis Risk Assessment." *Obstetrics and*

Gynecology. 103(3):440–446, 2004.

Chapter 6

Burry, KA, Patton, PE, Hermsmeyer, K. "Percutaneous absorption of progesterone in postmenopausal women treated with transdermal estrogen." *American Journal of Obstetrics and Gynecology*. 180 (6 Pt 1):1504–1511, 1999.

Campagnoli, C, Abba, C, Ambroggio, S, et al. "Pregnancy, progesterone and progestins in relation to breast cancer risk." *Journal of Steroid Biochemistry and Molecular Biology*. 97(5):441–450, Dec 2005.

Cicinelli, E, deZiegler, D, Alfonso, R, et al. "Endometrial effects, bleeding control, and compliance with a new postmenopausal hormone therapy based on transdermal estradiol gel and every-other-day vaginal progesterone capsules: a 3-year pilot study." *Fertility Sterility*. 83(6):1859–1863, Jun 2005.

Cooper, A, Spencer, C, Whitehead, MI, et al. "Systemic absorption of progesterone cream from Progest cream in postmenopausal women." *The Lancet* 351(9111):1255–1256, 1998.

Leonetti, HB, Wilson, KJ, Anasti, JW. "Topical progesterone cream has an antiproliferative effect on estrogen-stimulated endometrium." *Fertility Sterility*. 79(1):221–222, Jun 2003.

O'Connor, CA, Cernak, I, Johnson, F, et al. "Effects of progesterone on neurologic and morphologic outcome following diffuse traumatic brain injury in rats." *Experimental Neurology*. Feb 12, 2007.

"Role of progestagen in hormone therapy for postmenopausal women: position statement of the North American Menopause Society." *Menopause*. 10(2):113–132, Mar–Apr 2003.

Sitruk-Ware, R. "Routes of delivery for progesterone and progestins." *Maturitas*. March 17, 2007.

Chapter 7

Arlt, W. "Androgen therapy in women." *European Journal of Endocrinology* 154(1):1–11 Jan 2006.

Crenshaw, T. *The Alchemy of Love and Lust*. New York, NY:G.P. Putnam Adult, 1996.

Davis, SR, Guay, AT, Shifren, JL, et al. "Endocrine aspects of female sexual dysfunction." *The Journal of Sexual Medicine.* 1:82–86, Jul 2004.

Hofling, M, Hirschberg, AL, Skoog, L, et al. "Testosterone inhibits estrogen/progestogen-induced breast cell proliferation in postmenopausal women." *Menopause: The Journal of the North American Menopause Society.* 12(2):183–190, 2007.

Hogervorst, E, Bandelow, S, Moffat, SD. "Increasing testosterone levels and effects on cognitive function in elderly men and women: a review." *Current Drug Targets: CNS Neurological Disorders.* 4(5):531–540, Oct 2005.

Jacoby, Susan. *AARP: The Magazine.* August 30, 2006. Posted at http://www.aarpmagazine.org/lifestyle/relationships.sex_in_america.html Accessed 8/30/06.

MacLusky, NJ, et al. "Androgen modulation of hippocampal synaptic plasticity." *Neuroscience.* 138(3):957–965, 2006.

Miller, KK, et al. "Effects of testosterone replacement in androgen-deficient women with hypopituitarism: a randomized, double-blind, placebo-controlled study," *Journal of Clinical Endocrinology and Metabolism.* 91(5):1683–1690, May 2006.

Rako, Susan. *The Hormone Of Desire.* Epigraph. New York, NY: Three Rivers Press, 1996, page 14.

Shifren, JL, et al. "Testosterone patch for the treatment of hypoactive sexual desire disorder in naturally menopausal women: results from the INTIMATE NM1 Study." *Menopause.* August 22, 2006. epub ahead of print, abstract posted at: http://www.ncbi.nlm.nih.gov/entrez/query.fcgi?db=pubmed&cmd=Retrieve&dopt=AbstractPlus&list_uids=16932240&query_hl=4&itool=pubmed_docsum.

Chapter 8

Amy, JJ. "Hormones and menopause: pro." *Acta Clinica Belgium.* 60(5):261–268, Sep-Oct, 2005.

Bush, TL, Whiteman, M, Flaws, JA. "Hormone replacement therapy and breast cancer: a qualitative analysis." *Obstetrics and Gynecology.* 98(3):498–508, 2001.

Chang, KJ et al. "Influences of percutaneous administration of estradiol and progesterone on human breast epithelial cycle in vivo." *Fertility and Sterility.* 63:785–791, 1995.

Chen, W, et al. "Unopposed estrogen therapy and the risk of invasive breast cancer." *Archives of Internal Medcine.* 166(9): 1027–1032, May 8, 2006.

Domchek, SM, Stopfer, JE, Rebbeek, R. "Bilateral risk-reducing oophorectomy in BRCA1 and BRCA2 mutation carriers. "*Journal of the National Comprehensive Cancer Network.* (2):177–182, Feb 4, 2006.

Duncan, AM. "The role of nutrition in the prevention of breast cancer." *AACN Clinical Issues.* 15(1):119-135, Jan–Mar 2004.

Fournier, A, Berrino, F, Riboli, E, et al. "Breast cancer risk in relation to different types of hormone replacement therapy in the E3N-EPIC cohort." *International Journal of Cancer.* 114(3):448–454, Apr 10, 2005.

Levgur, M. "Hormone therapy for women after breast cancer: a review." *Journal of Reproductive Medicine.* 49(7):510–526, 2004.

Li, CI, et al. "Relationship between long durations and different regimens of hormone therapy and risk of breast cancer." *Journal of the American Medical Association (JAMA).* 289(24):3254–3263, Jun 25, 2003.

Natrajan, PK, Gambrell, RD. "Estrogen replacement therapy in patients with early breast cancer." *American Journal of Obstetrics and Gynecology.* 187(2):289–295, 2002.

Tamimi, RM, Hankinson, SE, Chen, WY, et al. "Combined estrogen and testosterone use and risk of breast cancer in postmenopausal women." *Archives of Internal Medicine.* 166:1483–1489, 2006.

Wood, CE, Register, TL, Franke, AA, et al. "Dietary soy isoflavones inhibit estrogen effects in the postmenopausal breast." *Cancer Research.* 66(2):1241–1249, Jan 15, 2006.

Chapter 9

Amore, M. "Partial androgen deficiency and neuropsychiatric symptoms in aging men." *Journal of Endocrinologic Investigations.* 28(11 Suppl Proceedings):49–54, 2005.

Amory, JK. "Exogenous testosterone or testosterone with

finasteride increases bone mineral density in older men with low serum testosterone." *Journal of Clinical Endocrinology and Metabolism*. 89:503–510, 2005.

Bedrood, S, Kimchi, A. "A High Cortisol to Testosterone Ratio Is Associated With Ischemic Heart Disease Mortality and Incidence." http://www.cardiologyonline.com/journal_articles/A_high_cortisol.htm accessed 9/12/06.

Benito, M. "Effect of testosterone replacement on trabecular architecture in hypogonadal men." *Journal of Bone Mineral Research*. 20(10):1785–1791, 2005.

Carson, CC. "Effects of testosterone on cognition and mood in male patients with mild Alzheimer's disease and elderly men." *Current Urology Reports*. 7(6):471–477, Nov 2006.

Department of Cardiology of Medical Faculty, Yuzuncu Yil University, Turkey. "Testosterone and coronary stenting." *The Institute of Nutritional Medicine and Cardiovascular Research*, June 2007.

Geerlings, MI, et al. "Endogenous sex hormones, cognitive decline, and future dementia in old men." *Annals of Neurology*. 60(2) doi:10.1002/ana.20918, 2006.

Gore, JL, Swerdloff, RS, Rajfer, J. "Androgen deficiency in the etiology and therapy of erectile dysfunction." *Urology Clinics of North America*. 32(4):457–468, vi-vii, Nov 2005.

Gruenewald, MA, Matsumoto, AM. "Testosterone supplementation therapy for older men: potential benefits and risks." *Journal of the American Geriatric Society*. 51(1):101–115, Jan 2003.

Harding, Anne. "Low testosterone common in middle-age men." *Reuters Health,* Wednesday, June 28, 2006. Study by Dr. Thomas Mulligan in the *International Journal of Clinical Practice*. July 2006.

Jones, TH, "Benefits of testosterone therapy on the cardiovascular system." part of lecture series posted at http://www.agingmale2004.com/transcript-Jones_Int.htm

Kolata, Gina. "Male hormone therapy popular but untested." *The New York Times,* August 19, 2002.

Lazarou, S, Morgentaler, A. "Hypogonadism in the male with erectile dysfunction: what to look for and when to treat." *Current Urology Reports*. 6(6):476–481, Nov 2005.

"Male scientists not so manly," http://www.scienceagogo.com/news/20040922054756data_trunc_sys.shtml, accessed 7/26/06.

Moffat, SD. "Effects of testosterone on cognitive and brain aging in elderly men." *Annals of the New York Academy of Sciences.* 1055:80–92, Dec 2005.

Moon, YJ, Wang, X, Morris, ME. "Dietary flavonoids: effects on xenobiotic and carcinogen metabolism." *Toxicology In Vitro.* 20(2):187–210, Mar 2006.

Morgentaler, A. "Testosterone replacement therapy and prostate risks: Where's the beef?" *Canadian Journal of Urology.* 13 Suppl 1:40–43, Feb 2006.

Pike, CJ, Rosario, ER, Nguyen, TV. "Androgens, aging, and Alzheimer's disease," *Endocrine.* 29(2):233–241, Apr 2006.

Rainone, F. "Milk thistle." *American Family Physician.* 72(7):1285–1288, Oct 1, 2005.

Raloff, J. "Estrogen's Emerging Manly Alter Ego." *Science News Online.* December 6, 1997. http://www.sciencenews.org/pages/sn_arc97/12_6_97/fob1.htm, accessed 7/26/06.

Rosario, ER, et al. "Age-related testosterone depletion and the development of Alzheimer's disease." *Journal of the American Medical Association (JAMA).* 22;292(12):431–432, Sep 2004.

Schiavi, RC, et al. "Effect of testosterone administration on sexual behavior and mood in men with erectile dysfunction." *Archives of Sexual Behavior.* 26(3):231–241, Jun 1997.

Shores, MM, et al. "Low serum testosterone and mortality in male veterans." *Archives of Internal Medicine.* 166:1665, 2006.

Chapter 10

Bemis, DL, Katz, AE, Buttyan, R. "Clinical trials of natural products as chemopreventative agents for prostate cancer." *Expert Opinion Investigative Drugs.* 15(10):1191–1200, Oct 2006.

Marks, LS, Mazer, NA, Mostaghel, E, et al. "Effect of testosterone replacement therapy on prostate tissue in men with late-onset hypogonadism." *Journal of the American Medical Association (JAMA).* 15;296(19):2351–2361, Nov 2006.

Severi, G, Morris, HA, MacInnis, RJ, et al. "Circulating steroid hormones and the risk of prostate cancer." *Cancer Epidemiology Biomarkers and Prevention.* 15(1):86–91, Jan 2006.

Chapter 11

Associated Press. "Never Say Die: Live Forever." Wired News, February 12, 2005, online at http://www.wired.com/news/medtech/0,1286,66585,00.html accessed 6/22/06.

Breslow, JL. "N-3 fatty acids and cardiovascular disease." *American Journal of Clinical Nutrition.* 83(6 Suppl):1477S–1482S, Jun 2006.

deGray, Aubrey. "We will be able to live to 1,000." BBC News, December 3, 2004, posted at http://news.bbc.co.uk/2/hi/uk_news/4003063.stm accessed 6/21/06.

Freeman, MP, Hibbeln, JR, Wisner, KL, et al. "Omega-3 fatty acids: evidence basis for therapy and future research in psychiatry." *Journal of Clinical Psychiatry.* 67(12):1945–1967, Dec 2006.

Havas, Magda. "Biological effects of non-ionizing electromagnetic energy: a critical review of the reports by the US National Research Council and the US National Institute of Environmental Health Sciences as they relate to the broad realm of EMF bioeffects." *NRC Research Press.* Oct 11, 2000. http://www.powerlinefacts.com/Canadian%20Review%20of%20NCR%20and%20NIEHS%20studies.pdf Accessed 9/15/06.

Kontogianni, MD, Zampelas, A, Tsugos, C. "Nutrition and inflammatory load." *Annals of the New York Academy of Sciences.* 1083:214–230, Nov 2006.

Olshansky, S. "Don't fall for the cult of immortality." BBC News, December 3, 2004, online at http://news.bbc.co.uk/2/hi/uk_news/4059549.stm; accessed 6/21/06.

Roberts, SB, Schoeller, DA. "Human caloric restriction for retardation of aging: current approaches based on preliminary data." *Journal of Nutrition.* 137(4):1076–1077, Apr 2007.

Touillaud, MS, Thiebaut, AC, Fournier, A, et al. "Dietary lignan intake and postmenopausal breast cancer risk by estrogen and progesterone receptor status." *Journal of the National Cancer Institute.* 99(6):475–486, Mar 1, 2007.

vonSchacky, C. A review of omega-3 ethyl esters for cardiovascular prevention and therapy of increased blood triglyceride levels." *Vascular Health Risk Management.* 2(3):251–262, 2006.

Chapter 12

"The Choice: Health Care for People or Drug Industry Profits." September 2005.

http://www.familiesusa.org/resources/publications/reports/the-choice.html . (A .pdf of the full report can be accessed for free at the above address.)

Index

About the Author

Ronald (Ronny) Brown, M.D. was born in Southern Pines, North Carolina. He is a graduate of Davidson College and the Medical University of South Carolina in Charleston, SC. He has been a physician and surgeon for over twenty-five years, and has been treating women with hormone replacement therapy since completing his residency in 1979. Today, at his Carolina Healthspan Institute, his focus is on wellness issues for women and men, with particular emphasis on nutrition, fitness, supplements, and bio-identical hormone replacement.

Dr. Brown's professional associations include: Fellow, American College of Obstetrics and Gynecology; Member, American Society of Reproductive Medicine; Member, North American Menopause Society; Member, American Academy of Anti-Aging Medicine; Member, International Society of Clinical Densitometry; and Diplomat, American Board of Obstetrics and Gynecology.

He lives and practices what he preaches full-time in Charlotte, North Carolina. When not helping his patients, Dr. Brown can often be found on the golf course or spending time with wife Susan, to whom he has been married for thirty-four years. The pair have two grown children, Spencer and Margaret. Dr. Brown is also an avid exerciser and wine collector.